IN THE WAY!

IN THE WAY!

Goalkeepers: A Breed Apart?

NICK HAZLEWOOD

MAINSTREAM
PUBLISHING

EDINBURGH AND LONDON

First published in 1996 by
MAINSTREAM PUBLISHING COMPANY
(EDINBURGH) LTD
7 Albany Street
Edinburgh EH1 3UG

ISBN 1 85158 798 5

Extract from *Hancock's Half-Hour – 'The Football Pools'* by kind permission of Ray Galton and Alan Simpson; extract from *Paddy Clarke Ha Ha Ha* by kind permission of Roddy Doyle and Martin Secker and Warburg Ltd; extract from *Speak, Memory – An Autobiography Revisited* by Vladimir Nabokov by kind permission of Weidenfeld and Nicholson; extract from *The Goalie's Anxiety at the Penalty Kick* by kind permission of Peter Handke and Eyre Methuen Ltd (an imprint of Reid Books); extract from *A Kestral for a Knave* by Barry Hines (Michael Joseph, 1968) copyright © Barry Hines, 1968, reproduced by kind permission of Penguin Books; extract from *Loneliness of the Long Distance Runner* by Alan Sillitoe by kind permission of Sheil Land Associates

A catalogue record for this book is available from the British Library

Typeset in Sabon and Bodoni Classic

Printed in Great Britain by Butler & Tanner Ltd

For Caroline

Acknowledgements

Many individuals and clubs deserve my thanks for the help they gave me with this book. They include: Terry Frost at Bradford City for pointing me in the right direction with Willie Foulke; Gareth Davies for his invaluable knowledge of Welsh football; Jim McAllister at Dumbarton; Graham Hughes at Wolverhampton Wanderers; Billy Simmons, the records officer at Sunderland, who was at Roker Park on the fateful day in 1936 when Jimmy Thorpe played his last; Paul Plowman at Swindon Town; Eric White at Brentford; Norrie Price at Dundee; Bob Matthews and Tim Beddow at Birmingham City; Jim Brown at Chesterfield and Andy Mitchell at the now defunct St Bernards FC. Also to: Arbroath FC; Bolton Wanderers; Charlton Athletic; Chelsea; Greenock Morton; Tottenham Hotspur.

Many thanks also to: Shuggy for getting me into cyberspace and for Tony Weir, Charlie Harvey, Peter Burns, David Frier, Alan Clark, Tommy Cannon, Dermot Houston, John Maxwell, Mike Furby and Ray Foran for replying down the internet. To David Barber at the FA; Ray Spiller at the Association of Football Statisticians; Margery Nimmo at the SFA; Phil Atkins at the National Railway Museum; Barbara Davies, assistant archivist at the National Library of Wales; Mr A. Willis, Birmingham Central Library; Graciela Gomez Garcia at the Mexican Embassy; Jim Craig, 'Lisbon Lion'; Jedd O'Brien; Jim Hossack; the Archbishop of Westminster, Cardinal Basil Hume.

To the goalies who responded, including Jimmy Allan, Peter Bonetti, Chic Brodie, Pauline Cope, Dai Davies, Shaka Hislop, David Icke, Pat Jennings, Eddie Niedzwiecki, Rosa Serra.

For their help with foreign translations and phone calls abroad, Maria Luisa Ricottini, Catherine Barral, Mimi Escudero and Roberto Cortes. For reading through much of it, Gary Pleasants and for both reading through and living through it, Caroline Annesley.

Contents

Prologue   The hunt for René Higuita   9
           Introduction   15

1   Once upon a time in the nets   27
2   Greek to Greek   55
3   Sex and drugs and rotten goals   76
4   The holy goalie   107
5   . . . But is it art?   124
6   Débuts, disasters and Scotland   132
7   Days like these   159
8   A parting shot   183

           Bibliography   189
           Index   191

Prologue

The hunt for René Higuita

Wednesday, 6 September 1995

There was a small but frantic mêlée around the entrance to the Holiday Inn, Cromwell Road. A large ambassadorial limo was pulling away with a crowd of men waving and shouting at it.

Fate had taken what seemed like a bargain turn for the better. Up until two weeks before, England had been due to play Croatia in a friendly international, a warm-up for the host nation as it prepared for the 1996 European Championships. But then some quick wit in the Football Association, probably a cleaner, had picked up a newspaper and started reading from the front for a change – war in the Balkans? 'How long's this been going on? Serbs attack Croatians! Croatians attacks Serbs! Tens of thousands dead in Bosnia-Hercegovina! Christians against Muslims! Wide-scale bloodshed! Why didn't anybody tell us? We can't possibly play football against Croatia, people might get the wrong impression . . .'

And so it was that the Croatians turned out to be not the sort of Johnnies that little Bobby England wanted to play football against and, responding with all the speed of a Bert Millichip cup draw, the Football Association promptly split with the splitters from Split and pulled Colombia out of the bag.

Yes, Colombia, that oasis of political stability where there have been 30,000 political killings since the early 1980s and where 600,000 people have been driven from their land by greedy landowners, drug barons, the army and guerrillas. Yes, Colombia where four presidential candidates were assassinated in one recent election, where more trades unionists are killed and more people

9

kidnapped than in any other country in the world. Indeed the Colombia where drug barons rule the roost, where private death squads root out so-called troublemakers, and self-appointed 'clean-up squads' stalk the night-time streets murdering prostitutes, urchins and homeless families?

Now that's more like it.

Not that I'm complaining. I've been to Colombia several times and love the place. The figures for violence are facts, the reputation deserved, but they do conceal a side that is shy at coming forward. Colombia is a beautiful country, populated with warm and indomitable people inured with a fighting spirit and a sense of humour and fun that pulls them through the daily grind.

They also have, in René Higuita, one of the great eccentric goalkeepers of all time – and today he's in London, which saves me another trip to his homeland and the cost of an airfare from a book advance that was spent before it was received.

My appointment with him is for 12.30 p.m. and I push my way through the bustle on the steps into the lobby of the hotel – only realising when I get to the top that in my haste to be punctual I have just bumped two of the world's most famous footballers, Carlos Valderrama and Faustino Asprilla, out of the way.

I am ten minutes early and find the lobby awash with young Latinos videoing their mothers hugging international football stars and getting signatures on inflated plastic footballs. Against one wall there's a gaggle (well, three anyway) of badly dressed hacks, fags in mouth, pens behind ear, notepads clamped under the arm.

'He's still in bed,' says the man from the FA. 'He only arrived last night and so I haven't seen him or spoken to him.'

'So he doesn't know I'm coming then?'

'That's right. You'll have to grab him when he comes down.'

So much for organisation, my first ever celebrity interview in Spanish, my first ever celebrity interview, and the celeb doesn't even know he's got an appointment. I wait.

The man from the Football Association assures me: 'There's no problem, they're a great bunch of lads, very friendly, easy to get on with, very free with their interviews. Now the Brazilians, when they came over for the Umbro Cup, now they were a different story . . .'

My problem is that Higuita, like all good keepers, has narrowed my options. His team-mates had arrived five days earlier without him, owing to 'passport problems'. I never found out what these were; somebody said that he hadn't enough space for a visa stamp in his book and had to wait for a replacement. Whatever the cause, the result is that he arrived on the Tuesday night – last night – and missed training. He plays tonight and leaves tomorrow at six in the morning. This is my only chance.

Thirty-five minutes pass without a sniff of the man, when suddenly there's a shout and a spontaneous scrimmage at the door to the lift. The hacks are there, the kids with the video cameras are there, their mothers are there. In fact the only one who's not there is me. At the centre of it all is a man with a chubby tanned face, black perm and Zapata moustache. I don't need this, there's no need to panic, I've got an appointment.

'Mr Higuita, over here. That's right, here I am,' I shout as the scrimmage rushes past me, past reception and out onto the street. The world's most famous goalkeeper is pinned against the railings of the hotel like a cabbage white in a young butterfly collector's first box. But it's all right, he'll be in in a moment and then I'll grab him.

And I was right, he was in in a moment, but the problem was that the in that he was in was a taxi speeding away from the hotel.

I slump into a chair and the atmosphere in the lobby calms down again. The hacks return. One, a Billy Bremner lookalike in his mid-50s, is very pleased with himself. Another, a fatter, younger man in acrylic trousers and a light-blue v-necked jumper that went out of fashion with Stig of the Dump, wipes a small river of sweat from his brow and boasts proudly to his mate:

'Brilliant, just two more to get and that's the lot. Anyone want to see my Seve Ballesteros 1989?'

Billy Bremner nods eagerly. Fat man flicks over a page of his big book.

'And that's Jack Nicklaus, oh and look at that one, that's Faldo. What do you think? I've got darts too if you want to see them.'

They're not hacks at all. They're autograph-hunters. Menopausal males spotting scribbles rather than choo-choos.

'He'll be back by two – he has to be back by two or he'll be in trouble with his manager,' says the man from the FA.

Two comes and goes, unlike Higuita; 2.30 and 2.40 pass, 2.45 comes and then he's back. Striding through the lobby in his blue-

and-white Cerveza Aguilar tracksuit. Like a video being rewound, the scrimmage reforms and transports him back to the lift from where he had been spewed two hours earlier. The autograph-hunters demand one more. In Spanish I demand my interview, but as the doors close behind him the only words emerging from behind the Zapata are 'Not today, not today.'

I wait in the bar with his manager's promise of an interview at 4 p.m., but I call his room every 20 minutes just in case.

In one corner of the bar a group of young Colombians sing drunken songs as a prelude to a noisy and violent ejection from the premises. In another, the soccer agent Eric Hall, trademark cigar in mouth, top button of his pink shirt undone, does business with clusters of grey-suited Colombians.

The autograph-hunters slump over a shared bottle of mineral water, talking confusingly of Wilf Mannion, Kevin Keegan, Eric Bristow and Sheena Easton. At the next table sits a woman with long straggly hair, wild staring eyes and woolly mauve leg-warmers. Five years ago she saw a picture of Higuita and had become infatuated. But her love at first sight, expressed in four sides of A4 air-mailed to Colombia, had been unanswered and now she's up from Torquay to throw herself at his feet. She had caused a bit of a stir on Saturday by refusing to believe that Higuita was not with the team. On Tuesday night – the night of his arrival – she had been found asleep in the doorway to his room and forcibly removed from the hotel. Now she's back again and waiting in line with the rest of us. Was that 'Misty' I could hear playing over the bar speakers?

Four o'clock passes and becomes five o'clock. The team coach arrives out front and is immediately booked for parking on a yellow line. Colombian footballers are ejaculated one by one from the elevator; bets are taken among the groupies on which one would be the next to appear: Valderrama, Rincon, Valencia, Alvarez, Asprilla . . .? The autograph-hunters rise to a frenzy, 'Play Misty for Me' twitches nervously, staring into the lift doors like they were the portals to heaven.

Finally, yes finally, Higuita emerges and cuts a brisk walk in the wrong direction – towards me. I take his arm, thank him for agreeing to the interview. He looks puzzled. The penny drops. He looks around him, snatches his arm back and turns on his heels towards the sanctuary of his team-mates, talking tactics behind closed restaurant doors. Flashlights light up the lobby like distress flares, young kids mob the disorientated keeper and 'Play Misty for Me' walks by his side, looks into his eyes and slides silently out of the hotel alone.

Next day the papers are full of it. 'HE'S FLIPPED HIS LID!' says *The Sun*. 'Keepers won't risk his party-piece.' In a well-contested game, in front of a near-empty Wembley, Colombia and England had fought out a skilful 0–0 draw. But not for the first time that 'fearless nutcase' Higuita had stolen the show with 'his save of the century' – the by now internationally acclaimed 'Scorpion Kick'.

> OLÉ! Colombian clown René Higuita is always game for a laugh and he proves it at Wembley with the amazing save he calls The Scorpion.
>
> At first the fans think that Tricky Higgy has made a right cock-up . . . but Colombia's flippin' marvel launches into his deadly donkey kick and leaves the fans in a state of Collapse . . .
>
> But just a word of warning from the crazy Colombian: 'Don't try it at home kids, you could end up giving yourself a nasty injury.'

From a Jamie Redknapp shot, that was probably intended to be a cross, Higuita had foregone the easy option of simply pluck-ing the ball from the sky with his hands. Instead, in what looked like a terrible misjudgement, he dived, arms outstretched, to the ground, swung his legs to the heavens and with the heels of his boots whacked the ball to safety. It was a remarkable moment from a remarkable keeper.

Introduction

'In my youth,' Father William replied to his son
'I feared it might injure the brain;
But now that I'm perfectly sure I have none
Why, I do it again and again.'
FROM *Alice's Adventures in Wonderland* BY LEWIS CARROLL

Sunday morning, 11.29 a.m.

And the question is . . .

Why?

Why am I here? Not in a Carl Sagan, Jesus Christ, Mayan Prophecy sort of way, but why am I standing here propped up by a flaky white post on a mud-drenched Clapham Common? There's no two ways about it, this is grim, bloody grim. Playing goalkeeper for the less than glorious Brixton Munchengladbach – an experience that has all the pleasure potential of a night out clubbing in downtown Grozny.

It's a cold and drenched Sunday morning, the sort of Sunday morning when I could be tucked up under my duck-down duvet, drinking a cup of steaming tea, skimming *The Observer*, reading the *News of the World*, preparing to remove *The Archers* from my airwaves and getting excited at the prospect of a repeat episode of *The Little House on the Prairie*.

It's the kind of Sunday that's made for a quiet stroll and a warm beer, followed by a cosy afternoon nap. But no, in the words of Martin Luther, here I stand. The pounding rain pummels my head. My legs and shirt, already ripped from the strain of previous incumbents, are caked in glutinous grey mud and I've let in six goals. Six! Real donkeys have beaten me half a dozen times and you know the worst thing? We're winning. Yes, it's that sort of game.

Fifty-five minutes gone and if I've touched the ball more than ten times, I'm Peter Schmeichel – I'm not, and more than half of those touches were to retrieve the ball from the back of the net. The fingertips of my right hand throb – purple from the smack of the ball as I bravely tipped an abysmal shot into the top netting, out of the easy reach of my own defender.

'Nick, you silly t**t, that was going out!' was just about the nicest thing anyone said to me at the time.

And now, as a man lets his dog cock its leg over our bags at the side of the goal and, as I berate him, I kid myself that I don't know why I'm here.

I'm standing here, dreading the thought that the ball might come my way, that somebody might shoot, that I might be called into action, for the simple reason that nobody else would go in goal. I'm in goal because it's my turn and it was goalie or wash the kit for the third week running. I'm in goal because I'm 36 and, it is said, a bit of a responsibility in the outfield these days. I'm here leaning on these posts, listening to myself talking to the crossbar, because I've got Achilles tendons so tight they hum G-sharp when I run, knees with the solidity of pease pudding and a stomach that has, in recent years, developed an independent and not totally inexpensive lifestyle all of its own. In the words of our captain: 'The thing about Nick is, his speed is deceptive – he's slower than he looks!'

But so what? This is not Wembley, it's park football, with pitches so narrow the corner flag's nearly in the penalty box and the next pitch is so close I could probably score in somebody else's game.

My goal-line has been obliterated by a horrible great puddle; any bigger and you'd need a permit to fish it. I made myself a promise at kick-off that whatever else happened I was not diving into that. But it wasn't a dive that got me in the end, it was a slip and a panic as the ball came towards me, sticking and slowing deceptively. It skimmed the water, passing through my sadly parted hands and legs as I closed my eyes to keep the splash out. Perhaps, if I added a little dive to the slip I might get away with a 'Hard luck, Nick' or a 'Don't worry mate, it was a rotten bounce. It can happen to anybody'. But no, it was a raised eyebrows and despairing, slapped thighs conversation, made worse by the laughs – yes, the laughs – of the opposition.

Why, oh why, be a goalkeeper?

In the line of fire

The first goalkeeper I ever came across was Jim Herriot, a gaunt, sharp-faced man, fit and agile but with the look of a 45-year-old even though he was probably little more than 26. Catch, bounce, bounce, bounce, bounce, run, bounce, kick he would go and the ball would sail off to the safety of the halfway line. In those Birmingham days of the mid-'60s the goalkeeper seemed to be more about standing, hands on hips and watching, than stopping shots. I don't remember Herriot being particularly spectacular, though I do remember the frequency with which he retrieved the ball from the back of the net. But he must have been quite good, because I can still recall the pride I felt when he played for Scotland and the feeling that I should perhaps as a mature six-year-old change my national allegiance.

He was a keeper, and it was a pride that I'd forgotten until a few years back when the other Herriot died. The one who always seemed to have his hands shoved firmly up some cow's bottom, who was forever drinking tea with Neanderthal northern farmers and who would incessantly row with a man called Siegfried about the spiralling cost of worming tablets. For the man who penned such classics as *All Creatures Great and Small* and *It Shouldn't Happen to a Vet* wasn't really called James Herriot – he was called James Wight OBE. He'd taken his name after watching Birmingham City, my Birmingham City, on one of their infrequent appearances on *Match of the Day*. He didn't name himself after a centre-forward, he didn't name himself after a full-back. No, the man who immortalised the Yorkshire Dales and its hyperactive sheep chose the name of a goalkeeper. Thank God Chelsea weren't playing; *Vets Might Fly* by Eddie Niedzwiecki doesn't have the same ring about it somehow.

Yet it should come as no surprise that the writing vet named himself after a goalie, for in so doing he was recognising what we all know, deep down, to be true – the most interesting character on a football field is the man between the sticks. For here is a position that over the years has attracted the daft and the divine, the intellectual and the dumb, the athletic and the obese. And even today in a sport that takes itself far too seriously for its own designer bootlaces, the goalkeeper's jersey provides an often gaudy vision of the absurd – a multi-coloured splash of hope.

It's something that some people have worried over for a long time. As far back as the last century one soccer manual, terrified at what goalies might get up to, was warning: 'Above all, never resort to "gallery play". The goalkeeper who does fancy tricks to "show off" before the spectators, or to obtain cheap applause, should be kicked out of any team. He is a conceited, selfish man, who sooner or later will make his side suffer while pandering to his own vanity.'

Thank God for the fact that goalkeepers have had the strength or possibly the ignorance to disregard such advice. Without such 'conceited' and 'selfish' play the game would be so much duller, since the bizarre accident, the freak injury, the spectacular blunder and the over-the-top showmanship that one has come to expect of the 'last defender', are what makes the goalkeeper one of modern sport's most flamboyant and startling inventions. Eccentricity and controversy gather at the goalie's feet like Tory ministers to a board meeting of a privatised public utility.

But what is it that is so special about playing between the posts? What is it about a profession that has united the likes of Banks, Shilton, Jennings and Yashin with Grobbelaar, Higuita, David Icke and the Pope? A profession that unites the great and the straight with the flaky and the often slightly wobbly.

When rival Colombian drug barons needed a kidnapping sorting out, was it any surprise that they chose none other than the nation's best and most renowned goalie, René Higuita, to act as their go-between? Is it a shock that Higuita found it more difficult getting out of jail than he did out of his penalty box?

Where else on the field would one have expected to find the football mad, but slightly asthmatic, revolutionary leader Che Guevara strutting his stuff other than between the posts?

Nowhere. Exactly!

For in both British and world soccer, the position of keeper has beguiled, and continues to beguile, some of football's strangest, most interesting and most entertaining players and some of its strangest and most unfortunate occurrences.

The story of goalkeeping is a story of glorious saves that have defied death and, on occasion, glorious saves that haven't. It's the story of keepers who design their own shirts and keepers who fight with their own defenders. It's about keepers who try to kill referees and keepers who become vicars, existentialist authors or smooth Spanish balladeers. Above all, it is about keepers who refused to change their underpants between games.

It is a tale of honest players and dishonest players, tricksters and athletes, show-offs and eccentrics and it is the tale of Lurch, the Clown, the Cat, El Condor, El Loco, the Black Octopus, the Black Spider, the Man in Black, the Flying Pig, Fatty and Little Willie.

Even now in these high-money, high-stake days, with modern goalkeeping a highly pressurised profession demanding skill and athleticism, concentration and judgement, there is still a place reserved for the oddball character or oddball moment. 'You don't have to be mad to work here, but it helps' applies only marginally more to alligator-wrestlers and significantly less to children's party entertainers than it does to goalkeepers.

After all, where else on the field could you expect to have a hand-grenade lobbed at you?

Ask Chic Brodie, he should know. Here was a man standing innocently keeping goal for Brentford against Millwall at Griffin Park in 1965 when, as half-time approached, he spotted a standard army issue grenade lying in the back of his net. He didn't see it coming and he didn't see it land and he was mightily relieved that he didn't see it going off. 'Jesus Christ, eh ref!' he screamed and did a runner. A bucket of sand was called for and PC 472 Pat O'Connell gingerly handed the bomb over to a Mr George Hill who – being a bit shocked when he saw what the policeman was holding in his hand – buried it in the bucket.

As it happens, the firing mechanism had been removed from the grenade and so no damage was done. The police later pointed out that the grenade was far from harmless: 'It weighs over a pound and that's solid iron. It could have seriously injured Brodie if it had hit him.'

Brodie was to have more perilous things to worry about than hand-grenades, but that's another story and we'll come to that in due course.

19

But if it's easier to be a goalkeeper if you don't mind re-enacting scenes from *All Quiet on the Western Front*, it's also a bonus if you are prepared to be lonely.

Outfield players may share and interchange kits and positions, but goalkeepers do not. They stand alone, detached from their colleagues and identified to the world by the different colour shirt they wear. In a world of soccer theory that talks of teamwork as 4-4-2s, 4-2-4s or 4-3-3s, it is easy to forget that there are actually 11 players to a side. Even the so-called 'total football' expounded by the Dutch is really only ten-elevenths total. Yet the keeper is further isolated by the fact that he is the only person who cannot escape his mistakes. It's a loneliness and a vulnerability that the goalie shares with few other sportsmen – though perhaps the cricket batsman would understand – reliant at the crucial moment not on the sustenance of others, but on pure reflex and wit.

Is there any greater illustration of this isolation than that drawn by Charlton keeper Sam Bartram? Back on Christmas Day 1937, Charlton were playing Chelsea at Stamford Bridge when all of a sudden, with half an hour left on the clock, a blanket of fog descended on the ground. With football impossible, the two managers walked onto the pitch and called their players off, and the game was abandoned. But only 21 made it back to the changing-room for, as the *Kentish Mercury* put it, 'Everybody knows where Moses was when the light went out, but where was Sammy Bartram when the fog came down on Christmas Day at Stamford Bridge?'

It's not as if there was a sudden realisation that there might be something untoward. Sam Bartram was left standing guard in his goalmouth for fully ten minutes, believing that his attackers were doing a grand job and that the ball was probably, even now, speeding towards his opposing number's goal. His team-mates were half-dressed and the 40,000 crowd all but out of the ground before, according to the same paper, 'someone shouted, "Oi! Where's Bartram?"' and a search party was despatched to find him. The *Mercury*'s reporter was puzzled. 'Whether he had lost his way in the fog, or whether he had not been told that the game had been called off, I don't know . . .'

Bartram was escorted home via the touchline, according to a report in the *Woolwich Gazette* headlined 'PHANTOMS AT STAMFORD BRIDGE — GAME ABANDONED WITH BARTRAM MISSING'. The headline says it all. This was Stamford Bridge, it wasn't a plane crash in the Amazon with 147 passengers missing, nor was it a boat capsized in the darker reaches of the Baltic Sea. It was a bit of fog sitting over a football game at a modern stadium. Yet nobody thought to tell the keeper that they were going off. Sam Bartram, in his lonely vigil as the last defender, was left standing on a deserted pitch in a deserted stadium, thinking that there was a game going on and that any moment now he might be called upon to intercept a cross.

And when things go wrong don't expect any sympathy – if you do, Alex Stepney can put you right. In his first season of professional football with Millwall he was playing away at Shrewsbury. The score was 1–1 and there was less than two minutes of the game left. All he had to do was take a goal-kick, but sometimes the simple things just aren't that simple. He placed the ball, retreated, measured his step, ran forward, swung his leg and caught a clump of earth with his boot. The ball rolled straight out to a Shrewsbury forward who returned it, as they say, with interest. Millwall had lost the game and the players had lost their bonuses. Stepney relates his particular loneliness in his imaginatively entitled autobiography *Alex Stepney*: 'On the field and in the dressing-room, the Millwall players gave me hell. They called me everything. There was nothing I could think of to say. I started to say "I'm sorry . . ." but they just looked at me with contempt.'

You also have to be prepared to be an undeserving scapegoat like, well, like Muamba Kazadi of Zaire who was substituted after letting in three goals against Yugoslavia in the 1974 World Cup finals. How can one be certain that it wasn't his fault and that he was a scapegoat? Well, because his replacement Dimbi Tubilandu conceded three more in his first 16 minutes and a further three by the end of the game. Zaire 0, Yugoslavia 9. Kazadi was back for the next game.

So my question is – and for what it's worth, I'm not sure there's a real answer – what sort of person becomes a goalkeeper? Does the position, with all its potential for public mockery and indignity but sometimes, conversely, instant glory, attract oddballs, mavericks, show-offs and dare-devils as well as athletes, or are they created by the game? Does the bravery and constant vigilance of the job with its fierce cut and thrust necessitate a modicum of craziness? Or the mentality of a psycho? Can standing within feet of thousands of baying and abusive fans send the goalie a little bit peculiar or bring on a dash of panache to keep them quiet? Is there something in the psyche of goalkeepers that makes them willing sacrificial lambs to very real and sometimes mortal dangers? Does having all that time between action give them the space to become more contemplative or withdrawn?

There are those of course who would deny that there is a case to answer. Frank Swift, the popular Manchester City and England keeper in the 1930s and '40s, was ardent in his objection. Writing in his autobiography *Football from the Goalmouth* he commented, 'I once heard it said that a goalkeeper was either born crazy, or else worked himself into that state. I must have been an exception. I'm not crazy, except at myself sometimes when I've made a silly mistake. Goalkeeping is just like any other position on the field. You just make up your mind to be a goalkeeper, and you either become one, or give up the game and take up ludo.'

But is it really such a long way from Big Swifty, the goalie who started his working life as the coke keeper of the Blackpool gasworks to Higuita the goalie who finished his as the coke keeper of the Medellin drugs cartel? Swift, who had huge 'frying-pan' hands and who, standing on tiptoe could touch his head on the crossbar, was an acknowledged character of his time. People would go to football matches especially to see him play and, anyway, as if to disprove his claims on sanity, he'd indulge in 'near-miss' boxing bouts with England's distinguished centre-forward Tommy Lawton – to the great amusement of the crowds and the terror of the national selectors.

It is very possible that the seeds of this madness, known in the medical world as *lunaticus goalkeeperus*, are sown at a very early age – and always have been.

In the last century picking schoolboy goalies was a cruel process, saying as much about your social standing as your ability, as one observer commented on football at Westminster School: 'The small boys, the duffers and the funk-sticks were the goalkeepers . . . If any player who was playing out showed any sign of funk or failed to play up, he was packed off into goal at once, not only for the day, but as a lasting degradation.'

A hundred years later in Birmingham's Lakey Lane Junior and Infants School, the school of my early childhood, little had changed and the procedure was still simple and clear cut. Break and dinnertime were begun with the ritual selection, a sort of fantasy football for seven-year-olds. We, the rabble, would line up against the crumbling brick wall, while the two best players alternately selected their teams. The bullies and big ones were called first, followed by the best players:

'I'll have Lee.'

'I'll have Barry.'

'Tony.'

And as the roll call went on and the selected prepared for kick-off, the butterflies fluttered in your stomach and disappointment grew, with each name that was not yours being a personal slur. Eventually (and after I'd been picked) we reached the dregs. The last two chosen could surmise several things about themselves: they almost certainly wore glasses, they were probably on the plump side, they were definitely unpopular and they were crap at soccer . . . oh and yes, they were in goal. Thus even at this tender age being goalkeeper was already a position for the outsider.

For some, at this age, keeping goal helps to resolve and work through childhood problems, ending up with them enjoying or needing the experience. David Icke, for one. The man in the turquoise tracksuit, otherwise known as former goalie, former broadcaster, former leader of Green Party and current number two in the Holy Trinity, is enlightening when it comes to explaining the pivotal role that goalkeeping played in his childhood. As he wrote in his autobiography *In the Light of Experience*, while living through a troubled and lonely childhood, 'the biggest boost to my self-respect and confidence, my salvation in so many ways during this period, was about to make its first appearance in my life. It was the game of football . . . I took to goalkeeping immediately and the more I played the more confident I became in myself as others recognised that I was pretty good for my age.'

Nothing is quite so straightforward in Icke's life, though. 'My growing self-confidence was not just due to the influence of football . . . I came under the influence of Mars' energies which not only led me into sport, but also activated feelings of determination and ambition . . . There was no doubt in my mind. I wanted to be a professional footballer and what's more I would be a professional, no question.'

The problem with Icke was that he wasn't really very interesting while he was a goalkeeper. When he retired at the age of 21 with rheumatoid arthritis, there were no shockwaves, no news flashes, not even any testimonials. As Jasper Carrott commented: 'David Icke says he's here to save the world. He saved bugger all at Coventry City.' Nor was he a great pitch entertainer in the way that, for example, Grobbelaar is – no swinging from the bar, no gambols along the goal-line or forays into the crowd. Nevertheless, while Icke was the journeyman goalie, it's clear that the seeds of his later eccentricity were there long before he had signed up as a professional.

So if it is true that young goalkeepers are very often poor athletes, bullied, loners or simply unpopular, at what point does one choose to become a keeper? At what point does the professional athlete step forward and claim this seemingly unglamorous role? At what point does one decide they want to be a goalie as opposed to being a doctor, a sheet-metal worker or even a centre-forward?

When the top Belgian team Standard Liege signed Michel Preud'homme at the age of five in 1964, their faith was rewarded – Michel went on to become not only the Belgian international keeper, but also 'the World's Best Goalkeeper'. But most keepers are a little more potty-trained than that when their moment arrives. So what is it that eggs them on? And, if the possibility exists that goalkeeping attracts characters, it is also certainly true that the nature of the job can mould and influence the nature of the player.

Goalkeeping is about beating the ball away from your goal by any means necessary. It's about standing up to opposition attackers and living with opposition supporters. No other position on the field carries such responsibility, nor such exposure – a defender who ducks out of a tackle will be forgotten, a striker who fluffs a chance may get another go, but a goalkeeper who misses a save will usually find a ball in the back of his net.

Yet in that moment when catastrophe is so near at hand, the game can also give to those it chooses. Gordon Banks' dazzling save against Pele of Brazil is still talked about by footballing anoraks over a quarter of a century later. Jim Montgomery's stunning double save back in 1973, which helped win the FA Cup for Sunderland against the near invincible Leeds United is still remembered affectionately by all those who hated the professional cynicism of Don Revie's all-conquering 'whites'. And a Polish goalie called Tomaszewski will live long in the hearts and minds of English fans for the night in 1974 when he prevented

England qualifying for the World Cup finals with a wonderful one-man show.

Where success and failure are such close colleagues, building a strategy for survival becomes the essence of quality goalkeeping. Courage and professionalism are one side of the goalkeeping equation, showmanship, eccentricity and a touch of the psycho are often the other side – I couldn't save that goal, but here's a glimpse of my bottom! Yes, I know I'm not particularly good in goals, but if I wear this strange hat I'll go down as a character. I'm sorry, ref, I'll go and fetch the centre-forward's head from the crowd now.

In a rather unscientific way this book intends to take a look at many of the incidents and characters that have plagued and populated the goalnets over the decades. It will look at the way the goalkeeper has had his role and his freedom eroded by watchful authorities and will ask whether the modern game, with all its tactical sophistication and its need to eliminate the erratic, has finally killed off the madman on the line.

It isn't a compendium of silly goalkeeping fluffs and nutty keepers. Many of us have our own favourite daft goalie story. There is a possibility that it is in this book, but there's a greater possibility that it isn't. A book that included all, or even the majority of such stories, would be almost impossible to write and not necessarily that entertaining to read. Instead *In the Way!* is a look at the trials and tribulations that have afflicted and will continue to afflict keepers. It takes a look at the special pressures that keepers face, the lives they lead and asks questions about the sort of person who is minded to don the gloves.

I Once upon a time in the nets

Sing ho! for the dauntless Goalie,
   Brave old Goalie!
     For shots galore will never score,
Sing ho! for the dauntless Goalie!
     Rushing out to meet his man,
       Greek to Greek!
   Showing judgments' reason'd plan –
       Never weak!
FROM 'THE GOALKEEPER' IN *At the Football Match – a wreath of lyrical poems and songs* BY S. HENRY EACHUS, 1910

Lord Arthur Fitzgerald Kinnaird was a half-back, a centre-half, a centre-forward and, with his fulsome red beard, athletic frame and reputation as a hard man, one of the great figures of 19th-century football. He also occasionally put in an appearance between the posts.

It was in this capacity, as custodian of the Wanderers in the 1877 FA Cup final that he made what was possibly the very first recorded goalkeeping gaffe.

It wasn't his favourite position by a long chalk, but Wanderers were short of a keeper and Kinnaird, being of an obliging nature, donned the gloves. As he stepped onto the field, though, the one thing he wasn't prepared for was a public humiliation. Sadly for him it's what he got. With the game barely a few minutes old, Oxford University's half-back Waddington fired a long ball into the box. Kinnaird collected it neatly and stepped back – too far.

Inadvertently his lordship had crossed his own goal-line. There was an appeal, a consultation of umpires and a goal awarded.

It wasn't disastrous – the goal added much-needed vigour and determination to the Wanderers attack who squared the game and then won it 2–1 in extra-time, but Lord Arthur couldn't take the stigma.

Not being the duelling-pistols-at-dawn type, nor the suicide-by-hanging-from-the-rafters-of-the-country-seat type, Kinnaird wasn't too proud to beg. As a man of influence he pleaded with the Football Association not to leave him with the lasting infamy of having scored an own-goal in a cup final. At a specially convened meeting a few days later it was agreed, the score was altered and 2–0 to the Wanderers became the official result. As Stalin was to airbrush Trotsky from Lenin's side, so too did this most noble of footballers arrange for his own personal history of the cup to become the accepted version. Kinnaird o.g. was erased from the FA's records and to this day does not appear in them.

Kinnaird went from strength to strength, winning five FA Cup-winner's medals, rising to the dizzy heights of President of the Football Association and, in 1912, being presented with the trophy for keeps. What the letters L-o-r-d before your name could do back then.

In those early days of organised soccer, Kinnaird's reluctant willingness to play keeper typified the uncertain and uneasy status the position of goalkeeper enjoyed – a status that in some ways it retains right down to the present day. For the goalkeeper was a newcomer at the ball game, an invention born out of necessity; but unlike the telephone, the radio or penicillin, there was no father claiming paternity.

For a brief period in the 1860s there could have been a Victorian music-hall joke that went something like 'What's got 22 legs and two behinds?' To which the answer, amid spontaneous and uproarious laughter, would have been 'An association foot-ball team'. Admittedly it hardly ranks alongside such classics as 'Why did the submarine blush?' 'Because it saw the *Queen Mary*'s bottom!' or 'Mary had a little lamb, she also had a bear; I've often see her little lamb, but I've never seen her bear!', but at least it's true.

For in the eight years following the formation of the Football Association in 1863 there was only one type of football team, that with nine forwards and two behinds. Not for the early pioneers were there to be technical discussions on the relative merits of 4-4-2 as against the diamond formation; no 'Christmas Tree' preferred to the sweeper system. And most importantly, no officially recognised goalkeeper.

Not until 1871 did goalkeepers appear on the statute book for the first time – a player specifically, but reluctantly, created to act as the last defender, who could handle the ball anywhere in his own side's half.

In the previous eight years the Fair Catch rule had allowed any player to catch the ball and, provided they made a mark in the pitch with their boot, take a free-kick. It did not, however, permit running with the ball in the hands, nor scoring from a throw. Nevertheless, for a brief period in history, 'We are all goalkeepers' was a popular sentiment.

This is not to give the impression that the idea of goalkeeper was plucked from the firmament in a 'Eureka!'-style moment of Victorian clarity. Oh no. Goalkeepers had been hanging around the periphery for some time. At that crucible of early soccer, Westminster School in the 1840s, a tradition was being born: 'Two of the biggest boys would choose sides, and when the best players had been called alternately to either side, the second-class performers would range themselves on which side they pleased. The small boys and beginners were posted as goalkeepers . . .'

In Sheffield too, where football was played to its own rules, goalkeepers were recognised at a much earlier stage: 'Any player between an opponent's goal and the goalkeeper (unless he has followed the ball there) is offside and out of play. The goalkeeper is that player on the defending side who, for the time being, is nearest to his own goal.'

In 1871, with the recognition of goalies by the Football Association, the lid was taken off a Pandora's Box that was to set loose on an unsuspecting world a whole vast array of oddballs. If hope was the only commodity left in Pandora's casket, perhaps sense was the last remnant in football's equivalent.

Yet the early goalkeepers were just so respectable – proper gentlemen like Lord Kinnaird, like Captain (later Colonel) Merriman of the Royal Engineers, like C.E. Hart, future treasurer of the FA, and like Major Sir Arthur Francis Marindin.

Marindin was the founder of the Royal Engineers Football Club and president of the FA from 1874 to 1890. He was captain and full-back of the Engineers, but he also played in goals for Old

Etonians. When his two clubs met in the 1875 FA Cup final, he did the only thing a true gentleman could do and withdrew his services from both.

Marindin and Kinnaird with their abundance of positions were examples of an inevitable early confusion over just who exactly was a keeper and who wasn't. The great Scottish keeper H.G. Rennie began his career as a half-back; fellow Scot George Gillespie was a full-back. As late as 1930 Roy John was transferring from Swansea to Walsall as a full-back, but after going in goals in an emergency he decided that he liked it so much that he made a career out of it, becoming the Welsh international keeper.

Dramatically, the Dumbarton keeper James McAulay who, during the 1880s was the first custodian to earn the nickname 'Prince of Goalkeepers', had before that built a successful career as a centre-forward, winning his first international cap for Scotland as an outfield player and actually scoring for Dumbarton in the 1883 Scottish Cup final.

It was only after that match, with the regular keeper John 'Diver' Kennedy suffering a terrible loss of form, that McAulay tried his hand between the posts. A legend was born. In the following years, until work forced him to go abroad in 1887, McAulay was Dumbarton's number one and won a further eight caps for Scotland in that position.

When he left the country in 1887 the press lavished his all-round abilities with fulsome praise: 'As a back he kicks and tackles brilliantly, as a forward most judicious and sometimes a very good shot. But it was as a goalkeeper that his greatness was revealed on taking up the position. Intrepid, cool to the point of nonchalance and maker of numerable saves with hands and feet.'

And when you weren't a gentleman with extensive lands in Perthshire like Kinnaird, you had to be able to make a bob elsewhere. This period, when goalkeeping was establishing itself, coincided with the fight for professional football. Goalkeepers, being the most vulnerable players on the field, had to make sure of an income by filling in with another trade. McAulay supplemented his footballing by working as an engineer for the Irrawaddy Navigation Steam Company in Burma, which may have been a bit extreme, but Jack Baynton of Wolves was a teacher, Robert Downie of Third Lanark a calico printworker and Welsh international Leigh Richmond Roose was an unqualified doctor and bacteriologist.

The reluctant acceptance of professionalism by the football authorities gave the game an attraction to a groundswell of men who had made their names in other sports too, men ideally suited to a life between the posts. Kinnaird had excelled at tennis, athletics and canoeing; Queen's Park and Scotland keeper Archibald Rowan was a famous cricketer; and John Sutcliffe, who made a career at Bolton, was a former England international rugby player.

Sutcliffe had won his rugby cap against New Zealand in 1889, but later that year he was suspended from the game for professionalism. Turning to soccer, his like of the rough and tumble, his ability to catch and dive, plus his speed (he was Bolton's fastest player over both 120 and 440 yards) made him a natural keeper, and within four years he was England's number one. He kept goal for Bolton for 11 seasons and in the process became their first player to be sent off, for dissent in a game with Sheffield Wednesday.

With time the keeper's jersey was to attract other sportsmen. William Foulke played a season of cricket with Derbyshire, scoring a whirlwind 53 on his debut against Essex; Howard Baker of Chelsea and England was six times high-jump champion of Britain; and Hibernian's William Harper was a heavyweight boxing champion in the Scots Guards.

As one might expect, professionalism and goalkeeping were not always free from controversy. The case of James Trainer shows that even as early as the 1880 a good goalkeeper was a thing worth fighting for.

Trainer, who was also a coach-builder, took to goalkeeping with some reticence, but at the age of 19 he played his first game for his home town, Wrexham. A year later he was on the run from the Welsh Football Association after a ferocious FA Cup tie with Oswestry. During the course of the game he was alleged to have insulted the referee. The English FA kicked Wrexham out of the tournament and called on their Welsh counterpart to sort out Trainer, but by the time they had got their act together he was gone. The Great Lever Football Club of Lancashire had tempted him with the mouth-watering offer of 30/- a week and, having failed to find him work, they struck the revolutionary deal of paying him 13/- a week over the summer to retain his services.

He was, however, soon the subject of competing clubs desperate for his signature. Bolton won. They paid him 50/- a week and then to end the auction handed him a fiver and sent him packing with his girlfriend to the Isle of Man until the new season started. As the 1885–86 season began the angry chairman of Great Lever publicly condemned Trainer: 'I hope when he's coming home his boat will go down, and everybody will be saved excepting him'.

Trainer played two seasons for Bolton before being snapped up by the 'Invincibles' of Preston North End, who considered him 'as safe as a sandbag' on the basis of a Bolton v Preston game in which he had conceded a mere 12 goals!

Trainer's Preston career was to extend beyond his playing days and for a while he enjoyed great success. Twenty caps for Wales whilst playing, director of the club in later years, but let down by his personal life. In 1904 he separated from his wife and ten children and thus began a slippery slide into oblivion that would become familiar to many a keeper in subsequent years. He resigned his directorship of Preston, took on a dodgy soccer business enterprise involving an indoor exhibition at London Olympia, got himself banned by the FA when the scheme collapsed, and died in poverty in 1915. Contemporary stories talk of his arrival at the hotel of the Welsh national side on international match days and hanging around the lobby to cadge money from his old team-mates.

It is sometimes difficult to reconcile these facts with a description of Trainer in 1899 as 'one of the most gentlemanly of players and a good sportsman to boot'. Trainer was clearly a charmer.

In the meantime, new rules and new practices were changing the goalkeeper's on-pitch activities. In 1875 goalposts were topped by a bar instead of a tape and the normal practice of swapping ends after each goal was abandoned. New laws on barging keepers were designed to relieve the fear of grievous bodily harm every time the goalie went for the ball. In January 1891 goalnets, supplied by Brodie of Liverpool, were used for the first time in an important game, The North versus The South, and on 6 June 1891 James Connor of Airdrieonians faced the first ever penalty, taken and scored by a man called McLuggage who played for Royal Albert.

At this time penalties were taken, as now, from 12 yards out, and a line six yards out marked the limit to which the keeper could come to save the shot. After 1905 keepers were forced to stand on their goal-line for penalties, and in 1929 they were made to keep still until the kick was taken.

If nothing else, rule changes gave new opportunities for keepers to cover themselves in glory. On 13 February 1909, for example, Grimsby Town faced Burnley away and Walter Scott, Grimsby's keeper, found himself on the receiving end of four penalties. Amazingly, Scott saved three of them and, as the *Grimsby Daily Telegraph* reported, 'This remarkable feat, which we believe is unequalled in league football, greatly astonished the crowd, but they warmly appreciated Scott's performance, and he was the hero of the match.' None of which prevented Grimsby losing 2–0!

Changes in the laws of the game were frequent in these, the early days of football. Goalkeepers often found themselves on the butt end of such amendments, none more so than in 1912 when new rules banned the keeper from handling the ball outside a newly marked penalty area. Having been accustomed to handling the ball at will in their own half it may, to some keepers, have seemed like a form of imprisonment. In many cases, though, practice was running ahead of theory and this was one example. For a number of years team-mates and team managers had been discouraging what was seen as a dangerous and risky tactic. The *Edinburgh Evening News* clearly believed so in 1907:

> Nine out of ten goalkeepers do not take many risks in the matter of running out of goal, but this is obviously a policy which must be dictated by the circumstances of the game. It is, however, generally disparaged, and there is reason to believe that the extent to which your favourite Rennie practises it has lost him the confidence of the Scottish Football Association selectors.

The pace of change also allowed keepers to be instrumental in the creation of new laws. In December 1894 Herbert 'Herbie' Arthur, the good 'but somewhat excitable keeper of Blackburn Rovers', was just such a custodian, whose actions in another astonishing game involving Burnley led to alterations and controversy.

The problem was the weather, and it would, according to the *Burnley Express and Advertiser*, 'be almost impossible for a football match to be fought out under more unfavourable conditions'. Torrential rain and freezing wind throughout the week had turned into a snowstorm without mercy on the morning of the game. But a big crowd had turned up at Turf Moor for the local derby and officials were reluctant to disappoint the supporters, so 'Rovers started out downhill in the teeth of a heavy snowstorm made worse by the strong wind behind it . . .'

Fierce local rivalry compounded by the awful weather made it an ugly and vicious contest. One correspondent called it 'the roughest match I have witnessed, and I hope it will never fall to my lot to see another such'.

Burnley were the superior team, but from the outset Arthur was up to his tricks, most audaciously trying to take advantage just before half-time when Bowes scored a third Burnley goal: 'The Rovers' custodian, who seemed to take the ball from underneath the net from the outside, was placing the sphere for a goal-kick, but Mr Clegg [the referee] had no hesitation in allowing the goal.'

Thoroughly demoralised, soaked to the skin and desperate to abandon the game, the Rovers team spent half-time negotiating with the referee and Burnley officials. Their offer to give Burnley two points for a victory was to no avail. Having listened to 15 minutes of whining, the referee restarted the game; four of the Blackburn players lingered in the changing-room, straggling on minutes after the restart.

Trouble was not long in coming. Blackburn's winger Lofthouse and Stewart of Burnley were involved in an unnecessarily crude clash and it was snowballs at five paces. Mr Clegg jumped in and ordered them off the field, but the game was about to descend into deep farce.

Whether in protest at the dismissal, or simply fearing the imminent onset of frostbite, the whole of the Blackburn Rovers team seized the opportunity and walked off – the whole of the Blackburn Rovers team that is, with the exception of one Herbie Arthur. 'Rambler' of the *Lancashire Evening Express* takes up the story:

> The affair was not totally void of the comical. Arthur alone of the Rovers, remained on the field. The referee blew his whistle for play to proceed, and Burnley threw the ball in from the touch-line, that being where the row occurred. Arthur ran towards his goal surrounded by opponents, and I wondered what he would do. When within a few yards of the mouth he stopped, and turning round

coolly appealed for offside. Roars of laughter greeted him from all quarters of the field.

Clegg granted the appeal, Arthur rolled the ball into his net and the game was abandoned.

A couple of weeks later the FA met in special session, suspended both Lofthouse and Stewart and then passed a resolution prohibiting players from leaving the pitch without the referee's permission.

The goalkeepers were beginning to take the piss, and it was having an effect. The Football Association had noticed.

Fat Willie and the Archdeacon

As football grew in popularity during the 1890s and the first decade of the new century, so too did the seriousness with which the players took their task. Goalkeepers were no exception and, as a whole cottage industry developed publishing football annuals, so the 'expert advice' for keepers increased. Some stuck to the field of play:

> As a rule he is a spectator during most of the game, but the short spells of occupation he has bring into play qualities which are not a *sine qua non* for any other position in the field. He must be cool, quick-witted, without hesitation, and free from flurry. He should be sturdy and strong in body, arms and legs.

Others, such as England international keeper Jack Robinson, acted as premature, turn-of-the-century Claire Rayners with words of warning on lifestyles:

> SELF-DENIAL
> Eat well, but never be gluttonous. Don't spend your time and money in the many light-refreshment rooms which flourish in our towns, to the ruination of many a good digestion. Sweets, ices, pastry and other such rubbish are not natural foods and indulgence in eating them is bound to clog the muscles and produce shortness of wind . . .

All of which was ever so slightly ironic in view of Robinson's famous craving for rice pudding. 'No pudding, no points' was the warning that rang in the ears of Robinson's Derby County team-mates, and on the one match day that he missed his favourite indulgence, Sunderland put 11 past him.

Some keepers turned to science. At Greenock Morton Scottish goalie Harry Rennie was the first to mark his area out and to calculate the angles from which crosses and shots could be hit at him; off the pitch he risked severe personal damage by spending as much as 30 minutes a day locked in the dressing-room, diving on to piles of rough boards to harden his torso for the fray.

But as the crowds grew and the stakes rose, others turned to superstition. Robinson had a custom of hanging his watch on a special nail at the back of the goalposts, until one day an away supporter jumped the fence before the teams entered the field and removed the makeshift hook. Oh, how they laughed as his little routine was thrown into chaos. Elisha Scott of Liverpool would arrive two hours before kick-off, change alone, warm-up and then, to the chagrin of his team-mates, bounce a ball against a wall for an hour. With minutes to go before kick-off he'd put on two more shirts and another pair of socks, irrespective of the weather. Perhaps he was just taking note of the motherly advice handed out to keepers in 1899: 'Be sure to keep warm. Have good warm woollen clothing, but leave the limbs as free and unencumbered as possible.'

Woolwich Arsenal's James Ashcroft, writing on goalkeeping in J.A. McWeeney's *Football Guide or how to play Soccer* in 1906, listed the necessary attributes to good keeping as height, speed and nerves of steel. He emphasised the need for robustness, but not just in the face of marauding centre-forwards: 'You must stand very frequently on damp grass, shivering with cold and inviting an onslaught from pneumonia or the influenza fiend. If you are constitutionally strong you can laugh at damp, colds in the head and rheumatic twinges.'

This would be helped by proper and developed concentration: 'Do not spend your time, when the ball is away up the field, leaning listlessly against the goalpost, or chatting with your friends behind the net.'

And the keepers were giving the crowd plenty to talk about, for there were already many characters playing between the posts and plenty of incidents to keep them chattering. These included 'Happy' Jack Hillman of Burnley and Manchester City who once won a £5 wager that he could keep a clean sheet with one arm tied behind his back; Albert Iremonger, who raced up the field to take a penalty for Lincoln only to see it smash against the bar and rebound over the halfway line, from where it was punted into his empty net; and Charlie Williams, whose unorthodox style may well have kept him out of the England team, and whose most famous moment was a phenomenal clearance that ended up in the back of Sunderland's goal.

But two men stand out as symbols of both the confidence and the showmanship that had become attached to goalkeepers, two men whom crowds would make a special journey just to get a glimpse of. They were William Foulke and Leigh Richmond Roose. The careers of Foulke and Roose have attracted their own mythologies down the years and more's the pity because the true story of these two titans of eccentricity needs little exaggeration.

William Foulke or Foulkes, or Fat Willie or Fatty Foulke or Baby, was a giant of a man, clocking in at the twilight of his days at more than 28 stone. He was simply the heaviest man ever to play for England and surely the largest man to ever make a successful career in goals. During his playing days, from 1894 to 1907, he was described as the most famous man of his time and was an exception that James Ashcroft was happy to make when describing his ideal keeper:

> Moreover, a goalkeeper must not carry too much flesh. The great Foulke may be instanced as an argument against my contention, but it must be remembered that the old Sheffield United man is a law unto himself. Take a thousand men of Foulke's bulk and you probably would not find one to compare with him for a moment in the matter of rapid agility and rapid action.

Foulke was born in April 1874, and as the illegitimate son of Mary Ann Foulke was taken at just a few weeks old from his mother's home near Telford to live with his grandparents at Blackwell in Derbyshire. It was here that he grew up and here that he went down the pit like any normal lad. That is until one day in 1894 when news of a young collier keeping goal for Blackwell spread like wildfire throughout the pit villages of north Derbyshire. The local team had given Derby County a run for their money and their marvel of a goalkeeper had excelled himself, despite (or perhaps especially when) mis-punching a ball and knocking out the two front teeth of Derby forward John Goodall.

Derby wanted him, but Foulke delayed signing on the advice of his brother, who said they'd be back with a better offer. In the meantime his reputation had reached as far as Sheffield, and, further bolstered by the glowing report of a Mr Swaine of Heeley who had refereed a game involving the soon-to-be big man, Sheffield United swooped. They offered Foulke £5 for signing and paid the Blackwell club a sweetener of £1 for each of the few days of the season left.

As United's representative Joseph Tomlinson left the room with Foulke's signature safely tucked away in his bag, he passed the Derby people in the corridor. They were returning with the predicted improved offer, but Tomlinson had a big smile on his face – he had pipped them at the post, Foulke was his. Later that week the management of Nottingham Forest arrived at the pit-head and summoned Foulke up from the coal-face only to discover that their journey too had been wasted.

Sheffield's efforts were well rewarded, for although Foulke was to become a human dirigible over the coming years – 14st 12lbs in 1895, 19st 8lbs in 1899, 22st 8lbs in 1902 and thereafter reaching as much as 28st – he was to provide excellent service to United for 11 seasons and to become one of the great entertainers of the game.

Foulke combined many precious talents: a genuinely gifted goal-saver virtually unbeatable on high shots and smart on low, hard shots, he was also incredibly powerful for his day, being able to punch or throw the ball further than most players could kick it. He was equipped with a marvellous sense of humour and would build a great rapport with the crowds, who turned up not only to see the giant that everybody was talking about, but also because when Foulke took to the pitch you never knew what to expect.

From the off he was a figure of some renown. In November 1894 Foulke was one of several United men carried off the field in awful conditions at Aston Villa. A bitter wind and freezing sleet ripped through the two teams as Ernest Needham, the Sheffield captain, later recalled: 'Even Foulkes was carried in completely exhausted. Several of the Villans did what playing they could in greatcoats, and one used an umbrella.' Needham was presumably thankful that this took place in the early stages of the keeper's career, while it was still just about possible to carry him from the field.

In February 1897, on a weekend when neither club had a fixture, the United and Sheffield Wednesday first teams took over a reserve-team fixture at Bramall Lane. More than 6,000 were watching when, just after half-time, a peculiar incident occurred: 'Brush sent in a long, dropping shot, which went straight for goal, and Foulkes jumped up to clear. He missed the ball and caught the cross bar, snapping it clean in two.' Foulke was left lying spread-eagled on the ground, covered in splinters and netting. 'Another bar had to be requisitioned . . . to the great delight of the crowd, who indulged in sarcastic remarks at the carpentering efforts . . . The first bar which was brought proved too short, and a second had to be brought, and this was fixed up amidst loud cheers . . .'

Against a team of black South Africans known as the Kaffirs, touring the country at the time of the Boer War in 1899, Foulke, bored by the lack of action in his own half of the field, evacuated his goal and rampaged up front like a rogue bull elephant. The *Sheffield Daily Telegraph* reported the next day that 'his ponderous thumps and throws were viewed with undisguised amazement and wonder by the dusky visitors'. Not to mention the two goals he put past the diminutive African keeper Thwayi.

As a bit of a joker it was often difficult to separate the totally necessary act from the desire to please the crowd. At Chelsea, to whom he moved in 1905, it was said that he once appeared wrapped in a white bath towel because his colours clashed with the opposing team and there was no other shirt big enough for him to play in.

In this role as club comedian, Foulke developed sensitive antennae to the state of team morale. Long after his retirement from the game in 1907 he gave an interview to the *London Evening News* in which he emphasised this:

Nobody is fonder of fun or 'divvlement' than I am . . . I don't mind admitting that I think I had as much as most men during my football career. To my mind almost the best time for a joke is after the team has lost.

When we'd won I was as ready to go to sleep in the railway carriage as anybody. All was peace and comfort then! But when we lost I made it my business to be a clown. Once when we were very disappointed I begged some black stuff from the engine-driver and rubbed it over my face. There I was sitting on the table and playing some silly game, with all the team around me, laughing like kiddies at a Punch and Judy show, when some grumpy committeeman looked in. Ask the old team . . . if a bit of Little Willie's foolery didn't help to chirp 'em up before a tough match.

Another illustration of his sense of humour was reported in the *Athletic News*:

Foulke was sitting in a railway carriage, eating bread and cheese with the relish of a Spanish onion and the aid of a clasp knife. A curate in the opposite corner, meaning to be friendly, remarked: 'My friend, I see that you are an epicure.' Foulke, stunned by the word, regained his speech and answered: 'Oh, am I? Then you're a —.' The final word was more unparliamentary than that which Mr Bernard Shaw employed once in *Pygmalion and Galatea*. The curate was silent.

The curate should have known better than to comment on the big man's eating habits. At Chelsea it was reported that his team-mates came down to breakfast one morning to find that all 11 meals had already been consumed. In the face of hungry abuse Foulke's reply was simple: 'I don't care what you call me as long as you don't call me late for dinner.'

But it wasn't all good humour. The flipside to Foulke's amiable nature was a short fuse and explosive temperament. He was a big man and, like all big men, was often seen as a challenge for others. It wasn't a sentiment Willie admired. He let fly at Trent Bridge in September 1898 when, during a Notts County attack, there was a pile-up in his area. Foulke took exception to the opposing winger and lashed out at him. It created a sensation, and irate County fans poured over the barriers onto the pitch and 'showed their feeling by hooting the big Sheffield custodian in very hearty fashion'. The disturbance lasted two or three minutes, during which time Foulke was cautioned by the referee. The whistle for half-time sounded soon after and the Sheffield keeper was booed to the rafters as he left the field.

A month later at Anfield there began an acute and abrasive rivalry with Liverpool centre-forward George Allan, a rivalry that was to spice up the many meetings between the two teams over the next few seasons. In an exciting match Sheffield took a 1–0 lead into half-time, but shots had rained down on their goal and they only remained in the game through a combination of

Foulke's brilliance and Liverpool's bad fortune. There are many versions of what was about to happen.

Apparently before the game the Liverpool forward Allan had 'sworn to knock Foulke into the back of the net' and Foulke was tiring of his attempts. While clearing a shot from Robertson, Foulke was charged heavily by Allan and, according to the *Liverpool Football Echo*, 'the big man, losing his temper, seized Allan illegitimately and turned him upside down'. Other accounts talked of Foulke standing Allan on his head and bouncing him up and down in the mud, or potting him in the penalty area like a wilting aspidistra.

The referee awarded a penalty which McCowie duly put away, equalising for Liverpool and providing the platform from which they would subsequently win the game.

The Allan–Foulke discord added an extra frisson to Liverpool v Sheffield United games for seasons to come, although nothing as dramatic occurred again despite the tension of a cup semi-final that year that took four games to settle.

Talking in 1913 about the incident, Foulke tried to play down the whole affair as a product of Edwardian media hype:

> You may have heard that there was a very great rivalry between the old Liverpool centre-forward, Allan, and myself; that prior to one match we breathed fire and slaughter at each other, that at last he made a rush at me as I was saving a shot, and that I dropped the ball, caught him by the middle, turned him clean over in a twinkling, and stood him on his head, giving him such a shock that he never played again.
>
> Well, the story is one which might be described as a 'bit of each'. In reality Allan and I were quite good friends off the field. On it we were opponents, of course, and there's no doubt he was ready to give chaff for chaff with me. What actually happened . . . was that Allan (a big strong chap, mind you) once bore down on me with all his weight when I was saving.
>
> I bent forward to protect myself, and Allan, striking my shoulder flew right over me and fell heavily. He had a shaking-up, I admit, but quite the worst thing about the whole business was that the referee gave a penalty against us, and it cost Sheffield United the match.

All of which might be a tad more believable if he didn't claim complete innocence every time.

A year before the Allan incident, in 1897, Foulke had provoked a mini riot against Liverpool's neighbours Everton. He'd played a major part in a thrilling game which Sheffield United won 4–1, but just after United had scored their fourth Everton broke through and forced a save from the big man. Everton fans claimed that Foulke bowled their forward Bell over, rubbed his nose in the mud and lifted him up with one hand for his trainer to sort out. Furious, they forced the game to be held up for several minutes as they pelted the United keeper with stones. Years later he once again dismissed the incident as a regrettable accident: 'Just as I was reaching for a high ball Bell came at me and the result of the collision was that we both tumbled down, but it was his bad luck to be beneath and I could not prevent myself from falling with both knees in his back.'

Foulke weighed 22½ st at the time and when he saw Bell's face he 'got about the worst shock I ever have had on the football field. He looked as if he was dead.' Thinking that he'd killed the Everton man, Foulke claims to have been overcome with fear. 'I picked him up in my arms as tenderly as a baby and all I could say was "Oh dear! Oh dear!"' In actual fact Bell was okay and lived to fight another day.

Foulke did, however, acknowledge in the same interview that at times it was all he could do to control his temper in the face of aggressive opponents anxious to get their name on the score sheet. 'You might have thought,' he said, 'that forwards would steer clear of such a big chap. Some did, but others seemed to get wild when they couldn't get the ball into goal and I suffered a lot through kicks administered when the referee wasn't looking.'

It was probably down to his extravagance, his showmanship and his irascibility that Foulke failed to make it big on the international scene. In truth there were few goalkeepers to match his ability and he was the victim of good fortune on the night he won his one and only England cap in 1897, for England thrashed Wales 4–0 at Bramall Lane. Foulke was called upon to do next to nothing and hence missed out on his one big opportunity to impress the international selectors.

With little to write home about in representational terms therefore (he did play for a Football League XI on two occasions against Scotland), helping to win the league for Sheffield United in 1898 by conceding only 31 goals and his three appearances in FA Cup finals were the centrepieces of Foulke's career.

Twice he walked away with an FA Cup-winner's medal. In 1899 Sheffield United cowed Derby 4–1 at Crystal Palace, the reporter from the *Sheffield and Rotherham Independent* noting the 'ripple of amused wonder as Londoners surveyed the dimensions of the United Mammoth as he stalked majestically to his place between the goalposts'. Foulke had sufficient breath left at the end of the game that, when the trophy was presented by the Leader of the House of Commons (and soon to be Prime Minister) A.J. Balfour, he was able to give him a mouthful and tell him he didn't think that he was up to the job. A few days later he confided to a journalist that he 'didn't think much of Mr Balfour'.

In 1901 Sheffield United were back, to take on the amateurs of Tottenham Hotspur in front of a huge crowd of more than 111,000. Spurs won 3–1 in a replay at Bolton after the first game was drawn. An upset Foulke walked away with his reputation intact, though a little tarnished after several erratic runs way out of goal that had sent tingles of trepidation down the spines of the United fans.

The following year, 1902, was a different story. It had been a rather shaky campaign in which the United team had won in spite of a series of hapless performances and a number of blunders by Foulke. They faced Southampton in the final. A very dull game was all but over, United were a goal up and the south-coast supporters were streaming out of the stadium when, with one last thrust, Southampton broke through and from an apparently offside position Wood beat Foulke and equalised. Referee Kirkham consulted his linesman and, to the dismay of the Sheffield players, ruled that the ball had hit United player Peter Boyle, putting Wood onside. He awarded a goal and shortly after blew for full-time.

Foulke was disgusted, and as the Sheffield team left the pitch trouble broke out around the mouth of the players' exit: 'The players had a little difficulty to reach their dressing-rooms. Foulke seemed irritated during his progress between the files of policemen, and Needham turned round on some objectionable person and promptly showed a desire to teach a lesson by physical force . . .'

As Lord Kinnaird, now the President of the FA, made a speech singling out the merits of the Sheffield keeper he could little have known that Foulke was, according to legend, at that very moment nakedly wandering the changing area stalking someone, anyone, to vent his anger on. According to this much told story, while soaking in the bath Foulke got so angry about the Southampton equaliser that he leapt up and, towel-less, went on a referee hunt. Meanwhile, Tom Kirkham, fearing the possibility that he might become Foulke's next meal, had locked himself away in a boot cupboard, but still only survived when various officials, including the secretary of the Football Association, dragged the crazed keeper away.

This seems a highly unlikely story, if not only because just a week later Kirkham refereed the replay with no fear and no obvious antagonism from Foulke.

However, at the replay 'Tityrus', the reporter of the *Athletic News*, was soon to discover that Sheffield's anger hadn't fully subsided. Scouting around the United changing area for information he was confronted by Peter Boyle, who demanded to know whether in his match report Tityrus had written that Boyle was to blame for the Southampton equaliser. Tityrus admitted that he had, and a livid Boyle prepared to pulverise him. Remembering the incident years later, the reporter recalled:

> Just at the crisis when Boyle might have carried his ultimatum into execution, who should step out of his cubicle, or dressing box, but good Master Foulke, 19st 7lb of perfect nakedness. He looked down at me, and with his lusty voice and a smile which would have set a Quaker's meeting in a roar, said: 'I'm your man for a fight. You're just about my weight.' As I was under 5ft and scaled less than 11st in the Turkish Bath, the reader can imagine this sally was the restorative of good humour, although Ernest Needham, wise as ever, took the precaution to open his door and pull me into his apartment, where reason ruled.

Foulke spent his most successful playing years at Sheffield United, but with his form beginning to slip he signed for Chelsea in 1905, a bargain at £50. It was there that it is said he spent the happiest days of his career. The big city held many attractions for Foulke and Londoners were fascinated by the big northerner. Invitations to social occasions flooded in, a motor-car was made available for his personal use and he became a familiar and popular figure at music halls all over town, where his presence would be announced from the stage.

Chelsea, in their first season, narrowly failed to get the

promotion to the top flight that they were so desperate to achieve. No blame could be laid at Foulke's door, since at one stage in the season he had kept nine clean sheets in a row and over the course of the year he saved no fewer than ten penalties – though this may have owed as much to an optical illusion he employed, whereby two ball boys stood either side of him behind the goal, creating an effect of no space for the striker to hit.

Foulke moved back to Yorkshire for a final brief spell at Bradford where for a joke the manager would make him collect his wages via a narrow gate leading to the club offices, much to the amusement of his team-mates and Valley Parade staff. In 1907 he retired at the tender age of 33, laid low by rheumatism and legs bearing the scars of 13 years' worth of campaigns. He had played just 24 matches for Bradford.

When Foulke left the game he wasn't a rich man. He'd played football before the big money of the £4-a-week man came along, and before cup and league bonuses became both common and legal. A testimonial game in 1901 against Celtic had raised £115, but his obituaries hint that had he made money he might have had difficulties hanging onto it.

In an interview in 1913 he looked back on his career with surprising modesty. 'It is a bit late in the day for me to begin to talk about myself. There were times when the papers used to say a fair amount about Foulke saving his side – when we'd won! But I do not wish to claim more credit than as a member of a great side, for United were wonderfully warm in my day.'

The final legend of Foulke's life came with his demise. It was said that he died of pneumonia contracted saving penalties from holidaymakers for a penny a go on Blackpool Sands. It's a sad image, but unfortunately the truth is even sadder. Foulke, strapped for cash, may well have supplemented his income in the summer months as a sideshow attraction, but it didn't kill him. There is a chance also that the big man did have a touch of pneumonia, developed from a chill suffered during a downpour at a Sheffield race meeting. More importantly, though, back in Sheffield, Foulke had become the landlord of The Duke Inn in Matilda Street – it didn't help him get any smaller and it effectively finished him off. On 1 May 1916, in the week when compulsory conscription was introduced to bolster the flagging war effort on Flanders Field, William Henry Foulke succumbed to cirrhosis of the liver and a fatty heart – two conditions that

45

he had suffered for more than two years. He was just 42.

In *Association Football – The Men Who Made It* by Alfred Gibson and William Pickford, Foulke is portrayed as 'A leviathan with the agility of a bantam. Abnormal yet normal. The cheeriest of companions; brims over with good humour; at repartee is as difficult to score against as when between the posts.'

Five months after Foulke's death a contemporary of his was to come to a very different end, mown down by the bullets of a German machine-gun as he climbed out of an infernal Somme trench. That Leigh Richmond Roose would die valiantly in war would come as little surprise to those who had seen him battle away between the posts over the previous 20 years for a succession of football clubs.

Along with Foulke, Roose had been one of the great goalkeeping and great footballing characters of his time. His wanderings up and down the pitch, sorties into the crowd, his insistence on playing in the same unwashed kit for Wales, his penchant for a practical joke and his hiring of trains for personal use at Stoke City's expense all made him an amusing and likeable celebrity.

Roose was an amateur who gave no particular long-term commitment to a single club. He epitomised a new breed of journeyman goalkeepers with a spirit of 'have gloves will travel'. From 1898 to the outbreak of war, Roose's career took him to a string of clubs stretching from Aberystwyth to Celtic. Along the way he took in the Druids, London Welsh, Stoke, Everton, Sunderland, Huddersfield, Aston Villa, Woolwich Arsenal, Llandudno and the Royal Fusiliers, with whom he was a lance-corporal when he was killed.

Like Foulke, Roose's sense of humour, eccentric goalkeeping and extravagant behaviour made him an instant hit with the crowds. And like Foulke he had to be a good keeper in order to get away with it. His 24 caps for Wales are testimony to his ability.

Roose was the son of the Revd Richmond Leigh Roose, a man for whom, when it came to naming sons, the word imagination had little resonance. The Reverend was the minister of Holt Presbyterian church in North Wales from 1875 to 1916.

Leigh was born on 27 November 1877, one of five children, in a household stiff with religion. One of his brothers, John Stevens Roose, was ordained into the ministry to the great joy and happiness of the father. There is no record of his reaction to another of his sons becoming a footballer.

In his early years Roose was educated at Holt Academy where for a while he was taught by the famous novelist and dilettante H.G. Wells. The man who was to become the author of such popular classics as *The War of the Worlds*, *The Time Machine*, *Kipps* and *The History of Mr Polly* may possibly have been quite an influence on the young Roose, who was to leave Holt to study science at the University of Wales, Aberystwyth, and years later his sister Helena was to stumble across her brother showing the music-hall star Marie Lloyd his etchings, something the great womaniser Wells would no doubt have approved of. But this unsubstantiated and unnecessary gossip should play no part in any serious study.

At Aberystwyth Roose's chance to shine came early on when the town team's keeper, Jack Jones, was signed up by Manchester City. The 'Old Black and Green', as Aberystwyth were affectionately known, were a moderately successful and moderately ambitious team playing amateur football against all-comers, from Welsh village teams to the likes of West Bromwich Albion and Walsall. In 1896 they entered the Welsh League and after a poor start eventually finished sixth. This was essentially a North Welsh league, and Aberystwyth's geographical isolation caused them to struggle. Travelling expenses rocketed and, with an average train journey time of ten hours to every away game, it became difficult to get a settled and committed team. One season after joining the league they dropped out of it and turned their attention to the proliferation of cups on the scene at the time: these included the FA Cup and the Welsh Cup, the South Wales Cup, the Tywyn Cup and the Leominster Cup.

Roose made a spectacular début in front of a large crowd against Whitchurch of Shropshire in October 1898. The 'Black and Greens' won by six goals to nil, with Roose distinguishing himself not only with excellent saves but also amusing dashes up field to help out his defence. Already his talents were showing through, supporters were startled by the strength of his kicks, the accuracy of his intuition and the firmness of his grasp.

In this first season, Roose was at the heart of a major triumph when Aberystwyth met Glossop North End in an early round of

the FA Cup. Glossop were professionals from the Midland
League and probably didn't relish their trip to West Wales
anyway. The future historian and librarian Tom Richards was a
young boy in the crowd that day and recalled in his autobiography, *Atgofion Cardi*, the arrival of the visitors who were:

> Big, strong lads from the Pennines, with hairy legs and in form to win
> the first-round tie in the English Cup, for that was the occasion.
> Their dreams were ended by that wonderful goalkeeper Roose, par-
> ticularly by his diverting a penalty into the middle of the gorse on
> Buarth hill . . . I saw him play dozens of times afterwards . . . but
> never with greater zest and effect than that first time at Vicarage
> Field.

Glossop sent another penalty wide of the post and the Welsh
team walked away victors by one goal to nil. Sadly they were
hammered 5–0 by Stockport County in the next round.

As Aberystwyth hit their zenith in 1900, winning the Welsh
Cup, Roose made the first of his many career moves, joining the
top Welsh team Druids and then moving to London to study
medicine at Kings College Hospital. Football, though, remained
the first love of his life and, although he took to bacteriology like
a microbe to penicillin, he never qualified as a doctor. This would
not have prevented him earning a living in the medical profession,
but it would not have been the big bucks available to a GP or a
consultant, and with Roose maintaining his status as an amateur
it is clear that there must have been some money in his background.

This more than suited Stoke City. These were years of financial
crisis for the Potteries club and the scale of their financial
desperation led them to look for capable amateurs. Step forward
Leigh Richmond. He spent two spells at Stoke during the years
1901 to 1908 (with a short period in 1904 at Everton) and
became something of a local hero. His arrival at the ground
would frequently be signalled by a buzz of excitement as he pulled
on the reins of a horse and carriage with crowds of admirers in
hot pursuit. It was at Stoke that his character began to shine
through, dashing here and there, rushing along the touchline with
the ball, having a joke with the crowd behind his net. Tityrus in
the *Athletic News* described him as 'dexterous though daring,
valiant though volatile', while another writer commented that he

was 'not a model custodian by any means – he would not be L.R. Roose if he were'.

As with most goalkeepers of his type, there was a price to be paid and the occasional mistake cost the club points, as for example in the first round of the FA Cup in January 1902 when he played against Aston Villa. The final score was a draw, but as the *Sheffield Daily Telegraph* reported, 'Villa again took a lead thanks to a blunder on Roose's part, a slow shot from Garraty slipping through his grasp.'

That same month the Welshman's medical background had badly failed him at Anfield. At the pre-match lunch the Stoke players had feasted unknowingly on rotten fish. The effects were taking their toll by kick-off and, despite his best efforts at tending his sick team-mates, Roose was the first to fall. After eight minutes Liverpool took the lead and Roose ran from the pitch in search of a toilet. His pulse rate was 148 and he was not to return. Meredith went in goal, but with only seven players coming out for the start of the second half and the dressing-room resembling 'the cabin of a cross-channel steamer in bad weather', Liverpool won 7–0.

About this time a curious incident occurred which, although resolved amicably, was to foreshadow events in Roose's later career. In February Bristol Rovers lodged an official protest with the Football Association against Roose's appearance in an FA Cup tie against them earlier that week. The goalkeeper's brilliant performance at Bristol had been central to Stoke's victory and had resulted in his being carried off the field shoulder high. The substance of Bristol's complaint was that Roose had already appeared in the FA Cup that season, in the first round of the qualifying competition for London Welsh against the Crouch End Vampires, and was cup-tied and therefore barred from further participation with another club.

Newspapers were critical of the Bristol appeal, for a team list had been given to them five days in advance of the game and no objections had been made then. It seemed like a bad case of sour grapes. The secretary of London Welsh spoke up for Roose, denying that he had played. He agreed that Roose's name had been in the programme, but it was a mistake and the programme was not official. To the contrary, W.S. Bound had appeared in goal for the Welshmen in every game up until Christmas. The explanation was accepted by all the parties concerned.

Not that Roose was a stranger to controversy. In March 1906 he was sensationally suspended for bad behaviour at Sunderland. According to Roose, he had complained to Roker officials about the offensiveness of some of the home fans behind his nets and police were dispatched to keep order. But when he was leaving the pitch at the end of the game, a Sunderland director had assailed him with 'an objectionable expression'. An altercation followed which, sadly for Roose, was witnessed by a member of the FA Council. He was banned for 14 days.

In the meantime he was playing well, Arsenal's Ashcroft singling him out as a good example of the courage and commitment needed between the posts:

> Last season when Stoke played the Arsenal at Plumstead, I watched the Reds swoop down on Roose like a whirlwind. There was a scrimmage in goal and Roose was down on the ball like a shot with a heap of Arsenal and Stoke players on top of him. It was all Lombard Street to a halfpenny orange that the Reds would score. Presently from out of the ruck emerged Roose clinging to the ball, which he promptly threw away up the field. I'll bet that the thrill of triumph which went through him was ample compensation for any hard knocks he received.

But he may have been costing Stoke dear. In the 1906–7 season following their relegation, the Potters went into liquidation and the following year were all but wiped out. Amateur he may have been, but Roose liked his comfort and would, according to some sources, deliberately miss the last train and then hire his own personal locomotive and charge it to the club. According to other sources, he only did it once and that was for a game at Aston Villa. Nevertheless, it was not cheap. In the years leading up to the First World War major railway stations would keep several trains steamed up and ready to go. The cost was 5/- (25p) a mile plus the fare at whatever rate was appropriate – first, second or third class. London to Birmingham being 120 miles, meant that Roose presented his club with an unauthorised bill of almost £31, a phenomenal amount at the time.

Parallel to his club record, Roose was carving a successful international career. At a time when internationals were far less frequent than today and when they were confined to the home countries, he picked up 24 caps for Wales. They weren't games, however, that he took any more seriously than his club outings. He arrived in Belfast for one international with his arm bandaged and firmly strapped, seemingly incapacitated. At an impromptu press conference he kept the assembled hacks on tenterhooks until standing up in front of them and removing it, no doubt with some witticism like 'Ha ha – fooled you!' He played a blinder.

It is said of his internationals that he played every game in the same undershirt, which he never allowed to be washed. But Roose's dress code has been the subject of dispute and the actuality lost somewhere in the mists of time. Some agree with the undershirt, others say he never appeared in a clean pair of shorts, others that he would only play in one particular long-bottomed shirt made in a particular way by a particular person. The *Dictionary of Welsh Biography* claims romantically that 'He played 24 times for Wales and legend has it that underneath his goalkeeper's jersey he would wear another coloured black and green.' An old Aberystwyth Town shirt.

Clearly, even at the time, Roose's dress sense was a topic of discussion. In March 1904, while playing for Everton, he conceded three goals for the first time in a year, but this was not the main talking point, as Bolton's *Cricket and Football Field* pointed out.

> Roose is one of the cleanest custodians we have, but he apparently is a trifle superstitious about his football garments, for he seldom seems to trouble the charwoman with them. Considerable amusement was created at Stoke on Saturday and again at Liverpool on Monday, when it was noticed that Roose alone had failed to turn out in spic and span garments. His pants, we should say, carried about them the marks of many a thrilling contest . . .

His record for his country was respectable considering the Welsh were regarded as the whipping boys of the international circuit. Under his custodianship Wales won nine, drew six and lost nine, and while his boys were scoring 36 goals he was conceding 46, a figure boosted by a couple of slaughterings at the hands of the English when six and seven goals flew past him.

Roose may have been a joker but he was also a gentleman whose perspective of sports was demonstrated by his amateur status and summed up by his opinion on sporting excess with the phrase 'a pinch of salt is a good condiment, but a spoonful becomes nauseating'. To illustrate this he offered to stand down and let Alf Edwards win his first full Welsh cap, after having been reserve keeper on eight occasions. Alf may have been delighted, but the Welsh FA were not and prohibited it.

From 1908 Roose went on something of a grand tour of football clubs, only ever really making a substantial impact on one other club, Sunderland, for whom he played 92 times. According to many fans of the day, Roose almost single-handedly saved the Roker team from relegation, but plans to honour him with a testimonial were squashed by the Football Association because of his amateur status, and in the end all he received was an illuminated address from the mayor.

Roose seems to have loved the travelling life and while still on the books of Sunderland there were sightings of him at grounds all over the country. In March 1910 he filled in for Celtic in the Scottish Cup semi-final, their usual keeper being laid low with pneumonia. It wasn't to be a happy day for Roose; Clyde put three past him at Shawfield in front of 37,000 fans and Roose never played for Celtic again. Two days later he was back in Cardiff playing for Wales in a 1–0 defeat by England.

In 1911 alone he appeared for Huddersfield, Aston Villa and Arsenal to name but a few. It almost ended in tears. On 23 April 1910 there was a little difficulty in Stoke. In the decider of the North Staffordshire League, Stoke Reserves were to play Port Vale. A remarkable crowd of more than 7,000 turned up to discover that Port Vale had beefed up their team with four notable ringers including Roose and Herbert Chapman. The crowd was upset and particularly resented Roose's presence, not only because he was a former Stoke player but because he was dressed in a Stoke shirt! Early in the game, following complaints from the Stoke players, the referee requested that Roose change his shirt, even suppling a white one for him – but in what must have been a deliberate wind-up Roose refused to change.

Stoke played well, but Roose was on form and before they knew what had hit them, the home team were 2–0 down. The crowd were seething. After an hour they could control their anger no longer. Roose made a splendid save from Horrocks and, as the *Argus* reported:

At this juncture the crowd broke on to the ground. The Stoke players as well as the police endeavoured to persuade them to return to the other side of the railing. They refused and surrounded Roose in the Vale goal. Additional spectators added to the number who crowded around Roose, and he was swayed from out of the goal towards the River Trent.

The Revd A.E. Hurst made a public appeal to the crowd to desist and, with the aid of the police and some of the Port Vale supporters, Roose was able to prise himself away from a watery grave and into the sanctuary of the dressing-room. As the crowd continued to swirl round the pitch like an angry mob, the Reverend made another appeal for the pitch to be cleared. As further progress proved impossible in the main match, two junior teams came out and started an exhibition game. The pitch cleared.

At a bad-tempered inquiry held the following Tuesday, the Port Vale secretary handed over a letter demanding that the game be awarded to his club. He refused to elaborate. The Stoke secretary accused Port Vale of being 'unsportsmanlike and contemptible', claiming that it was common knowledge that Vale had scoured the country for a week in an attempt to find players with whom to beat Stoke. As for being ill prepared for such a big and unruly crowd, the Stoke secretary refuted allegations of neglect by pointing out that as it had been a championship decider the police presence had been increased from three to eight; it was just unfortunate that they had all been 'new policemen'.

Speaking for Roose, the Revd Hurst told an incredulous investigation that the keeper had believed that the game was just a friendly and that he had had no idea that there was a championship at stake. It transpired that he had, however, been properly registered with Port Vale after a hasty transfer from Kidsgrove Wellington, though what he was doing there when he should have been on Sunderland's books is a mystery. There was a hint that the transfer was not totally above board and that Roose had been 'induced' to leave.

The League ordered the game to be replayed two days later with Roose eligible, but Vale didn't turn up, announcing that it was too dangerous, and a large crowd had to make do with another exhibition match, this time between Stoke and Stoke Reserves.

On the outbreak of the First World War Roose signed up immediately for the 9th Battalion Royal Fusiliers. He sent telegrams home to his friends under the jokey nickname 'The Archdeacon', but died a lance-corporal amid the carnage of France on 7 October 1916. He was awarded a posthumous Military Medal.

2 Greek to Greek

... sometimes their necks are broken, sometimes their backs,
sometimes their legs, sometimes their arms; sometime one part
thrust out of joynt, sometime another; sometime the noses gush out
with blood, sometimes their eyes start out ...
PHILLIP STUBBES DESCRIBES THE JOY OF FOOTBALL IN
The Anatomy of Abuses, 1583

To this day there are those who persist in their belief that the First
World War was caused by a gunshot in the Balkans. Admittedly
this is always a painful place to be shot. And, yes, it's fair to say
that there was a little local difficulty with Serbian nationalists
even back then – so what's new?

There are others, though, who know that the First World War,
that horrific conflagration that resulted in the slaughter of the
Somme, Passchendaele, Gallipoli and the eradication of a whole
generation of young men, actually began, not in August 1914, but
some three months earlier on the corner of a foreign football field
that is forever German.

Back in those days Spurs were in the habit of making summer
trips to the continent to play friendlies against decent opposition.
They had made a number of successful trips to Germany and in
May 1914 returned again. This time, however, the *bonhomie* had
gone and wherever they went they faced intense hostility. Abuse
followed in their every footstep and at one game stones were
hurled at them as they beat the home favourites. It was a moment
that serves to illustrate the particular vulnerability of the goal-

keeper located, as he is, next to the potentially hateful fans.

The Tottenham goalkeeper on that day was the ironically nicknamed Tiny Joyce. For if Foulke was the official 'king of the fatties', football's very own Zeppelin, then Tiny was his little baby barrage balloon – a mere 18st in socks and shin-pads. On a previous tour of Germany he had been called upon to take a penalty against Leipzig but the opposing goalie, on seeing the elephantine keeper pounding down the pitch, turned and ran, leaving his goal empty. But stature on this particular day in May helped Joyce none. As a section of the crowd applauded the stoning of the Spurs team, one maniac jumped the fence and pummelled Joyce with his umbrella, cracking the keeper's head open.

As such, if hooliganism is a problem endemic to football, then it is a very special problem for goalkeepers. When the crowd spills out onto the pitch, or when trouble erupts in the terraces, the goalkeeper is the nearest and therefore the most likely target. And sometimes the cause of a goalie's downfall comes from totally unexpected quarters.

When a small black-and-white terrier ran onto the field at Colchester, one crisp but sunny afternoon in November 1970, few could have anticipated the consequences, least of all our old friend Chic Brodie, Brentford's veteran and still popular goalkeeper, the man who had found a hand-grenade in his net five years earlier.

With most of the first half completed, Brodie could tell that it was going to be a bad day: two goals down to a Colchester United team now beginning to stroll their way to a ninth unbeaten match in a row. Even optimistic Brentford fans were already speaking the unspeakable – more than six months of the season left and a battle for survival looked on the cards.

Brodie's season had been a funny one. Sixteen years keeping goal and still as agile and acrobatic as in his early days. On several occasions his miraculous performances had been all that stood between Brentford and the fight for re-election to the Football League. But he'd been at the receiving end of some ill-luck in recent months. In August he'd tumbled into the net at Lincoln and the goalposts had collapsed, bringing the crossbar crashing to the ground. Brodie lay enmeshed with the Lincoln skipper Derek Trevis, the pair looking like a couple of flailing dolphins in a Spanish tuna net. The last three minutes of the game took a further three-quarters of an hour to complete, as both footballers and crowd alike awaited the arrival and construction of a new goal.

Brodie escaped unscathed this time, but in October he chipped a bone in his right arm and was forced out of action for several games. He had made his return just the week before the Colchester game and was now despairing of his team-mates as they put on a show so awe-inspiring in its ineptness that he was thinking about signing up the dog. The daft mutt was scampering all over the pitch, up-ending players, pinching the ball, barking at the linesmen. Despite appeals from the players, the referee refused to call a halt to the game. Now, as the centre-half Gelson knocked the ball back to his goalie, the dog joined in the race.

Whether driven on by the promise of the chipped bone still floating around in Brodie's arm or just the instinctive drive to score, no one will ever know. But as Brodie bent down to scoop up the ball, the hyperactive pooch took two bounds, a leap and crashed into the unsuspecting keeper. Before anyone in the crowd could utter the immortal words 'Nine out of ten owners say their dogs prefer Brentford keepers', Brodie's career was effectively over. The ball span out for a corner. Brodie sprawled on the floor, writhing in agony – clutching a shattered kneecap.

'I didn't see a thing,' he remembers now. 'I was keeping my eye on the ball, but as I went down to collect it, I thought I'm sure that's a bloody dog coming towards me! The next thing is it's hit me, right on the inside of my knee. My leg twisted, but with long studs on soft ground my foot was stuck and my knee shot up like a balloon. The bloody dog did a bunk over the wall and that was the last that was seen of it. My knee's never been the same since, even now, 25 years on, it aches like hell in the cold.'

The unfortunate victim of a bizarre accident, Brodie continued bravely until the end of the game, but was out injured for months. By the time he was fit again a new goalie had established himself and, despite a brief experiment in alternating keepers on a weekly basis, he was finished. He slipped into a footballing obscurity disturbed only momentarily when infamy once again knocked at his door. Persuaded out of retirement to play for Margate, he appeared in an FA Cup tie against Bournemouth and conceded 11 goals, nine from Ted McDougall. 'It was like the Charge of the Light Brigade. I've never been so fed up and so humiliated. It was pissing down with rain, it was cold and every time McDougall got the ball it just flashed past me,' Brodie recalls. It was only a matter of weeks before his boots were hung up again, this time permanently.

Brodie of all people should have expected the unexpected. Having had a grenade frighten the life out of him against Millwall, having had the goals tumble down around his ears at Lincoln, having had some crazed pooch end his career at Colchester, he really should have known better than to try and revive his career against a big Mac in Margate. As he says, 'Anybody ask you who's on the Palladium – Chic Brodie's on!'

Yet when under attack one of the most effective weapons of all can be the football itself – especially in the days when it flew goalwards like a heavy, water-sodden mortar bomb. Liverpool's Platt was to discover its true weight against Bury at the turn of the century, when Thorpe fired a fearsome shot between a dozen players: 'The leather finished its course by hitting Platt full "IN THE BREADBASKET" but he managed to clear before he doubled up.'

Undoubtedly, though, it is the opposing team which causes the keeper the most grief. A frequent complaint of today's supporter is that referees give goalies too much protection – you only have to breathe on them to find a yellow card flashing before your eyes. This has not always been the case, although the complaint of overprotection has an age-old resonance. The fact of the matter is that keepers often suffer serious injuries, more serious than anybody else on the pitch, and sometimes their injuries are fatal.

Back in the 19th century any player in an onside position could charge the keeper, and because whenever the keeper touched the ball he played everybody onside, he was frequently subject to attacks that would, out on the street, constitute a serious criminal offence. Many teams employed a 'rusher' up front who, as soon as a colleague took a shot, would make a dash for the goalie, aiming to hit him just as the ball reached him and drive both ball and keeper into the net. Naturally there were many mistimings that saw keepers fist the ball away only to find themselves crumpled in the back of the goal anyway.

By the 1890s the consequences were becoming severe. Too many keepers were being taken out whenever the ball approached goal and the laws of the game were amended so that the goalie could only be charged when he was actually playing the ball or obstructing an opponent. A football writer of the time commented: 'Since this amendment was passed the lives of goalkeepers have been much less liable to forfeiture.'

Still, one commentator might complain in 1899 that 'Goalkeepers of the present day have a much easier time than their predecessors had,' but the truth of the matter was that the problem hadn't really been tackled. Goalkeepers were subjected to sly kicks, hacks and digs when the referee wasn't watching, and the ability to be able to charge forcefully but 'fairly' up front became a crucial part of the job spec for attacking forwards. Most teams started to employ the Victorian equivalent of Scud missiles dressed in number 9 shirts to score their goals.

An incident in a game at Anfield in 1904, between Liverpool and Manchester City, illustrates how, despite changes to the laws, setting about the goalkeeper big time was still a legitimate tactic. Cotton, the Liverpool keeper fell on the ball under his posts, an action that would today end the play; however, as the *Liverpool Football Echo* reported,

> Then followed an ALMOST UNPRECEDENTED SCENE unless perhaps under the Rugby code. One after another of the Mancunians pressed into goal until the whole team was engaged and the Reds followed suit, so that it appeared as if a pyramid of 20 people were piled on top of Cotton, struggling and pushing the luckless custodian in or out of goal.

Cotton eventually escaped from the mêlée with the ball, only to see it whizz past him for a goal a few seconds later. At that moment the words 'why' and 'bother' must have bolted firmly together in his mind.

In the same way that tightening up track safety for Formula One Grand Prix races failed to prevent the death of Ayrton Senna, so too did new rules protecting keepers fail to cover every eventuality – besides, how can one legislate for accidents? Most of the serious injuries sustained by keepers were not as a consequence of foul play or fair charges (for which they could prepare themselves), but were received during the rough and tumble of the game.

Whatever the cause of injury, the 1920s and 1930s were among the bleakest of times for British keepers.

Dumbarton keeper Joshua Wilkinson had spent three years in the navy during the First World War and had survived everything the Germans could throw at him, even the torpedoing of his ship. But he didn't survive a Scottish league game against Rangers in 1921.

Wilkinson was a tall and slender young man who had gone to Glasgow University before the war and had returned to complete an MA. He played a season for Rangers Reserves before moving back to his home town where, as an only son, he lived at home with his parents while he tried to carve out a career for himself between the posts. On the afternoon of 12 November 1921 he earned his spurs against his old club Rangers, the local paper reporting that he had 'stood between his side and defeat', playing his best and most punishing game to date. How punishing was soon to be realised.

In the changing-room after the game he complained of feeling sick and as a special precaution he was motored home. That night, with his condition worsening, he was rushed to Glasgow's Western Infirmary, where he died of peritonitis two days later.

The young man's death came as a blow to the whole town. Wilkinson, being a local lad, had many friends on the terraces, which added to the tragedy. The club gave his family £100, the maximum amount permitted under Scottish League rules, and paid for his headstone. At Dumbarton's next match Wilkinson's team-mates wore black crêpe armbands and a man called Haggo took over between the posts.

Meanwhile, there was some attempt to exonerate football. It was stressed in the Glasgow press that Rangers had played fairly and not launched an assault on the keeper, that he had died of peritonitis, the implication being that this was a natural cause that could have happened to anybody. His father was having none of it and in a letter to the *Glasgow Evening News* refuted claims that his son had told his mother in the hospital that he had no complaints against the Rangers players:

Sir. – . . . His mother knew that her brave and generous son would not blame anyone, but he certainly met his death by a rupture of the small bowel caused by some blow received during the match. And, further, Joe went to Ibrox on Saturday in splendid spirits and perfect health.

W.H. Wilkinson

The 1930s were even worse. In February 1936 Chelsea visited Sunderland and treated them to a brutal afternoon's entertainment in front of 20,000 spectators. It was also an afternoon that witnessed one of the quickest bits of backtracking since Napoleon hit snow in Russia.

Sunderland had been winning 3–1, but in an ill-tempered and poorly controlled game Chelsea pulled back to share the spoils. Police protection was needed to ensure the safety of the referee, and local journalists had no doubt who was to blame – Jimmy Thorpe, the Sunderland keeper. At 3–1 Thorpe had misjudged a ball and failed to clear it from his line and then, two minutes later, worried by the Chelsea striker Bambrick who was haring in, he had taken his eyes off the ball when running to collect a back-pass and allowed it to run over his arm, giving Bambrick his second easy goal in as many minutes.

The *Sunderland Football Echo* that night told it as it was: 'Sunderland lost a valuable point and they lost it, I am sorry to say, through bad goalkeeping.' The following Monday in the *Sunderland Echo* 'Argus' continued the attack:

> Thorpe has shown some excellent goalkeeping this season, but he seldom satisfies me when the ball is crossed. On Saturday his failures had an entirely different origin, and I can come to no other conclusion than that the third goal to Chelsea was due to 'wind up' when he saw Bambrick running up.

Thorpe was scared said his critics; he'd turned chicken at the moment of truth. Little did they know that within 48 hours he would be dead. Knocked about on the pitch on the Saturday, Thorpe had suffered a recurrence of a diabetic condition that he had been treated for two years earlier, and which had lain dormant in his body ever since. He died in Monkwearmouth and Southwich Hospital at 2 p.m. on Wednesday afternoon. According to the newspapers there was not the slightest doubt that his death was due to blows received during the match. The sound of grovelling journalists was deafening and none were louder than Argus:

> I know many who would give anything now to feel that they had not uttered the harsh words they spoke in the heat of the moment regarding Jimmy Thorpe's failure to prevent the two Chelsea goals in

61

the second half last week. They did not know that the man whose failures were cursed was actually a hero to carry on at all. Neither did I know, and I confess now that I myself would give anything to have been in the position to have known and never to have given pen to what I wrote.

I do not think he was able to read them and if this is so I am glad that his last days were not saddened by anything I had written because I know he was sensitive about his job . . . Thorpe will not soon be forgotten.

In death Thorpe's ineptness was erased. Details of his 22 years were considered – how he was a good cricketer, a proud father and a staunch favourite of the crowd. 'It is said that all goalkeepers are mad: otherwise they would not be goalkeepers. Thorpe belied the adage. It was difficult to get a word out of him,' wrote Argus.

Other goalkeepers were killed during the 1930s. James Utterson, the bright and cheery Wolves keeper, with a reputation for being something of a 'crooner', died at the age of 21 from a kick over the heart during a Central League game. It took some months for him to fade away and for a while it seemed like he would make a complete recovery, but in December 1935 he was rushed into a nursing home, where he died two days later. The Wolves programme reported: 'That he had suffered uncomplainingly for some time is now quite apparent and his death is a shock to us all.' Utterson had joined the club a year earlier, but after an excellent start his form had slumped and he had had to make do with playing for the reserves or, as the club said in his obituary, he was gaining the necessary experience of the lower leagues when he took the fatal blow.

There was no legislating for the outlandish death of Charlton's keeper Alex Wright. He wasn't killed on the pitch, but nevertheless died as a consequence of the game. Wright had been a late starter in football owing to business reasons and his demise therefore brought to an end a relatively short career, which had taken him from Queen of the South to Irvine Meadow and then Charlton for £70 in 1932.

Back in those days, when trips to Marbella, Benidorm and Torremolinos were rarer than toasted Hovis with real butter, Wright took advantage of an away game with Torquay to enjoy the seaside and the sunshine. There was reason to celebrate –

they'd won 2–1 the night before – and Wright, standing atop a raft floating just off Torre Abbey Sands, demonstrated once again his match-winning saves. But it was one dive too many. Not realising the shallowness of the water around him, he plunged onto the rocks below and broke his neck.

He died 24 hours later, just minutes before the arrival of his parents, who had rushed down from his home town of Kilmarnock. Next day the teams, management, directors and crowd stood in sombre silence as a band played 'Abide With Me' before the start of Charlton's visit to Luton. Wright was 30 when he died in 1934, with 'death by misadventure' being the official verdict.

The death of a keeper can be a cathartic experience. Amid small, tightly knit working-class communities, the keeper's sacrifice led to spontaneous and genuine grief. In Dumbarton, people stood in deep ranks along the route from Joshua Wilkinson's home to the cemetery. Team-mates acted as pallbearers and senior pupils of the Dumbarton Academy walked in front of the hearse. Representatives of other teams from as far away as Blackburn Rovers turned up to pay their respects.

In Sunderland, too, the streets were lined for Thorpe's funeral cortège and a wreath, in the shape of a football field, was commissioned for the occasion. Similarly for James Utterson, despite his youth and lack of first-team experience, crowds turned out to witness his coffin pass by, topped as it was with another football-ground wreath – ferns forming the pitch, markings done in white chrysanthemums and black flags at each corner.

But no goalkeeping death was more traumatic than that of John 'Jock' Thomson, the Celtic and Scotland keeper.

Saturday, 5 September 1931, was a bleak day all round for Scottish football. In the Hibernian v St Bernards game, Hibs keeper Blyth had to be stretchered off with a fractured leg after rushing out to foil an attack. Airdrie keeper Paterson was also stretchered off at Falkirk. There was another broken leg at Dunfermline where Alloa's McPherson was carried from the field. At Hampden, Ayr's Turnbull smashed his nose in a collision with a Queen's Park opponent and Douglas of Motherwell had his face rearranged in a similar clash against Hamilton.

Off the field it was no better. At Tannadice, misdirected stones hurled at the referee badly injured a spectator, and at Kings Park police were called when a section of the crowd rushed onto the field with the intention of maiming the ref after he had awarded a penalty to Cowdenbeath. But by the end of the day all eyes would be turned towards Glasgow.

John Thomson was just 23 when he stepped out onto the Ibrox pitch that afternoon, but he was already considered one of the finest keepers Scotland had ever produced and had already played four times for his country. In a mediocre Celtic team it was Thomson's safe hands and spectacular heroism that had kept them in the running. A sensible young man, brought up in the grim Fife mining village of Cardenden, he was making the most of his career, but had already planned his life after football, with dreams of opening a gents' outfitters. He had recently got engaged and was excited at the news that Arsenal were interested in signing him.

Like any Old Firm game there was a genuine tension to the city in the build-up to the match. These games were, and continue to be, fierce struggles where no quarter is given. But Thomson was in an odd position for this most sectarian of battles, for he was one of those rare creatures, a Protestant in the team often known as Glasgow Irish. In an earlier encounter with Rangers he had complained to Celtic striker Jimmy McGrory that the opposing centre-forward kept calling him a papish bastard. McGrory had tried to placate him by telling him not to let it worry him – he was called one every week. 'That's all right for you, you are one!' had been Thomson's reply.

More than 80,000 were at Ibrox to witness an event that has remained imprinted on the Scottish football psyche ever since. With the second half barely five minutes old, Rangers striker Sam English broke free and lined up to shoot from near the penalty spot. He seemed certain to score, when Thomson launched one of his do-or-die head-first saves at the attacker's feet. It was Thomson's trademark save – in February 1930 against Airdrie he'd been injured doing exactly the same thing, fracturing his jaw and injuring his ribs. This time there was an even more sickening crunch, Thomson's head colliding with English's knee at the moment of greatest impact. It was no longer a do-or-die moment, it was a do-*and*-die. The ball ran out of play, English fell to the ground and rose limping, Thomson lay unconscious, blood seeping into the pitch.

The dazed English was the first to realise the seriousness of the blow and hobbled over to the unmoving keeper, waving urgently for assistance. Celtic fans were cheering the missed goal, Rangers fans were taunting the injured keeper, but the gravity of the situation was soon upon them. Rangers' captain Davie Meiklejohn raised his arms to implore the home fans to be silent. A hush descended over the ground. In the stands Margaret Finlay, Thomson's fiancée, broke down as she saw him borne from the ground, head wrapped in bandages, body limp.

In a probably apocryphal retelling of the moment, *The Scotsman* reported that as Thomson was carried away, 'he was seen to rise on the stretcher and look towards the goal and the spot where the accident happened'.

He died at 9.25 that evening of a depressed fracture of the skull.

What followed was an outpouring of public grief that, it is said, briefly united communities across the sectarian divide. In Bridgeton, Glasgow, traffic was brought to a halt by thousands of pedestrians walking past a floral tribute to Thomson, placed in a shop window by the local Rangers supporters club. And at Glasgow's Trinity Congregational Church there were unruly scenes when thousands struggled to get into Thomson's memorial service. Women screamed with alarm at the crush and only swift action by police cleared a passageway and stemmed the rush. Celtic right-half Peter Wilson, who was due to read a lesson, failed to gain entrance and found himself stranded outside the church for the ceremony.

Tens of thousands went to Queen Street station to see the coffin off on its train journey home to Fife. Many thousands more made the same journey: by train, by car and by foot. Unemployed workers walked the 55 miles, spending the night on the Craigs, a group of hills behind Auchterderran. In Fife, local pits closed down for the day and it seemed as if the whole of Scotland had swelled the small streets of Cardenden. Thomson's coffin, topped by one of his international caps and a wreath in the design of an empty goal, was carried by six Celtic players the mile from his home to Bowhill cemetery, where he was laid to rest in the sad and quiet graveyard populated by the victims of many, many mining disasters.

The following Saturday, matches all over Scotland were prefaced by memorial services to the keeper. At Parkhead, Celtic and Queen's Park players stood to attention while pipers played 'The Flowers of the Forest'. A bugler sounded 'The Last Post' to a crowd shrouded in silence, heads uncovered, and a band finished the ceremony with 'Lead Kindly Light'.

At the Fatal Accident Inquiry a month later, Willie Maley, the Celtic manager, in reply to the question of whether Thomson's death had been an accident or not, said: 'I *hope* it was an accident.' It was a mean-spirited reply. No blame could be attributed to English for what happened, but Maley's words ensured that the death of Thomson haunted the Rangers striker for the rest of his life.

And therein lies the rub. Goalkeepers can be protected, and are protected, from the deliberate foul, the misplaced barge, the kick, the dig in the ribs and the late hack, but so much of the goalkeeper's vulnerability is to the unpremeditated. The goalkeeper is an accident waiting to happen and it may as well be written into his contract when he decides to sign up as a professional.

There were too many deaths in Europe and Japan in the 1940s to worry about a few dead keepers, but the war years were important in the development of another major goalkeeping injury.

In the 1956 FA Cup final against Birmingham City, Bert Trautmann, keeper for Manchester City, did a 'Jock Thomson'. With 17 minutes of the game left and his team 3–1 up, Trautmann sped out to deprive Murphy of a certain goal. As he dived at the striker's feet his head crashed into his opponent's knee. He lay unconscious on the pitch, ball in hands, the goal protected and a broken neck for his efforts.

He didn't die – in fact he finished the game, having to make several more saves in the process. But then what was a broken neck to a man like Trautmann? Here was a man who had joined the Luftwaffe's parachute regiment and been one of only 90 (from an original 1,000) to survive the war, a man court-martialled and imprisoned for a casual and trivial act of sabotage, a German who was captured by the Russians, but who escaped, and was later captured by the French Resistance but escaped. A man who was one of only a handful of survivors of an allied bombing mission on the town of Kleve, who just days later had had a hand-grenade blow up in his face, giving him superficial scratches, but terribly wounding a friend. Here was a man who, according to Alan Rowlands' *Trautmann: The Biography*, had escaped from the Americans when two GIs pretended to execute him and who, in jumping a fence to escape them, had landed at the feet of a British soldier whose first words were 'Hello Fritz, fancy a cup of tea?'

Imprisoned as a PoW in Britain, Trautmann joined his camp's football team as a centre-half, but following an injury retired to the nets. It was a position he excelled in and made his own, putting down much of his ability to the training he had received as a parachutist. In 1949 he signed for Manchester City in the face of a threatened boycott of the club by Jewish and ex-servicemen supporters. 'When I think of the millions of Jews who were tortured and murdered I can only marvel at Manchester City's crass stupidity,' said one begrudging but typical letter to the press.

Racism was to be a continuing burden for Trautmann in the coming years. As late as 1956 the *Manchester Evening News* led on its front page, under the headline 'POISON PEN LETTERS TO TRAUTMANN', with a story that irate Spurs fans, claiming that the German had fouled one of their forwards in the dying moments of the Cup semi-final, had been sending him vile letters telling him to go back to his own country. Trautmann is reported as saying, 'They are very upsetting, but I am trying my best to forget all about them.'

By this time, though, Trautmann had done more than enough to win over the great majority of supporters and letters flooded into the *Evening News*. The Globetrotters from Ardwick summed up the feeling: 'It was a darn bad show and left a nasty taste in one's mouth. Both Manchester City and Manchester United fans are proud of Bert's record, both on and off the field. And if ever he walks into our pub – or any other pub for that matter – he would find that all the lads are with him and think a lot of him.'

When Trautmann broke his neck it was seen by his supporters as the ultimate sacrifice. In 1961 they showed their appreciation by turning out for his testimonial in huge numbers, almost 50,000 of them.

His survival had been touch and go, but by the time he knew just how bad it was, he was in safe hands. As his team-mates celebrated their victory throughout the night, Trautmann, believing that he had a muscle strain took an aspirin and sat watching the festivities in grim agony. Almost the worst of it had been on the final whistle when team-mate Bill Leivers supported him as he climbed the stairs to get his winner's medal, thousands of joyous fans slapping him on the back as he ascended.

Next day an x-ray revealed no damage and a few days later an osteopath, diagnosing five misplaced vertebrae, slammed Trautmann's head back and forth. Only when the pain became too much did the German go into Manchester Royal Infirmary for another x-ray – this time it showed that a cracked second vertebrae had split in two. Trautmann was only alive because the third vertebrae had been slammed against it and was wedging it into position.

And here's where the stupidity of the goalkeeper becomes sublime. There's an old John Wayne movie where the great man breaks his neck and spends the next few months repeating, 'I'm goin' ta move that toe'. Exhausted at the banality of his mantra, the paralysis breaks and the toe wiggles. Trautmann must have gone through a similar process. Despite having his skull drilled to provide bolt holes for a calliper, preventing the movement of his head, and despite having his back mummified in plaster and metal, Trautmann forced the pace. By November, just six months after his accident, he was training again. On 1 December he played for Manchester City Reserves and two weeks later he was back in the first team.

So goalkeepers are overprotected?

Well, they are undoubtedly more mollycoddled than in the past, for sure. But it's worth remembering what it felt like when a keeper did get seriously hurt. As far back as 1936, on the death of Jimmy Thorpe, the *Sunderland Football Echo* demanded a reform of the laws:

> It has frequently been advocated that a goalkeeper should be given protection from an opponent while in possession of the ball. In other words he should neither be charged nor kicked at in an endeavour to dispossess him.
>
> This rule has been in operation on the continent and there is no valid reason why it should not be made to apply in this country . . .
>
> That any man should be allowed to stand over a goalkeeper when he has made a save and hack away in the hope of kicking the ball from under him, or out of his hands, is diametrically opposed to the spirit of the game and a thing which Britishers should tolerate it [sic] no longer . . .

It is nevertheless inescapable that the threat of violence is a major aspect of the lunacy that it takes to become a goalkeeper. Danger goes with the job. Goalkeepers have given up their lives, others have suffered less serious blows: Foulke was stoned twice and took it in his stride, Stoke supporters ushered Roose to the Trent, Joyce had an umbrella snapped over his head by a crazed German with premature war lust, Brodie had a hand-grenade lobbed at him and was eventually ex-cruciated by a mad dog on acid.

If it's a career choice you make then it is as well to remember that you have effectively volunteered to become your side's human punchbag. You have volunteered to have a ball smashed at you with as much force as a centre-forward can muster. You have volunteered to receive head-butts and kicks from men intent solely on getting a small round object into the netting over which you stand guard. And, as if that wasn't enough, you have volunteered for the ridiculous accident or infuriated attack of the lunatics in the stand.

The keeper is in the firing-line and the job description requires either some kind of fearless nutter to put on the green shirt, a sort of Colonel H. Jones of football, or someone so sad that they have to prove to others that 'whilst you may think I'm a wimp, appearances can be deceptive!'.

Come and have a go if you think you're hard enough!

This, of course, is not to portray goalkeepers as innocent, fragile little treasures whose legs buckle every time they're hit on the back by a roll of last week's Andrex. Not at all; goalkeepers can be, and frequently have to be, a ferocious, self-preserving breed whose retaliation is very often slammed into the gullet of an opponent before the opponent has even had the chance of passing the time of day with him.

Indeed, it can be that a goalkeeper's latent aggression, coupled with his necessary lack of fear, is high on the list of reasons why every so often they end up with their heads in a different corner of the ground to their feet – John Thomson didn't get killed because he was running away, after all. John Thomson got killed because he dived head-first at the knees of an oncoming centre-forward.

Goalkeepers have to be hard, and nine times out of ten they can prove it: Scottish international William Harper was a heavyweight boxing champ in the Scots Guards who kept fit by working as a blacksmith; Spurs keeper Ted Ditchburn was handy in the ring too, the son of a champion pugilist, and it was said he could have made as good a living from fighting as he did in the nets; Bruce Grobbelaar was a jungle-fighter in Zimbabwe.

And while it's obvious that if there's got to be a hard man between the posts, you'd rather he was on your side, the reality is that it doesn't matter which team he's playing for – if there's a psycho between the posts then at some point during the match you're going to feel his wrath. This is because the canny goal-keeper is never in the wrong. The blame always lies elsewhere. The ball's in the back of the net – it strolled over the line while he was having a crafty fag against the far post; he didn't get down from the bar where he was sleeping quickly enough; he miskicked a back-pass away. Whatever the cause of the problem, ask yourself have you ever seen a keeper doubled up and sobbing into the turf with remorse? Have you hell! The canny keeper is just biding his time, charging his battery and before you can mouth the words 'Gary Sprake' he's up and tearing a strip off the full-back, the centre-half, the centre-forward, the centre-forward's mother and the man selling damp hot-dogs in the carpark outside.

It's a natural response from the occupant of a position where any mistake normally spells disaster, a defensive mechanism that allows the keeper to maintain an element of self-worth, that permits him to deflect some of the culpability to a beleaguered team-mate. Most of all it's a way of showing the punters in the stands that he's the only competent man in a team of utter nincompoops.

It doesn't have to be a goal. The ball goes out for a corner, the ball is saved, the midfield pass it back to him, his team score. Whatever the situation, it seems the keeper is invariably on the receiving end of a massive rush of blood, an impulse to holler, a primal urge to primal scream.

Cynics among us may feel that it's not only to exculpate himself, but that often it's a way of reminding everybody else that he's there. In a game where so much of the action is in the other half, shouting, bawling and hurling abuse are the keeper's way of proving to his mates in the cheap seats that he's not just come to reseed the goal-line, that he's actually involved and performing a crucial role in the game.

Not that they would admit that, of course. Goalies talk about keeping their colleagues on their toes, making sure they don't go off the boil, that they don't get complacent, berating them when necessary, praising them when deserved. Really. If Peter Shilton or Peter Schmeichel cast loud and very damaging public aspersions on your pedigree, are the chances high that your ego would receive a well-earned confidence boost? No. It's more likely to make you spend the rest of the match hoping and praying that the ball stays elsewhere – 'Not mine!' goes the shout from the right-back.

The phenomenon of the shouting keeper has had its more absurd moments. In 1975 Manchester United's Alex Stepney was carted off to hospital with a dislocated jaw after screaming too loudly. The second half had just started. The score was 0–0 and in what must have been one of the most remarkable goalkeeper interviews ever, considering his state, Stepney told the *Daily Mirror*, 'I just shouted for the ball, when my jaw clicked and left me in agony. It was ridiculous.' The *Mirror* reported: 'Stepney's team-mates were staggered when he went down, holding his face, with no one near him.' It didn't do them any obvious harm. Brian Greenhoff went in goal and they beat Birmingham City 2–0.

An even more startling example of a goalkeeper completely losing his rag occurred during the Merseyside derby at Goodison Park in September 1993. When Mark Ward put Everton ahead after 28 minutes, Bruce Grobbelaar went apeshit, and the target of his anger was the still-young Steve McManaman. Grobbelaar, dubbed by the Sunday press as 'Bruise Grobbelaar' or 'Bruiser Bruce', launched into his team-mate who he believed should have cleared a badly hit Everton corner. Within seconds he had chased McManaman out of his area and was at his throat, going eyeball to eyeball. Grobbelaar let fly with a mouthful of invective, a sharp push and an attempted punch. For once a player responded to his keeper's tantrum and McManaman tried to get a slap back in. Everton players and supporters looked on with astonishment and no doubt a degree of salacious pleasure.

The *Sunday Mirror* lapped it up: 'Liverpool finished up with faces as red as their shirts as they staged their very own version of *The Bruise Brothers* at Goodison. But it wasn't "Razor" Ruddock or "Terminator" Julian Dicks who threw the tantrum – it was nice guys Bruce Grobbelaar and Steve McManaman.'

The tension of the occasion had clearly got to the Zimbabwean goalie, even though it was his record 34th derby. Cracks were appearing in Graeme Souness's lacklustre Liverpool team and the 35-year-old keeper was the valve that blew. To his mind the corner should have been cleared, kicked upfield, into the stand, anywhere but to the feet of Mark Ward. Bruiser Bruce had been playing well, but he had been at Liverpool so long that he realised the special significance of the game and wanted visibly to exonerate himself. He said later, 'I have to live in this city and I don't like being on the losing side.' Liverpool lost 2–0.

Grobbelaar stormed away after the game, pausing only to give a brief comment to the waiting newshounds: 'I've been at Anfield for 13 years and never played in a derby like that – and I never want to again! We weren't just beaten, we were terrible. We were second best in everything,' he continued. 'Where was the passion? If people don't want to play for Liverpool, they should go and jump in the Mersey!'

Bruce later added that he had no regrets over the incident, but denied throwing a punch, adding with a dash of machismo, 'If I had come to blows with Steve he would be six feet under now.'

The incident was dissected and discussed across the country, and on that night's *Match of the Day* Grobbelaar was condemned by Alan Hansen as being irresponsible and irrational. Souness heard the criticisms of his goalkeeper but was nearer to condoning than condemning: 'I'm not planning any action against Bruce,' he said. 'I want players who show passion. I want a team of winners and a team who don't like losing. I wish I had more like them out there at Goodison.'

A few days later Bruiser owned up and admitted 'I was mad, but I play in a mad position.'

There's something not totally straightforward about the rather wanton thrill that goalkeepers get from the possibility of violence. It's something that comes up again and again when you talk to them. As far back as 1906 Woolwich Arsenal's James Ashcroft put his finger on it when, writing about the courage that was needed to play in goals, he penned the following:

'I don't know if you have ever been thrown into a fight which you did not seek. At the onset you are in a kind of a sliver of nervousness, but once you have had a smack on the jaw, your diffidence has disappeared, and you scarcely notice the hard knocks you receive in the fray. So it is in goalkeeping. The best incentive to good work is a rough-and-tumble early in the game . . . the harder the tussle the greater is your delirium of delight . . .'

Just to round it off he added, 'No one but a goalkeeper can realise the glorious sensation of such a happening. It is more than a sensation. It is an ecstasy . . .'

Indeed.

Naturally, there are those among the ranks of goalkeeping who are just plain troublemakers. Back in 1902 one such individual called Ridge managed to wreak havoc in a semi-final replay of the Hatchard Cup.

Ridge was in goal for Ecclesfield Town when, after 15 minutes, a misunderstanding between keeper and defence allowed a shot from opponents Roundel to go in off a post. According to the *Sheffield Daily Independent* there followed a most extraordinary scene in which Ridge and the Roundel centre-forward Griffiths became 'engaged in a bout of fisticuffs' which was the signal for mayhem. Around the pitch free fights broke out among the spectators, and officials had to rush in to break the players up. Ridge was sent off, but after only a few minutes of further play, 'amid cries of "Mob 'em" from different parts of the ground, a party of Ecclesfield supporters made a rush for the Roundel players, and Griffiths was the object of unpleasant attentions from a couple of the opposing players . . .'

It all settled down again, but there wasn't long left and on the final whistle 'an ugly rush' was made for the Roundel team and more skirmishes broke out around the ground. 'Several players attacked Griffiths and Hopkinson, while, with further cries of "Mob 'em", the spectators joined in the fray . . . Hopkinson and several of his comrades raced off with a howling mob at their heels, and succeeded in eluding the attack.' A couple of spectators were severely mauled – and all this because a petulant goalkeeper let in a goal!

But if none of this yet compares with the violence meted out to keepers, it's once again not because goalies are wide-eyed innocents in a big bad game. Keepers are strong men, capable of dishing it with the best, and in these days of professional athletes between the posts, the blind rush out for a ball or the mistimed punch can have dire consequences for anybody in their flight path. This is not to forget that at the end of the last century Foulke was first noticed after knocking out the teeth of a Derby forward and that on several occasions during his playing career, he feared that he had left some poor unfortunate for dead after bringing all 28st of his blubber down on top of them like a dead weight. No, the phenomenon of the pain-bringing keeper is nothing new.

In modern football two incidents stick out as examples of the psychopathic keeper on the end of a rush of blood and suffering from tunnel vision. The first came in the 1982 World Cup and involved possibly the most unpopular finalists ever – West Germany. In their approach to a semi-final clash with France, the Germans had been a public relations disaster. Algeria had beaten them in the first round, but the infamous 'Anschluss of Gijon' saw them beating Austria 1–0 in a most appalling game – it was a result that both teams knew would be sufficient to put them through to the next round at the expense of the plucky North Africans. In the second round they had refused to come out and play anything other than sterile football against England and then, sacrilegiously, they had knocked out the host nation, Spain. France, on the other hand, were winning friends left, right and centre. Their flair and dashing football was a delight and there wasn't a neutral that wanted Germany to win the semi-final in Seville.

Nevertheless, the match with its contrasting styles was to prove a thrilling affair – but in the final analysis the result hung on one ugly and unpunished incident in the second half. The substitute defender Battiston had only been in the game a few minutes when he latched onto a superbly angled pass from Platini that sent him rushing through the middle of a flat-footed German defence. He seemed certain to score, but as he slipped the ball round the oncoming keeper Harald Schumacher, the German flew through the air and hammered him into the ground with a terrifying forearm smash. It was a tackle of crushing cynicism and devastating brutality. The ball rolled out of play and Battiston lay lifeless on the ground. He was unconscious for more than three minutes and, after being stretchered from the field, he was put on an emergency oxygen supply in the changing-room before being taken to hospital. His jaw was shattered and two of his teeth were still lying embedded in the pitch.

It was a most blatant professional foul from the keeper, one of the worst and most dangerous ever seen. Yet the only person, of the millions watching the game that night, not to see what had happened was the referee. Not only was Schumacher not sent off, he wasn't cautioned. Not only was Schumacher not cautioned, the Germans weren't penalised – Dutch referee Charles Corver awarded a goal-kick! Schumacher, the butcher of Seville, had got away with it.

The removal of Battiston was crucial to the game. In extra-time France pulled away to a 3–1 lead only to watch hopelessly as their weakened defence caved in. West Germany pulled it back to 3–3 and then won on penalties. The next day Schumacher offered to pay for Battiston's teeth to be capped!

Goalkeepers are pretty good at successfully declaring their innocence. Sometimes they get away with such blatantly dangerous acts in public that it's a wonder they don't retire to lucrative law practices in Los Angeles. In January 1995 another German was involved in an incident highly reminiscent of the one in Seville. This time the German, Jurgen Klinsmann, was innocent and on the receiving end, but once again the referee saw fit to ignore the violence of a goalkeeper's frenzied attack. The game in question was Aston Villa against Tottenham, the keeper in the dock Villa's custodian Mark Bosnich.

Halfway through the first half the popular German chased a Spurs clearance deep into Villa's territory. But as he kept his eye focused on the ball, so too did Bosnich. The Australian keeper, anticipating a high bounce, charged out of his area and crashed, knees-first, into the head of Klinsmann. For anybody believing that this was an accidental clash, or an unavoidable bang, it should be pointed out that Klinsmann is neither a dwarf nor was he crawling on all-fours – Bosnich's knees were raised and flying fully five feet off the ground. It was a terrible, terrible blow, made worse by the combined pace of the two players. At the moment of collision Klinsmann's head jerked back with such a force that it looked to all intents and purposes like a mother ship preparing to detach from its booster rockets. Surely at the very least Klinsmann had shattered his head? The German forward, who had long overcome a reputation among English fans for faked dives and injuries, lay pole-axed on the floor. He had been hit smack in the face and was to lie unconscious for a full four minutes before being carried away on a stretcher.

Miraculously, the damage to Klinsmann was superficial, no bones broken and no harsh words from the master diplomat. As for Bosnich, naturally he denied allegations of reckless play, a claim apparently supported by the referee who again refused to award a free-kick.

3 Sex and drugs and rotten goals

Football is a fertility festival. Eleven sperms trying to get into the egg. Of course I feel sorry for the goalkeeper. But I've not had a boyfriend since October so I'm very sex-starved.
BJÖRK (IN *The Face*, JUNE 1995)

On 13 January 1995 two strangers approached Birmingham City goalkeeper Ian Bennett as he was preparing for early-morning training in Solihull. Second-division Birmingham were getting ready for an FA Cup replay at Liverpool following a stirring performance in the first game – a 0–0 draw. It had been a game in which 23-year-old Bennett had been acclaimed for his performance, his man-of-the-match show being capped by a brilliant save from arch predator Robbie Fowler.

It was ostensibly for this reason that the two men sought him out. Claiming to be from a Singaporean magazine, they requested an interview, taped their questions and took several photographs. Bennett was on something of a crest of a wave. He had just written himself into Birmingham's record books by keeping seven successive clean sheets and his manager, Barry Fry, had recently described him as one of the best six keepers in the land. He had shut Liverpool out despite still recovering from a car crash only three days before the game. Journalists turning up on spec were therefore nothing new and there was nothing suspicious about their unexpected approach.

Nothing, that is, until Bennett was left on his own with them. With no one else to witness it, the two strangers dropped their façade and offered Bennett £20,000 in cash to ensure that Liverpool won the replay by two clear goals. The startled keeper refused and ran to Barry Fry, but by the time they returned the men were gone, along with their offer.

Bennett had done the decent thing. As Fry was to joke later, the keeper should have taken the money because Birmingham were probably going to lose by a couple of goals anyway (as it happens they lost on penalties) and Bennett could have been £20,000 richer without doing anything.

The incident happened at a crucial moment for British football. With allegations of match-fixing hanging over two other goalkeepers, Bruce Grobbelaar and Hans Segers, the last thing that was wanted was another scandal. Players Union boss Gordon Taylor expressed his horror in the *Sunday Express*: 'I wake up every morning wondering what next? . . . When the Grobbelaar allegations originally broke there was a great deal of shock. Football has a tight grapevine and nothing of that magnitude has ever been hinted at before.' Taylor went on to implicate Malaysian and Far Eastern betting syndicates and suggested that nobbling keepers wasn't the most logical of acts: 'There are more significant people you can bribe – like a referee.'

But I've got news for you, Gordon. Firstly, football does have a problem with corruption, whether in Britain or abroad. It's sometimes on a small scale and it's sometimes on a massive scale, but it's there. And, secondly, the assertion that there's little point in getting to the keeper – for how can he guarantee a result? – may have all the logic in the world, but try telling that to those who would pervert the game.

It was a point heavily discussed when allegations were first made against Grobbelaar and co. Much of the gossip down the pub, on the terraces and, sadly, probably in the bedroom, focused on a goalkeeper's ability to (a) throw a match and (b) throw a match by the desired amount. Questions were raised along the lines of: supposing it's agreed that Newcastle will beat Liverpool by three clear goals and millions of pounds are wagered on it in some Kuala Lumpur gambling-den, how can the keeper stop his own team-mates from scoring too many to spoil the bet? What happens if the keeper lets in the required amount and Ginola or Ferdinand break through again? What if the opposing forwards, despite the opportunities that you present them with, keep missing?

Such discussions are normally terminated by 'Nah! There's no point in nobbling the goalie, there's too great a risk of failure involved and the odds don't justify the means.'

This conclusion is sensible. Anyone staking a pile of money on the back of a bent keeper would be taking a seriously major gamble on lady luck. Not only does the history of football betray an astonishing amount of corruption, however, it also shows that in many cases there was either a concerted attempt to get at the keeper or there was a maverick goalkeeper acting as the core of a bad apple.

The reason is obvious. The goalkeeper has significantly more power than any other player on the field to alter the course of a match. The keeper is the linchpin of the defence, for whom the dividing line between spectacular success and abject failure is frequently wafer thin. It doesn't take the acting talents of a Laurence Olivier (or even a Sylvester Stallone) for a goalie deliberately to let the ball fly into the top corner of the net while looking for all the world like he was within an inch of a stupendous tip over the bar. It does take a certain amount of front. If, just to top it off, he can couple that with the ability to give the defenders in front of him a huge bollocking for causing the goal, then he's away.

On the other hand, while nobbling a striker is undoubtedly a possible means of perverting a game, a centre-forward can never guarantee scoring a set number of goals, nor for that matter can he guarantee missing a set number of goals.

In terms of the actual play, therefore, the keeper is always most likely to be the culprit. But apart from the sheer fact that he can if he wants to, is there anything else that sets him up as the man most likely to take a dive? It is possible that the flamboyant, show-off element that makes the position so special, also makes it the position most likely to be involved in some naughtiness or other. Firstly there's the maverick element: 99.9 per cent of goalkeepers are as decent, honest, truthful and clean as a Persil advert, but these are men who take risks for a living, they calculate the odds, work out the angles and then plunge on in whatever the cost. Give the maverick keeper a good enough offer and he is liable to throw caution to the wind, along with his career.

There's another advantage, too – there's only one goalkeeper. When you nobble a goalie, you nobble one man. What would be the point of bribing Tony Adams (indeed!) without also bribing

Steve Bould, Nigel Winterburn and Lee Dixon? Not only is it more expensive to bribe an entire back-four, it also means that there are more people in on the scam – a dangerous thing.

Presumably Far Eastern (and we may just be talking about Bethnal Green here) gambling syndicates know what to look for when it comes to their man for the job. With Ian Bennett they clearly made a mistake, but what are the qualities and skills that they would seek out?

Firstly, their keeper must be a bit of a showman, generally popular with the punters, someone able to cover his tracks, hide his mistakes, be able to look genuine. He must be Robin Reliable, considered a safe pair of hands, though ever so occasionally prone to clumsiness or mistakes – the odds wouldn't be very good on a poor goalkeeper letting in goals, would they? Likewise, the keeper should play for a good team, generally expected to beat the opposition of the match in question (hence Bennett really was an aberration).

But the goalie must also be thick-skinned, contemptuous of his team-mates, have an overarching desire for even more money than he is already receiving and be prepared for the shit to hit the fan and start fertilising far-flung corners of his dominion when one day Sniffer of the Yard comes knocking at the door.

There is an alternative to nobbling the keeper, and that's removing him from the field of play all together.

Kidnapped!

In 1898, in an article in the *Football News*, an unnamed goalkeeper recalled a series of incidents that had befallen him years before. Although written anonymously, he leaves a trail of clues that any half-wit detective could follow up should they so desire – he had played for a Lancashire club referred to only as B– , they were the best club in the country, he had played for England and at the time of the events B– were preparing for a cup semi-final in 'a town noted for its cutlery'.

Ten days before the big match, with the team training near the 'town noted for its cutlery', the goalkeeper received a letter in a 'feigned hand asking my terms to throw the match away'. Having no interest in the offer, he reported the matter to the club secretary and was thanked for his honesty – here the story notes that the keeper in question had been a lifelong abstainer and hence 'no fear was manifested in his abilities'.

But bad luck was about to strike. One night, returning from town on his own, the keeper came across a well-known 'sporting publican' from B– , which for the sake of ease shall from now on be called Blackburn, and was enticed into a local hostelry.

'He would have me go into a wayside public house to drink success to the result,' notes the keeper, 'and after drinking a lemonade my mind was a complete blank. When my senses returned I was in a small room in the company of two powerful-looking men.'

He had been kidnapped and had no idea where he was, but from a window he could see what looked like moorland. One of the men told him that he was their prisoner until he agreed the terms of the letter. To his threats of bringing in the police they simply laughed.

It's then that he got his lucky break. The two men left him alone, locked in the room and 'To my joy at night I found out that the window frame was not very good, so by patience, and with a strong pocket knife, I managed to loosen the mortar and take it out.' With a strong pocket-knife? It pays not to ask too many questions.

In the darkness he could hear the rumble of a train and made in the direction of the track. Soon he had reached a small station where he roused the stationmaster and, after explaining his predicament, he was given the sofa to sleep on. In the morning a telegram was despatched to the club secretary who promptly turned up. As they chatted, one of the two 'powerful-looking' captors strolled into the station and turned out to be not quite so powerful as he appeared, for the stationmaster pounced on him.

Now that the tables were turned, the kidnapper, revealing himself as a bit of a sissy, pleaded for his liberty and blabbed like a new-born baby – the publican had been set to make a fortune on the game, the second-team goalkeeper was lame, the centre-forward had been nobbled, all they needed was to ensure that the first-team keeper was out of the picture.

Back in town the publican was summoned 'and I never saw a man so taken in in all my life. He promised to clear out from B– altogether, and give £20 to charities and £10 to the club for expenses.' His offer was accepted.

The goalkeeper now asked in private for the club secretary to forgive the wayward centre-forward, a plea that was agreed to. Blackburn won the semi-final and the final, with the centre-forward playing splendidly to make amends. And they all lived happily ever after.

Except that, in this era, still many years before gambling was totally legal in Britain, it seems that cup matches with their sudden-death element and penchant for surprises were particularly appetising targets for betting syndicates . . .

A right Villan?

The Cup final of 1892 between Aston Villa and West Bromwich Albion was one such match. Villa, who were pushing for the double, were odds-on favourites to hammer an Albion side which was languishing at the foot of the table. But things didn't go according to plan. A week after the final, Villa's goalkeeper, Jimmy Warner, his reputation destroyed by allegations that he'd fixed the game, had absconded with a servant girl, his career in tatters.

Serious questions about Warner, and in particular the company he was keeping, had been asked privately in the days leading up to the big game. Warner was a 27-year-old with a reputation for spectacular goalkeeping ability and a safe pair of hands. His performances in the league and earlier rounds of the Cup had been widely acknowledged as instrumental in putting the Villa in the strong position they now found themselves in. But at Holt Fleet, where the Villa team had been in serious training, it was said that he was not pulling his weight, missing schedules and, worst of all, socialising with a dodgy local boxer called Overton.

On Cup final day 30,000 people made their way to Kennington Park expecting to see a Villa romp in the sun, but they didn't have to wait long for the first of a series of shocks. Three minutes into the game Albion pushed forward, Geddes sent in a shot and 'Warner received it, but the ball seemed to spin out of his hands, and the first goal was scored for the Albion.'

Twenty minutes later Warner had the opportunity to make amends, but muffed a catch and Albion were 2–0 up. Ten minutes into the second half Warner was caught horribly out of position and the Albion were steaming. As much as Villa pressed for some consolation, they failed to get it. Albion returned triumphant to Birmingham, winners by three goals.

It wasn't long before the privately asked questions turned into public accusations. At a post-match dinner in St James Hall, Piccadilly, organised by the MP Captain Grice-Hutchinson, there had been a nasty incident resulting in a walk-out by an abusive Warner and 'friend'. Later on he was removed from a train for behaving 'scandalously' and using foul language. Once off the train, according to one report, he 'behaved in such a fashion on the platform as to bring discredit on himself and the club'.

Back in Birmingham the local *Daily Mail* reported that one man presented himself at the Villa and 'mentioned the name of a bookmaker who is said to have been told by Warner not to lay against the Albion . . . There are dozens of people who have "been told" that Warner openly boasted that he had made more money over the match than he had lost in bets . . .'

Not long after the final whistle a group of men attacked and 'blackguarded' Warner's wife. That night the police were called to contain a vengeful mob bent on smashing the windows of The Old College pub in Spring Hill where the goalkeeper was the landlord. On opening up on Sunday another mob entered and 'hissed' Warner, making insinuations and accusations against the keeper. 'You're enjoying your winnings, are you?' was the big cry. 'Twister' was another.

Next day the *Birmingham Daily Mail* fuelled the fire further with an article headlined 'THE DEFEAT OF ASTON VILLA – a sinister rumour', detailing the 'lamentable exhibition' of Warner which it said had discouraged the Villa side. Warner in goal had been 'absolutely feeble', the paper asserted; had he played to his normal ability 'he would have saved the whole of the goals scored by the winners'. And had the teams swapped goalkeepers, 'The Villa would have had eight or nine goals'.

Villa executive G.B. Ramsey had heard the rumours that Warner had bet on the Albion to win and denied their validity. 'First of all,' he asked, 'is it possible for one man to sell a game?' Interestingly, he also reported that after the game there had been terrible acrimony in the Villa changing-room.

Warner himself vehemently denied any wrongdoing, threatening to pummel anyone he caught bad mouthing him: 'I only wish I could get hold of anyone who would accuse me of anything shady. I meant writing [*sic*] to the papers to contradict the assertion that I sold the match; I wouldn't do such a thing for £1,000. I have too much respect for my own town. The defeat has made a lot of difference to me. I bet £18 to £12 against the Albion winning, and I even bet an even £1 that they would not score against me.'

The worst thing about the whole business, Warner told the *Mail*, was the fact that losing the game meant that he was constantly being taunted by Black Country people making a special trip to his pub. 'I'd rather have been licked by a team of schoolboys than by the Albion,' he told the *Mail*'s reporter.

Warner knew why the accusations had been made. 'I think it has a lot to do with my acquaintance with Overton,' he said. 'I backed Overton for £30 to £20 when Stanton Abbott beat him, and now people say that I had sworn to get some of my Overton money back again. I am told some say he actually saw me and Overton dividing the money in London. Why, I actually had to borrow a couple of pounds on Saturday night to carry me on till I got back home.'

The allegations, Warner reported, were hurtful and he repeated his threat of violence: 'I shan't stand them much longer. I know I am innocent, and if the remarks are repeated the one who does it will either have to thrash me, or else I'll thrash him and soundly too. I know there's no ground for saying I sold the match and I shan't be able much longer to keep my hands off whoever suggests that I have played false with the team.'

By Tuesday there was a backlash in the keeper's favour, with loyal Villa supporters rushing to his cause in the letters column of the local paper. 'It is very unsportsmanlike to "kick a dead horse" and the slanderous assertions against Warner . . . should be immediately silenced, or evidence brought forward to prove them no slander,' wrote WFD, and WSS waded in with 'All right-minded people will agree with me in condemning the cowardly remarks made respecting the Villa goalkeeper . . . The Villa have only themselves to thank for the defeat, not Warner, and it is to be hoped that no more will be said by people who very likely lost a little money and were chagrined in consequence.'

Another letter, signed TRUTH, maintained that the blame lay elsewhere: 'Sir, the uncertain form shown by the Villa club during the past few years is unmistakably due to the fact that several of the most prominent players are, or have been, managers of public houses . . .'

The newspaper itself rallied to Warner's side, stating that they were prepared to believe Warner's 'flat and manly denial' of impropriety, adding that Villa's performance had been an honest but ineffectual display by the whole team. The paper took the opportunity to rail against betting on football matches which it claimed had halved the respectability of a blue ribbon game and 'simply shows that some of the patrons of the game are convinced that there is no higher level of morality in football than there is to be found on the turf or in the prize ring, or at the card table'.

But with the tide seemingly turning in his favour, Warner's fortune suddenly slumped. Ordered to a special training session on Wednesday to prepare for a big game with Sunderland, he failed to turn up although he had been spotted in town in the afternoon. Summoned to a meeting of the Villa committee that evening, he once again snubbed the board. Not present to answer allegations of misconduct, of discrediting the club and of associating with unsavoury characters, Warner was suspended forthwith. There were no allegations of match-rigging, though the exercise looks very much as if the committee, knowing that such charges would be difficult to make stick, were out to get their keeper in whatever way possible.

The odds now stacked against him, Warner responded in Friday's paper by claiming that he had trained harder than any other player in the squad and that the unpleasantness at the dinner was caused by a director: 'I was accompanied by a friend who had purchased a ticket, and who was objected to by one of the members of the committee, under the impression he had not a ticket. I felt hurt and we both left the room. This was the commencement of the words which subsequently ensued.'

But it was a Canute-like action on the goalkeeper's behalf. Already rumours were sweeping the city that he had run away with a servant girl and a week's takings from the pub. Whatever the truth of the matter, Warner had played his last game for the Villa and the mystery of whether he had thrown the Cup final was never resolved. He disappeared without trace, popping up only briefly to make a few appearances for Newton Heath (Manchester United) in the next season.

Happy Jack

Fourteen years later, in 1906, 17 Manchester City players were suspended, along with the club's manager, chairman and two directors, for bribery and corruption. A commission of enquiry had found that the club had literally bought the 1904 FA Cup – through the use of irregular and highly illegal bonuses. In addition to a seven-month ban, the players involved were fined and prohibited from playing for City ever again.

At the centre of the storm was Manchester's captain Billy Meredith, but not far behind him was the goalkeeper Jack Hillman – 'Happy Jack Hillman' – one of football's most colourful characters at the turn of the century, and a man for whom controversy was no stranger.

Hillman had already been suspended from football once before, in 1900, on charges of attempted bribery, and before that he had been kicked out of Dundee FC for apathy and allegedly not trying hard enough.

At 6ft tall and 16st in weight, it was said that Hillman was second only to Foulke in stature and second only to Sutcliffe, the England keeper, in ability. The *Who's Who of Football* for 1901–2 says of the big man, who once won a bet by keeping a clean sheet with one arm tied to his side, that 'he is a goalkeeper of much talent, but in other affairs he has been most unfortunate'.

The 'unfortunate' began with his days at Dundee, a club he joined in 1896. It was to be the start of tempestuous times for Hillman. In those days Dundee could field a good side, but the club staggered from one financial crisis to another. When it became a limited company in 1897, only a quarter of the 2,000 £1 shares were taken up. By the end of the next season most of the club's top players had walked out, their wages unpaid.

As part of a package to help both himself and Dundee, Hillman went on loan to Burnley, but even this proved troublesome, for the club's directors refused to pay an agent the agreed fee for the transaction. A history of the club records that, having complained at his treatment, the agent was 'debarred from the ground, great amusement being caused by the engagement of a noted heavyweight pugilist to keep him out'. The agent wasn't finished there, though, for he hired a hansom cab and drew it up to the ground's palings and watched the games in true comfort.

When Hillman returned to Dundee he found a team both dispirited and fatally wounded by the walk-out of players. Only himself and the Scottish international Keillor, remained from the previous season. The events that followed are open to dispute, but what is certain is that, after two friendlies, Hillman was suspended *sine die* and, following an acrimonious bust-up, he once again left Scotland for Burnley.

The flashpoint was a pre-season friendly with Dundee's local rivals, Wanderers. Dundee were losing 5–3 with five minutes to go when the referee awarded Wanderers a penalty. The incensed keeper vacated his goal and leant against a post as Wanderers tapped in a sixth. The local paper reported: 'Hillman thereafter declined to allow the ball to be taken to the midfield, and it was only after some wrangling between a number of players, including Hillman and the referee, that the ball was centred . . . Immediately on the whistle being sounded a large crowd surrounded the referee. The police, however, interfered before any violence took place and escorted Mr Smith to the pavilion.'

The board of directors suspended Hillman for his misconduct, but the suspicion remains that they had engineered the situation in order to reduce their wages bill.

At an appeal, Hillman maintained that the incident was merely a pretext for the directors to cut his wages from £4 a week to half a crown. But in a long statement the board responded vigorously, claiming that on Hillman's return from Burnley he had offered to buy himself out of his contract for £100. When the club refused he had yelled at the directors, 'You can go to —; I won't play for you.'

The board insisted that it was more than just the Wanderers game that had pushed them into their actions. When he had returned from Burnley, they said, Hillman had sulked like a disconsolate schoolboy at the club's refusal to release him. Among his friends and colleagues he had put it about that Dundee would be 'burst within six weeks'.

His true intentions had first come to light in another preseason friendly against Kilmarnock, said the board. At a time when all fouls were indirect, Hillman deliberately handled the ball from a free-kick as it sped into the net, giving Kilmarnock an unnecessary goal. Later in the game he had ducked his head out of the way of a shot to deliberately sink his team's chances. Finally, it was alleged, he screamed at club officials after the game: 'Pay the men and they'll play. You can't expect the men to play if they're not paid.'

The Wanderers game was the final straw, during which, according to the board's version, 'Hillman altogether acted like a fool. He was repeatedly rushing out of his goal to the referee and entering into disputes with him. He cursed and swore at his backs and put one of his backs through this into such a state that he hardly knew whether his head or his heels were uppermost. Later he left his goal and started to walk off the field, but evidently thought better of it and returned to his position.'

Of the penalty, this version states: 'Hillman was seen to come out of his goal, place his hands in his sides, lean against the outside of one of the posts and magnificently view the opposing forward kick into an undefended and open goal. The public were astonished, and the Directors saw that their fears were well founded . . .'

The statement ended by pointing out that the club was the master and Hillman the servant. Hillman had 'tried to assume the role of dictator, but if he was coolly – because he liked golfing in the summer at Carnoustie – to take his wages all summer, it was only fair that he should play for Dundee in the winter.'

In a far from amicable way, both sides in the dispute got what they wanted. Burnley moved for Hillman and he was off; Dundee scrubbed him from their wages bill and received £175 in transfer fees.

It was at Burnley that 'Happy Jack' was to get himself into really deep schtumm. As the 1900 season drew to a close, the Clarets needed to beat Nottingham Forest to stave off relegation – they lost 4–0. A few days after the game the Forest secretary made an official complaint to the FA, reporting an attempt by Hillman to bribe the Nottingham skipper to throw the game. It was said that as the teams came out onto the pitch for kick-off, Hillman offered Forest's MacPherson £2 a man to lose. He refused. At half-time, with Forest 2–0 up, Hillman repeated the offer, upping it to £5 a man. Again it was refused and again it was ignored. Burnley were relegated.

When questioned later Hillman admitted putting the proposition to MacPherson, but said it was only a joke. The joint commission of the Football Association and the Football League failed to see the funny side and slapped a season's ban on him – a lenient but nevertheless very costly punishment, as he lost a promised benefit match that would probably have earned him £300 as well as his year's wages.

His suspension completed, it wasn't long before Hillman was involved in more trouble. It's difficult to judge just how important a part he played in the Manchester City scandal – a club he joined rather than returning to Burnley. Meredith certainly took the lion's share of the blame after it was found that he had offered Leake of Aston Villa £10 to throw a game. But illegal bonuses of at least £931 paid to the City squad during their successful FA Cup run of 1904 and no doubt Hillman was only too willing to accept the extra cash.

For his part in the scandal Hillman received a fine of £50. In an auction of the banned City players, after the suspension period was over, he moved to Southern League Millwall Athletic for a short spell, but a nasty blow to his elbow ended his career and left him with a crooked arm. How appropriate.

Throwing it all away

As one might expect, football has been plagued by minor disgraces throughout its history. But in modern times, while scandals have been sporadic, they have, nevertheless, also been shocking. When exposed they have rocked football to its very roots. This may be partly because of the size of the cancer, but it may also be because the era in which we live, while proclaiming itself more liberal and less inhibited in its outlook, is in actual fact both more puritanical and more hypocritical than days gone by. It may also be because the pace and face of public concern, in the absence of any genuine public interest, is increasingly set by the muck-raking morals merchants of the tabloid press.

Drugs, alcohol, violence and depravity have all invaded the modern sporting arena, frequently scandalising the country's moral sensibilities. But each of these vices can be picked off: temporary bans, life bans, rehabilitation centres, prison. The offenders can be removed from the scene. All of them can be handled and, with the possible exception of drug abuse, none presents a conspiratorial threat to the fabric of sport. Gambling syndicates, however, do.

The thought of large numbers of footballers actively involved in throwing games for financial gain is a continuing nightmare for soccer's administrative élite. Football, without parallel in any other sport, has a dedicated mass following of committed and often unquestioning support. Not only would the throwing of games be corrupt, illegal and immoral, it would also severely undercut the almost religious zeal of the modern fan. For supporters to suspect that their team, the team they have followed through thick and thin, through rain and dog-burgers, and for whom they have shelled out hard-earned cash, was not trying as hard as perhaps they could, would fatally undermine their faith in the undying purity of the game.

This was the prospect that British football found itself faced with in the early 1960s, in the so-called 'Soccer Conspiracy'. The plot might at times have gone under a different name ('The Swan, Layne and Kay affair' after its three most famous participants from Sheffield Wednesday), and it may have had a little-known Scottish forward Jimmy Gauld at its heart, but the first man caught was a goalkeeper and so was the worst offender.

One can't help feeling sorry for Esmond Million, Bristol Rovers' goalkeeper: his was a particularly sad case. He failed to throw away a game, but successfully threw away his career and in the process didn't make a penny.

Rovers were due to play Bradford Park Avenue in April 1963 when Million received a mystery phone call offering him £300 to ensure that the Yorkshire team won the game. Million, who was in debt following a transfer from Middlesbrough and the lack of a buyer for his bungalow on Teesside, saw a way out of his troubles – 'It looked so easy,' he later told *The People* newspaper. 'I thought I'd be £300 better off without having to do anything for it.'

At a secret rendezvous in Doncaster, on the night before the game, he was given an advance of £50 in cash. It was money that was handed over with an undertone of menace. 'We want Bradford to win. If they lose we want our money back,' was the message drummed into the keeper. Million was quite clearly already a little uncertain of what he was letting himself in for and he is reported as saying 'I got the impression I was up to my neck in a deal with a tough crowd. I knew there would be "reprisals" if I didn't do as I was told. But it was too late to back down.'

From that point on, though, it was all downhill for Million. At Bradford he watched in anguish as his team-mates excelled themselves and took an early two-goal lead – all without him touching the ball, never mind being able to engineer a victory for Park Avenue. So desperate did he become that he had to take his chances on the rare occasions that they presented themselves: firstly a humble back-pass was deliberately allowed to slip through his fingers. Then, a matter of a few minutes later, he ran out to meet a lob and, pretending to punch it away, watched it as it ended up in the back of his net.

It was two-all at half-time, but that was the end of it as far as Million was concerned. In the second half the Bristol defence stood firm and no more opportunities came for the keeper to lose the game. 'When the final whistle went I realised that I had taken this terrible risk for nothing,' he told *The People*. He posted his advance back and waited for the repercussions. It wasn't long in coming. Million's flirtation with soccer-fixing was effectively finished at training on Friday morning, when the session was halted and all the players were ordered to the boardroom. Here, in front of his team-mates, Rovers' manager Bert Tann accused Million of taking a bung. The goalkeeper confessed. That afternoon he was suspended and reported to the Football Association.

It seems that Million had probably blown his own cover. In order to ensure that the bet came off he involved other players and it is likely that somewhere along the way someone opened their big mouth in the wrong place. Million persuaded his inside-forward, Keith Williams, to join the scam and gave him half of the advance, but although Williams took the cash, he had a last-minute crisis of confidence and played to the best of his ability. The goalkeeper had even less luck with his full-back and friend, Gwyn Jones, who refused point-blank to have anything to do with Million's plot. Not only that, Jones was clearly suspicious throughout the Bradford game that his mate was up to no good and there were a couple of confrontations as Million admitted. 'Two of the worst moments of the game came for me when Gwyn Jones twice walked over, stared angrily into my eyes and said, "I hope you are not trying to throw it, Es." I didn't say a word.'

Williams was suspended along with Million and both appeared at Doncaster Magistrates Court in July 1963 charged under the Prevention of Corruption Act. Alongside them stood Brian Phillips, a footballer with Mansfield Town, the man who had handed Million the £50 down payment. All three were found guilty and fined £50. Three weeks later they were banned for life from football and football management.

It had been a bad career move and one made worse for Million by the fact that three days after the acrimonious meeting in Bristol's boardroom, the wayward keeper's bungalow was sold and a cheque arrived in the post. 'If only I'd known,' he said. 'I would never have accepted the bribe. All our troubles would have been over.'

Meanwhile, another goalkeeper still had a few months to go before being outed.

Dick Beattie was an accomplished custodian who had played for Scotland at both junior and under-23 level. His career had taken him to St Mirren, Peterborough and Portsmouth and he was considered by some to have been the finest goalkeeper of his generation. But on 19 April 1964 he was exposed by *The People* newspaper – he may have been one of the best at saving, but he doubled up as the undisputed king of not saving. In an article by Michael Gabbert and Peter Campling headed 'I took bribes to let goals through', Beattie was named as the 'worst offender in the whole gigantic scandal of bribed soccer players'. The newspaper went on to say: 'He was the most persistent of those who have "thrown" matches, and the most successful in making it appear that he was playing to win. And he certainly made handsome profits in direct bribes and in betting on matches that he had fixed . . . He could have been the finest goalkeeper in Britain. But he was a big spender and greedy for money. He was easily tempted.'

In a confession extracted by the *People's* investigative team, Beattie was to admit to a whole litany of malpractices. According to the keeper, another footballer at Portsmouth had introduced him to a bookmaker who promised good money for every Portsmouth game that the Scotsman could throw. One example Beattie gave the paper was a match against Peterborough in April 1962, when his bookie watched from the stands as Beattie contrived to let in three goals. Sitting in the bookie's car outside Bedhampton Station, Portsmouth, Beattie was handed £100 in used fivers.

There was a big irony here, too, for so impressed with Beattie's performance were Peterborough, that two months later they splashed out and bought him. Not that this instilled in him a new-found sense of loyalty – the Scotsman continued to throw games and *The People* sympathised with Peterborough by paying Beattie a backhanded compliment: 'He was an artist at deliberately letting in goals while appearing to have unluckily missed making a miraculous save.' How were Peterborough to know?

Jimmy Gauld, the 'Mr Big' of the fixed-odds scandal, didn't know of Beattie's connection with the bookmaker. Beattie's involvement with Gauld was in addition to the fixed games and involved straightforward betting on matches. Players fixing scores for Gauld would be obliged to bet on the matches in which they were playing, using their own money. In this way bribes could be disguised and the players involved became more committed to keeping their word. It was a very lucrative practice. For fixing the Portsmouth v Peterborough game, Beattie received £100 from his own bookmaker and a further £300 from Gauld – for his very own bet that he could help Portsmouth to lose.

Conversely, there was also big money to be lost if things didn't go right. Beattie was betting £50 a time, a huge amount that was probably the equivalent of half his match fee. It made him all the more hungry to make sure that things went to plan – but it wasn't always easy. One weekend Gauld and Beattie bet on the result of the Peterborough v Queens Park Rangers game in which Beattie was playing and doubled it up with a bet that Brentford would beat Exeter, a game in which they had absolutely no influence. The latter half of the double was a straightforward bet on current form, and it was the part of the bet that went to plan. The part involving Beattie wasn't so simple, as *The People* pointed out: 'It was touch and go whether he could contrive a defeat for Peterborough. At one point the score was 1–1 with only a few minutes left to play. Then he managed to throw the ball straight to the feet of a QPR player who banged it into the net. "It was a very near thing," said Beattie, "and there was a hell of a row about it in the dressing-room afterwards."'

After the game Beattie met Gauld outside a hotel in Nottingham to receive another £200. Gauld told *The People* that the keeper was 'flat broke' when he arrived – 'he didn't even have the money to buy petrol to get him home if I failed to turn up'.

Beattie was eventually sunk when Gauld started blabbing to the press. Any honour among thieves rapidly evaporated when the newspaper offered soccer's Mr Big £7,000 to name names. A registered letter from Beattie to Gauld connected the goalkeeper to the case and a recording Gauld made of Beattie finished him off. The goalkeeper went to prison for nine months and, banned from the game, took up a new trade on his release. He spent many years away, working as a welder in Saudi Arabia and Iran among other places, but died of a heart attack in Scotland in 1990. He was 52.

The story of Tina and a bit of Rough

As if things weren't bad enough on the pitch, off the pitch life often gets worse. For if there has been one thing that footballers have never been able to resist, it's temptation itself. And why should they? Athletic young men, with an ever-growing wodge of money, access to all the country's best and worst nightspots, constant recognition and time to kick about. Pass me that sherbet, Herbert, here I come!

And goalkeepers are no slouches when it comes to tickling the sleaze and salaciousness scale of the tabloid press. Sex, drugs, booze, cards, horses – you name it and somewhere there's a keeper with his gloves off getting down to it.

Who can forget the night of 25 September 1980? Certainly not Peter Shilton. Nor for that matter can red-haired mother of three Mrs Tina Street, wife of 'irate husband' Colin.

'Soccer star Shilton and "Naked Wife",' headlined *The Sun* on its soaraway front page. 'England goalkeeper Peter Shilton was last night at the centre of an amazing row over a date with a girl that ended with a car crash and sex allegations from an angry husband . . .'

Angry Colin takes over the story, claiming that he saw his 27-year-old wife and Shilton leaving an Indian restaurant together. He followed the goalkeeper's Jag and found them on a remote dirt-track near Nottingham racecourse where his wife was 'almost naked'.

'I put my headlights full on the Jaguar. They were definitely making love. I knocked on the window and shouted, "I know you, Shilton. I've got you." I heard Tina say "It's my husband," and Shilton slid back on to the driving-seat and roared off.'

According to Mr Street, so flummoxed was the Nottingham Forest keeper that he.drove straight into a nearby lamp-post. 'I went to the police. When we got back to the scene, Shilton was doing up his trousers and my wife was struggling to get back into her clothes.' Yes, these must have been the days of exceptionally difficult fly buttons, and really swift bobbies.

Of course, Shilton denied it. 'Nothing sexual took place . . . I was out late last night, which is unusual for me. Towards the end of the evening I met a woman. I was on my own and felt like some company and I asked her if she would like to have a meal. It got very late and I asked her if she wanted a lift home. She accepted.'

Shilton's luck was right out: later that night he had stitches put in his jaw and gave a positive breath test. If that wasn't bad enough, things were soon to get worse. The day after *The Sun* broke the story, Forest met Arsenal at Highbury. It was Shilton's first public appearance since the crash and the fans had a ball. To the tune of 'Bread of Heaven' the words 'Peter Shilton, Peter Shilton, does your missus know you're here?' resounded around the ground, along with countless other unseemly chants. The *News of the World* reported that when 'he flexed his muscles by touching his toes there were shouts of "Haven't you done enough press-ups?"'

Shilton was sanguine enough about his barracking. 'I knew I was going to get some stick from the crowd, but it didn't affect my game. Things happen in life like in football. You have to accept them, and stand or fall by what you have done.' But the taunts were to pursue him for many a season. More than two years later Shilton was playing for Southampton against Tottenham when, one Saints fan remembers, 'Shilts came out of the tunnel and ran down the pitch. The Spurs fans all applauded him in unison (we all thought as a mark of respect for his ability), but as soon as he reached his goal and put his hand up to acknowledge the Tottenham fans, they all started chanting, "TINA, TINA, TINA". He was really embarrassed and turned away.'

Shilton is an example of an enormously successful keeper who fails to match expectations in his non-footballing life. As we have already seen with the demise of James Trainer and the death of Willie Foulke, this is not uncommon. In 1995 the press delighted in reporting Shilton's latest off-the-field woes when his wife Susan was fined for not having a television licence. *The Guardian* took out the great keeper's dirty washing and hung it there for us all to see: suspended from his job as Plymouth Argyle manager following a £50,000 dispute over an unpaid tax bill; a holiday home in Bigbury repossessed; facing eviction from two other properties in the Midlands; owing former team-mate John McGovern £7,000 on a loan; and forced to repay racehorse trainer Martin Pipe £3,000 after bankruptcy proceedings were started. Shilton, *The Guardian* informed its readers, 'is a known gambler' – which probably explains why even now, well into his 40s, England's finest is still looking for a game.

All of which make the problems faced by Alan Rough seem rather trivial.

The tune that hounded Roughie wasn't 'Bread of Heaven', it was 'My Darling Clementine' and the words went something like this: 'Where's the mincebeef? Where's the mincebeef? Where's the mincebeef, Alan Rough? It's in your pocket, in your pocket, in your pocket, Alan Rough.' And it was perhaps the cruellest chant of all.

In 1990 one of Scotland's finest was seeing out his days at Ayr United. Alan Rough's career had seen him keep goal for Partick Thistle, Hibernian, Celtic, the Orlando Lions and, most importantly, Scotland. A popular player and a bit of a card, Rough was nevertheless robust enough to survive such notable débâcles as Ally McLeod's disastrous Argentinian World Cup campaign of 1978 and in particular the 3-1 drubbing by the 'old men' of Peru – though he did feel the need to vindicate himself when confronted with criticism over Peru's equaliser, a long-range free-kick from Cubillas: 'I have studied this goal over and over on the video and there was no chance for him to score if the wall had not shied away from his head-high shot,' he claims.

It was in Alta Gracia, Argentina, that, after a night out at a local casino with some of the lads, Rough was caught taking a short-cut through a hole in the hotel fence by heavily armed security guards. Without any form of identification, the players were frogmarched back to the hotel to have their claims of innocence verified. At the moment of capture, fearing that he had been mistaken for a camp intruder, Rough was supposed to have uttered the immortal line, 'Don't shoot, I'm the goalkeeper!' If only the remark had had equal success against the forward-lines of Peru and Iran, Scotland's stay in South America might have lasted longer.

In his entertaining autobiography, *Rough at the Top*, the former international goalkeeper seems to be forever getting into trouble, although never in a particularly serious fashion. The pinnacle of Rough's career came during Jock Stein's reign as Scotland supremo; it also appears to be a period when Rough had set himself an undeclared challenge to see just how much he could get away with without being punished by the strict disciplinarian. In truth the answer is not very much.

When the Scotland team assembled in Troon on a Saturday night, in preparation for a Wednesday Home International match, Roughie and George Wood, another goalkeeper, inadvertently forgot the 11 p.m. curfew that Stein had imposed. Having successfully sneaked back into their room apparently without their manager noticing, they proceeded to push their luck by ordering sandwiches and two pints of milk. As the midnight snack arrived so too did Stein, and before he knew what had hit him, Rough was covered in milk. The next morning, when squad training was over, Rough and Wood were made to run and run and run until they were physically sick.

Stein evidently liked pouring cold liquids over his goalkeeper. On another occasion, this time in Belfast, when he correctly suspected that Rough was sipping a coke laced with whisky, he once again burst into the keeper's room and chucked the contents of the glass over him.

Animals played a large part in Roughie's career – and by this I don't mean Billy Bremner and Willie Young. Just before a close-season game against Poland he was stroking a horse when it spotted a rabbit and bolted, stamping on Rough's foot in the process. Jock Stein agreed that he would be able to play despite severe bruising, if the keeper's boot was cut. In order for this to work, though, Rough had to paint his sock black so that the Polish attackers wouldn't notice. Of more significance to Rough were the cows belonging to his predecessor in the Scotland goal, David Harvey. Harvey was a farmer and when a couple of his cows started giving birth he withdrew from an international, giving Rough his big break.

So where's the beef? Well, the beef had been on the shelf of an Ayr Safeways store, but as the goalkeeper left the shop it dropped, unpaid for, from the bottom of his trolley. He was picked up and charged with theft. It was a body blow to Rough, who always insisted that he was innocent. Three months of hell followed, deflating his usual resilience – his nine-year-old son was ridiculed at school and his wife abused in local shops. Ludicrous versions of what was supposed to have happened started to sweep Ayr, including one which said he had stashed the beef in his soccer kit and another that he had hidden it up his jumper and made a guilty dash from the store.

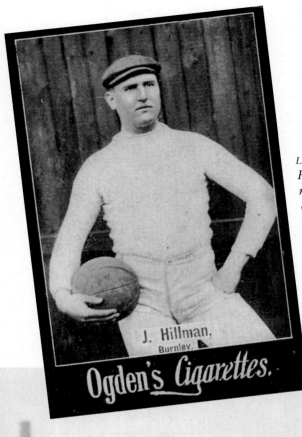

J. Hillman,
Burnley.

Ogden's Cigarettes.

LEFT: 'Happy Jack Hillman', a talented but maverick keeper, who in other affairs was 'most unfortunate' (Hulton-Deutsch)

BELOW: John Thomson's last 'do-and-die' save – the Old Firm game, 5 September 1931 (Caledonian Newspapers Ltd)

CERTIFIED COPY OF AN ENTRY OF DEATH

	REGISTRATION DISTRICT				Ecclesall Bierlow	
1916	DEATH in the Sub-district of				Ecclesall West Central	...in the Ca...

Columns:—	1	2	3	4	5	6
No.	When and where died	Name and surname	Sex	Age	Occupation	Cause of death
383	First May 1916 426 Glossop road U.D	William Henry Foulkes	male	42 Years	10 Matilda street Sheffield U.D. a Publican (retired)	(1) Cirrhosis of L... (2) Fatty Heart Certified by J. Dunlop

...ed copy of a Register of Deaths in the Distri...

...the Seal of the said Office, the ....

Fo...

LEFT: *A pre-gargantuan Willie Foulke in 1895, the early 'slim period' at Sheffield United (Popperfoto)* . . .

RIGHT: *. . . and as a cartoonist later saw him, the effects of eating his team-mates' breakfasts beginning to show (Hulton-Deutsch)*

LEFT: *Contrary to popular myth, Foulke did not die of pneumonia (Crown copyright; reproduced by permission of the Controller of the HMSO)*

e SHEFFIELD
GOAL KEEPER

F A KICK

Goal No. 1—Robson ... No. 2—Greaves ... No. 3 — Greaves ... No. 4 — Douglas ... No.

Greaves dazzles in rout of Scotland

ENGLAND 9 SCOTLAND 3 : by ALAN HOBY

SCORERS: Robson, Greaves (3), Douglas, Smith (2), Haynes (2): Mackay, Wilson, Quinn.

...shine. Dancing and prancing ..., the white-shirted Wizards ...highest-ever score against

Good Evening Gazette

GOALS THROUGH

No. 6—Haynes...   No. 7 — Haynes . . .   No. 8 — Greaves . . .   No. 9 — Smith

TOP: *The man who let nine goals through – the lonely vigil of Frank Haffey (Sunday Express; reproduced by permission of the British Library: LD42)*

ABOVE: *Dick Beattie makes another fine effort to stop a goal (Hulton-Deutsch)*

LEFT: *Mad dog forces Chic Brodie to take a bow-wow out of the game (Hulton-Deutsch)*

FAR LEFT: *The Return of the Mummy. Bert Trautmann gets in some comeback training (Hulton-Deutsch)*

ABOVE: *The Gorsedd of Bards, Dai Davies, playing for Swansea City, 1982 (Popperfoto)*

INSET: *A very green David Icke, Hereford United, 1975 (Mirror Syndication International)*

OPPOSITE
TOP: *Out of goal and out of the 1990 World Cup – Higuita tackled by Cameroon's Roger Milla 40 yards off his line (Popperfoto)*

BOTTOM: *El Condor splattered – Roberto Rojas apparently laid low by Playboy model 'Rosy Rocket' (Popperfoto/Reuter)*

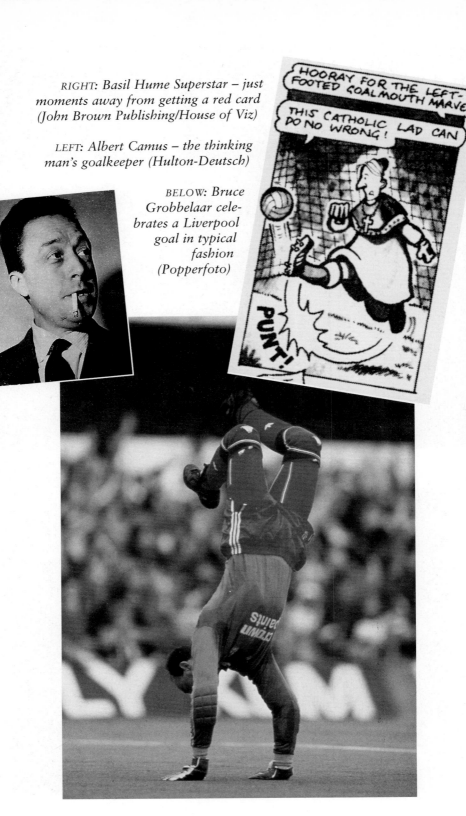

RIGHT: *Basil Hume Superstar – just moments away from getting a red card (John Brown Publishing/House of Viz)*

LEFT: *Albert Camus – the thinking man's goalkeeper (Hulton-Deutsch)*

BELOW: *Bruce Grobbelaar celebrates a Liverpool goal in typical fashion (Popperfoto)*

It was difficult for the goalie to understand how his standing as one-time national hero could take such an instant and crushing blow. In the Scottish *Sun* he tried to garner sympathy for his predicament. Under a story headlined 'THEY SAID I STOLE TO FEED MY FAMILY', he told how a simple mistake had turned his life upside down. 'I was careful to put the bleach in the front of the trolley and the meat at the back. But as I was packing the stuff into a carrier-bag at the checkout I missed the butcher meat and sat a carrier-bag on top of it by mistake.' As he left the shop one of the bags tipped over and everything spilled out. 'I stopped to put all the stuff back in the bag – including the meat which I assumed I had paid for with everything else. But as soon as I stepped outside a woman store detective stopped me and said I hadn't paid for everything.'

He was held in the store for over an hour and then taken down at the police station for a further two before being released. Over the next three months, as he waited for his case to progress, Rough's agony increased as friends called him to let him know the latest version of the story they had just heard down the pub. 'The court case hanging over my head has been the worst nightmare of my life,' he told *The Sun*. 'I just want everyone to know I'm no thief.' All charges were eventually dropped, but not without leaving the keeper with major scars.

But not, one suspects, as large as those etched into the psyche of the chubby-faced Colombian, René Higuita.

El Patrón, el Loco and a schoolgirl called Claudia

It may be a footballing cliché that nothing raises the temperature in Latin America like soccer. Sex and salsa may quicken the pulse, but nowhere does Bill Shankly's old witticism, 'Football's not a matter of life and death. It's much more important than that,' have greater coinage than in Colombia.

I first experienced this in December 1992 when I had arrived in Cali, Colombia, on the night that the city's major team, América, were playing for the big prize. If they beat local rivals, Deportivo, they would be crowned champions; lose, and arch-enemies, Atletico Nacional of Medellin, would steal their crowns.

And they did it – thank God they did it! América won 3–1, the championship was theirs. All we needed to do now was celebrate

– and what a celebration. The whole town jumped into the nearest car – it didn't seem to matter whose it was – and headed downtown, for the happiest traffic jam on the planet.

Motorcycle packs soared by, *hinchas* – fans – danced on rooftops and the incessant chant of 'América, América, América' filled the air. A sea of red flags, bandannas, handkerchiefs flooded the streets like a Bolshevik revivalist rally in Red Square. Aguardiente bottles flashed from mouth to mouth and a man with a revolver pointed it drunkenly at me. I found a red tea-towel on the car floor and waved it. He smiled and fired into the sky. We escaped down a backstreet, lives intact, thankful that my friends never do any washing-up.

The following morning, as dawn broke on the city's Avenida Quinta, the result of the joyous carnage was there for all to see – the burned-out shell of a bus was a clue. Newspapers reported at least two, and possibly more, murders, four dead in car accidents, 135 critically injured and dried-up bloodbanks in the city's and region's hospitals. I repeat, thank God they had won.

But here it's not only popular fanaticism that has deadly consequences. Rival mafia groups with far more organised methods of death and destruction have both cashed in on and simultaneously hijacked the game. Betting syndicates and drug laundering operations have corrupted football and turned it into a front for men who never stop short of murder.

Early mob involvement was crude and sometimes farcical. When Argentina needed to beat Peru by four goals in the 1978 World Cup, Miguel Rodriguez Orjuela, one of the capos of the Cali drug cartel and future owner of América de Cali, sent more than $500,000 in cash to Buenos Aires as a bribe to the Peruvian team. Sadly, the bags containing the money were lost in transit and were opened by a surprised customs official in New York.

The 1980s saw the drugs cartels muscling in on the game in a previously inconceivable fashion. In rivalry to the Cali mob and its América team, the notorious Pablo Escobar, a man with a passion for football and a penchant for death, homed in on Atletico Nacional, his local team and lifelong love. Footballers became commodities, wages were hiked and transfer fees spiralled.

The result was an intense and deadly rivalry between América and Atletico Nacional, a rivalry enjoined on a smaller scale by teams such as Millonarios and Santa Fé de Bogotà. Matches were thrown, referees bribed, players murdered and, in 1989 the season was abandoned in disgrace when referee Daniel Ortega was assassinated outside the ground of a game that he had refused to fix.

When the national team failed in the 1994 World Cup, the murder of defender Andrés Escobar was a sad and almost inevitable outcome. Escobar had scored an own-goal in Colombia's 2–1 defeat by the USA. The odds on a US victory were 19 to 1. Somebody made a financial killing that day; somebody else planned a real one.

On 21 July 1992 Pablo Escobar, king of the murderous Medellin drug mafia, escaped from his prison. Known as *La Catedral* – the Cathedral – it was a prison like no other, built to his own specifications with jacuzzis, football pitches, good food and fast women. Escobar had slipped away like a phantom in the night through an army cordon, when he feared that he might be about to be transferred to a more conventional, less luxurious gaol.

Thus began a protracted and desperate hunt for the 'world's most wanted man'. Having amassed a huge fortune in narco-dollars, Escobar was able to evade capture by calling in old favours, but as the police closed in on him and his access to the banks was severed, he became increasingly desperate. Even while still in prison he had organised the execution of former colleagues who had refused to lend him $1,000,000. Their bodies were buried under the soccer pitches of the prison. Now, in an equally monstrous act, he arranged for the kidnapping of 15-year-old schoolgirl Claudia Molina.

Young Claudia was the daughter of Carlos Molina Yepes, one-time ally of Escobar, but by early 1993 an avowed enemy and adversary in the lucrative cocaine trade. As Claudia played in the streets of Medellin she was lifted by Escobar's henchmen and held to ransom.

Kidnapping is a national disease in Colombia, as good a way of raising money as asking your bank manager for a loan. But the abduction of Claudia brought to the surface the very intimate relationship between the drugs barons and football. Like Escobar, Carlos Molina was a soccer fanatic and a major investor in

Atletico Nacional. He was a familiar figure with the players and in this moment of crisis turned not to the police, but to the goalie they called el Loco.

Raised in the poor Medellin barrio of Castilla by his grandmother, René Higuita had idled away his youth playing soccer, his head no doubt filled with what others believed to be ridiculous pipedreams of future fame and glory in front of crowded stadia around the world. Even in these early days, when the young René still aspired to being a centre-forward, the name of Pablo Escobar would have been known and in part revered. In Castilla he was a Robin Hood figure, el Patrón, who built houses for the poor and, more importantly for some, erected floodlights for the kids to play under.

At the age of 17 Higuita joined Millonarios in Bogotà before moving back to his home town to play in goal for Atletico Nacional. Here his youthful experience as an attacking forward gave him an exuberance that the penalty area could barely contain. Black curls flowing behind him, Higuita strode down the pitch at the slightest excuse, joined in on attacking moves, took penalties and scored goals – more than 30 in top-class games.

He was soon in the top flight of international keepers, and as his status grew so too did his audacity. Not that there were too many complaints. His excursions downfield are not only tolerated by his team-mates, they are integrated into their play. He is a skilful passer of the ball, with a deft touch and a good footballing sense.

'I think goalkeepers should get more freedom of expression,' he told one newspaper. 'If we are attacking, I like to move into the centre circle and exchange a few passes.'

Picked for the national team on the strength of his undeniable goalkeeping talent, Higuita became a national treasure, a symbol for Colombia – flamboyant, spectacular, vibrant, funny.

The Wembley 'Scorpion Kick' may have made him famous in Britain, but it was only one example of the man's philosophy, which must surely be that it pays to take risks. While his team-mates prepared for a free-kick against the USA in the 1995 Copa America, Higuita dashed the length of the field and crashed the ball against the bar. Asprilla tapped in from the rebound.

His flipside is, of course, Colombia's flipside too. Higuita, nicknamed by the masses 'el Loco', the mad man, is erratic, vulnerable to mistakes – flamboyant, spectacular and very often very funny mistakes. They were also frequently catastrophic and humiliating. Against Brazil in the same Copa America, Higuita fisted a corner into his own net, a typical botch that every so often serves to undermine his reputation.

Most famously, he screwed up big time in the Colombia v Cameroon game during the Italian World Cup of 1990. Colombia's progress to the second round of the tournament had exceeded all expectations and had been achieved in startling fashion when Freddie Rincon pushed the ball through the German keeper's legs in the final seconds of their ultimate round-one game. Colombia could have hoped to have beaten Cameroon, but the decisive moment came when Higuita, receiving a pass 40 yards from his goal, was caught by the Africans' prolific goalscorer Roger Milla, who raced away with the ball, leaving Higuita hopelessly chasing the Cameroonian back to the empty goalnet. He lost and so too did Colombia.

Despite returning under a cloud, the Colombian coach Francisco Maturana refused to blame him, saying that Higuita was 'without doubt the saviour of Colombia and not the crazy goalkeeper that some believe him to be. He brings the ball out with competence and great security.'

As Higuita made a name for himself on the football field, so el Patrón, Pablo Escobar, began to take an interest in him. Escobar was a soccer fanatic and even in hiding, in the days before his incarceration in *La Catedral*, he wished to be associated with his heroes. In 1987 he summoned Higuita to meet him for the first time. They talked soccer and, according to the goalkeeper, Higuita suggested to Escobar that he give himself up.

Their next meeting was four years later when Escobar was locked away in his luxury prison. Although invitations from el Patrón were difficult to refuse (how do you say no to one of the most powerful and ruthless criminals in the world?) this meeting scarred Higuita badly. Photos of him sharing a joke with Escobar were published and the impression created, of a couple of old pals together, was difficult to counter. It was for this reason that Carlos Molina solicited Higuita's help.

It all began with a phone call, a car to Molina's home and a demand for el Loco's intercession. To be charitable to the keeper it was, once again, one of those requests that are difficult to refuse. Molina was a powerful drugs boss; he too was suspected of ordering and carrying out assassinations. To refuse help was to refuse to live.

Higuita left Molina's house with $300,000 bundled into a briefcase and waited for a call. The money was to be given to the kidnappers in exchange for the girl. Days passed before the word finally came through and he was ordered downtown to a secret location. The operation went like clockwork. The case was passed over, Claudia was released and her father delighted. So delighted that he rewarded the goalkeeper with a thank-you gift of $64,000.

El Loco claims that the money was forced on him, that he tried to refuse it, that he had no choice but to accept, but even as he boasted naïvely in the press and on the television about his glorious part in securing the release of a young schoolgirl, the police were moving in on him. Hoist by his own petard, Higuita was imprisoned in June 1993 without trial, under Colombian emergency powers that prohibit anybody enriching themself from the proceeds of a kidnapping. He was to be in gaol for seven months, being released in January 1994 after going on hunger strike. Even by the time of his release he had neither been formally tried nor even indicted.

Imprisonment almost ruined his career. It certainly curtailed any hopes that he harboured of representing Colombia in the 1994 World Cup. His journey back to fitness and form was not without its problems, but having succeeded he has also re-established himself in the public imagination as one of the great showmen of football.

Higuita has already gone a long way to securing his future among the great names of the game and he has already written his own epitaph: 'When I have finished my career, my name will stay on people's lips and in their minds as a player who brought a bit of magic into the lives of ordinary people.'

El Condor splattered

One of the most audacious acts of footballing sabotage occurred in South America, during 1989's World Cup qualifiers. While it is a widely held stereotype that South America is a hotbed of back-handers, bribes and bungs, it seems that the continent is not particularly fertile ground on which to propagate a corrupt goalie. Or at least there are very few that have blossomed sufficiently to need pruning. Indeed, sometimes keepers are completely innocent victims. Take Juan Carlos Maciel of Colombia's Independiente Medellin club, who was banned for six matches in 1995 when traces of a prohibited substance were discovered in his urine. It appears that Juan Carlos, or Juanca to his friends, suffered at the hands of both the bad guys and the good guys. The high levels of Lidocaine that were found in his sample were an anaesthetic that would have slowed him down. They were hardly a performance enhancer and the likelihood is that he was doped by a rival team. When the authorities kicked him out of the game, the dopers effectively won.

In the years before 1989 the largest upset had been caused by Peru's Ramon Quiroga, a wild keeper who had quite possibly been an early role model for Higuita, and a man who was quite possibly innocent. Quiroga had been born in Argentina, but was a naturalised Peruvian and played for his adopted country during the 1978 World Cup finals. It was here that he too earned the monicker el Loco, enhancing his reputation with long runs into the opponents' half, sliding tackles miles from goal and, ridiculously, against Poland getting booked for a rugby tackle on Lato, nearer the Polish nets than his own.

The 1978 finals were held in Argentina and were critically important for the home side. Success on the football field meant the continuing political survival of an ailing and violent military dictatorship. The head of the ruling junta, General Videla, knew that victory would see 60 per cent of the population happy and dancing on the streets; he also knew that defeat would see 60 per cent of the population baying for blood and dancing on his grave.

Peru and Argentina met in the semi-final, with the home team knowing that they needed to win by at least 4–1 to progress to the final. If ever a game was fixed, it was this one. Argentina put six past a team that had earlier hammered Scotland and Iran and drawn with Holland.

The result incensed many. Brazil, who went out of the competition on goal difference, cried foul, and in the search for scapegoats Quiroga's Argentinian connections were held to be key. Recriminations piled on top of recriminations and, personally wounded, he made public declarations of his innocence, even writing a letter of self-exoneration to the press for continent-wide publication. It was met with a wall of disbelief.

There is, however, no doubt about the guilt of Chilean keeper Roberto Rojas – he's owned up. Unfortunately for him, he is also banned for life from football.

In the run-up to Italia '90, Chile and Brazil were due to meet each other twice. It was not a gentle pairing. Two years earlier in the Copa America, Chile had thumped Brazil 4–0, making them the last team to beat Brazil anywhere in South America. Now Pele, safely in retirement, was already declaring to an adoring nation that it would be a disaster if Brazil failed to qualify for the World Cup.

A controversial first leg in the Chilean capital Santiago had finished 1–1, the home team equalising deep into injury-time. Hyped up by both press and team officials as a full-scale war, it had been a ferocious game that had lived up to its near-hysterical billing. Romario had been dismissed, a Chilean had been sent off and six more players had been booked. Over ten minutes of injury-time were played and the crowd had rained missiles down onto the pitch.

Forced into action by the crowd trouble, FIFA moved in and closed Santiago's national stadium. Chile's next home game had to be played in Mendoza, Argentina.

By the time of the second meeting of the two, this time in Brazil's Maracana stadium, the South American league system had worked itself out: Brazil knew a draw would be enough; Chile knew they had to win to qualify.

But until Careca scored for Brazil, early in the second half, the game had been a complete contrast to the first match. Yes, the Chilean national anthem had been drowned out by boos before the game, but only two players had been booked, remarkably few for such a potentially explosive game. As the ball hit the back of the net, however, the party began. Minutes later, from out of the crowd, a firework hurtled aggressively from the hand of a glamorous young secretary called Rosemary. Amid a fog of smoke and the sharp cackle of a flare, Roberto Rojas, 'El Condor', hit the ground, blood pumping from his head like a newly drilled oil-well.

The Chileans walked off, their goalie straddled between them like the sacrificial kill in a Brazilian deer hunt. Twenty-five confusion-filled minutes later, the game was abandoned, the boys not from Brazil refusing to return to the field.

Back in Santiago, thousands of furious Chileans gathered in front of the Brazilian embassy. The windows of surrounding buildings were smashed and the flag of Brazil symbolically burned.

There was already talk of a replayed match on neutral territory, but there were also rumours of a faked dive by el Condor, a fall to void the game and give Chile another crack of the whip. Inevitably enough, it was started by the Brazilian team doctor: 'I am absolutely certain he was not hit,' Dr Lidio Toledo told the press. 'I also can guarantee that the red liquid they said was blood was just mercurochrome. The flare that fell is for signalling and is not explosive.'

Examination of photos taken of the incident showed that the firework had landed over a metre away from the prostrate keeper; examination of the gash to his head didn't appear to be the result of a burn or an explosion – more likely it came from a sharp instrument.

The problem was handed over to FIFA to sort out. Their ruleboook was clear: any team abandoning a game forfeits it by two goals to none. But there were other precedents for the Chileans to cite, most notably from 1987 when the goalkeeper of Cyprus had been hit by a smokebomb thrown by a Dutch supporter. That game had been restaged behind closed doors in an empty Amsterdam stadium. This was what the whole of Chile wanted, but it wasn't what they got. Days later, with Rojas still swathed in bandages and offering words of forgiveness to young Rosemary, FIFA awarded the game to Brazil. Chile were out of the cup, Brazil were on their way to Italy.

'FIFA has done something totally wrong, which bears no relation to what happened in the Maracana,' said Chile's midfielder Pizarro. 'I saw Rojas bleeding and now they are doubting his injury.'

A Chilean official waded in with the conspiracy theory that Brazil were too powerful to kick out of the cup. 'The decision was expected,' he said. 'There are too many economic interests involved.'

For his part, el Condor was ordered to Zurich to explain himself to the authorities. With the evidence piling up against him, FIFA barred Rojas from every level of football for life, while Chile were banned from future World Cups.

In Brazil a blonde, 24-year-old secretary with an electricity company achieved overnight celebrityhood. Rosemary de Mello – normal salary $100 a month – appeared on the news, on chatshows, in a television ad for a travel agency and finally, for $10,000, across ten pages of *Playboy Brazil*. In Chile she was known as *Mujer Bengala*, 'the woman of the flare'. In Brazil she was known simply as *Rosinha Fogueteira* – 'Rosy Rocket' – and she was a national hero.

As for Rojas, in subsequent years he was to admit carrying a scalpel in his glove, ready to take advantage of any opportunity as and when it inevitably presented itself on that heady night in the Maracana. The ban devastated him. His old club Colo Colo and friends helped him to make ends meet as much as they could, and, eventually, after much soul-searching, he got himself a job as goalkeeping coach with another of his old clubs, São Paolo in Brazil.

In February 1995 he told *World Soccer*, 'In the heat of battle you tend to do things which you then regret for the rest of your life.' El Condor's way through the mire into which he had dragged himself has been religion, his faith leading him to become an evangelist preacher for a little known group called The Sportsmen for God. 'The first thing you have to do to be able to live in peace with your mind is to realise that you were wrong,' he told the magazine. 'I accepted this and that is why I am not so worried about the future now.'

4 The holy goalie

The kingdom of heaven is like unto a net . . .
MATTHEW 13:47

'Two-four-six-eight, who do we appreciate? His Eminence Cardinal Basil Hume.' This was the chant of adoring fans when the football-mad Archbishop of Westminster played goalkeeper some time in the early 1990s. But as much as the followers of Fulchester United loved him, he was to blow his chances of ever getting the papacy that afternoon. His disgraceful behaviour might have been sanctioned 500 years ago, and it may continue to be popular in certain parts of Belfast and Glasgow, but when his 'goaliness' nutted Walford Town's centre-forward, little Bobby Runcie, the then Archbishop of Canterbury, his career went up in a puff of white smoke.

Dismissed from the field of play, His Eminence was heard to complain, 'Verily it's a real sickener.'

Sadly, though, I'm being rather unecumenical with the truth – this scene was little more than a comic strip from the fevered imaginations of the writers at *Viz* magazine. Nobody had ever really shouted 'Hooray for the left-footed goalmouth marvel', and Basil Hume never really replaced that goalmouth artiste Billy the Fish. Indeed, His Eminence tells me that, despite a great enthusiasm for soccer, he used to be a rugby player.

Nevertheless, in placing him between the sticks, the writers at *Viz* touched upon a football phenomenon – the keeper as Holy Goalie. And it's not just because Jesus was, until recently, making saves for Vitoria Guimaraes of Portugal. Whether taking their lead from the Bible – 'and on him they laid the cross' (Luke 23:26) – or from other celestial sources, there is something about the keeper that often makes him the spiritual touchstone of the team.

It could be something to do with all the spare time that they get to spend doing nothing while the ball is at the other end of the pitch – some twiddle their thumbs, some flex their buttocks, others contemplate the meaning of life. It could be the natural sensitivity of the goalie, a man who feels every goal conceded like an arrow through the heart and who, but for strong laws and strict admonitions from parents against killing people, would probably receive them. It could just be the number of kicks he gets in the head.

It's definitely there, though. His Eminence Basil might not in reality have ever put on the green jersey, but his immediate boss, the one with the white cap, most certainly did. Pope John Paul II, when he was a mere Karol Joseph Wojtyla of Wadowice, Poland, was a great one for a bit of pre-transubstantiation 'shots in' – and, on those icy Polish playing-fields, he was always keen to be the one with the gloves.

As an apparently athletic youth, in the days before he joined the 'Living Rosary' prayer group, the young Karol loved to swim in the flooded waters of the River Swaka and enjoyed all sorts of games, sports and stage plays. But his true love was playing in goals, according to one of his official biographers, Lord Longford: 'He was not only outstandingly good at his books, he was also very popular with his schoolmates. Powerful of build, he was one of the best footballers, usually playing in goal.'

However, for those seeking concrete evidence of the Man Who Would Be Pope's footballing abilities, time has not been too kind. No secret footage of miraculous saves, no black-and-white shots of young whitecap divinely intervening at the foot of a burly Polish forward, no post-match interviews with Karol declaring himself 'as sick as a prelate'. For at that moment when Karol was playing football at school and university and possibly (but only remotely possibly) considering the relative strengths of offers from Legia Warszawa and Jagiellonia Bialystock, history intervened in the form of a German tank column. Karol's college was overrun by the invading Hun, his seminary went underground and the nearest the Man Who Would Be Pope was to get to topflight football from then on was stopping volleys from young choirboys in the Vatican gardens.

But goalkeeping isn't just a Catholic thing. In the last century G.B. Raikes of Oxford University was a top-class keeper. While still at college he was playing well enough to earn himself a place in the England team and was probably the last goalkeeper to captain England before Frank Swift did so in 1946. After graduating, though, he took holy orders and didn't play again.

The Church didn't prevent Leonard Small eking out a successful career in goals, but it eventually came down on him like a ton of swarming locusts and banned his on-field antics. Small, who was ordained a minister of the Church of Scotland in 1931 and who rose to the heady heights of Moderator of the General Assembly and chaplain to the Queen, captained Edinburgh University football team and after leaving college became the amateur keeper of the Scottish second-division club St Bernards. His ability was recognised in 1929 when he was capped for amateur Scotland in a 3–1 defeat by England at Elland Road. Shortly after being ordained, though, the authorities in the Church took him aside and gave him a quiet talking-to. He had become the minister of St John's Church, Bathgate, and was playing for the local team when, as he recalls in his autobiography *The Holy Goalie*:

> Come the Saturday before New Year, I dashed out and dived at the opposing centre-forward's feet and got his boot across the forehead. I went into the pulpit with a suitably liturgical cross on my brow, but made of sticking-plaster. The office-bearers came to me and said: 'We know you got it respectably, but it doesn't look good. We think you had better stop.' So I did.

Nevertheless, it had been an interesting time for the reverend, teaching him more about his flock than any of his postgraduate studies in Rome, Berlin and Zurich. It was through football that he received an early education in politics: when Prime Minister Stanley Baldwin visited Edinburgh, to be installed as rector of a college hall, Small and the university shinty goalkeeper were drafted in to defend him from 'bags of flour, soot, pease meal along with a few codheads, even a live cockerel' that were thrown by disgruntled students.

Small recognised, too, that players and crowd alike responded differently to him than to each other, perhaps even a little uneasily. As a divinity student he had played with a team full of miners, most of whom showed him a great deal of warmth and respect.

What was normal language was carefully moderated, and the same attitude prevailed among the spectators. Once, when playing against Raith Rovers at Starks Park, Kirkcaldy, there was a mix-up in the goalmouth and the ball went past – no one was sure if it was a goal-kick or a corner-kick. There was a voice from behind the goal: 'Hey, referee . . . ask the goalie. He's a meenister . . . he'll no' tell ye a lee.'

In spite of the ban on his footballing activities, Small remained a soccer fan until his death in 1994. In the austere surrounds of the Scottish Church his enthusiasm was not without its problems. When, as a senior churchman, he was both seen having a kick-around with apprentice boys in Govan and also known to have refereed a match at Elgin he was accused of lowering the dignity of his office. When he accepted an invitation to a game at Ibrox he left the ground to find a picket-line bearing placards that proclaimed 'SMALL MUST GO' and 'JOHN KNOX WOULD TURN IN HIS GRAVE'.

As Small received his CBE in 1975 he would probably have understood the dilemma that had recently confronted another Scottish goalkeeper. In February 1974 Britain was held firmly in the grip of industrial action by its coal-miners. Their ban on overtime as part of their battle for improved pay and better conditions had reduced industry to a three-day working week. The miners' militancy, soon to be expressed in an overwhelming vote for strike action, had snared the Conservative government in a trap from which it could not escape. Within days Ted Heath had called an election and within a month he was no longer prime minister.

Up and down the country, power cuts were the order of the day. Blackouts closed schools and removed *Crackerjack* and Cilla Black from the television, candle sales reached an all-time high and neighbours gathered together to share cold dark nights of lukewarm milky tea from cracked flasks, wartime songs about bluebirds and Dover, and increasingly aggressive games of Scrabble.

To avoid the need for floodlights at football matches, kick-off times were brought forward and some games were allowed to be played on a Sunday – a revolutionary innovation designed to lessen the strain on the national grid.

In Swindon falling gates already had the club in the doldrums. They were frequently getting barely a quarter of the 19,000 that they needed to pay their bills passing through the turnstiles. Now, with the shift of local industry to an emergency Thursday-Friday-Saturday working roster, the outlook was bleak. In mid-January, hoping it would give the club a boost, the club jumped on the Sunday football bandwagon.

It took some time to find opponents willing to switch their fixture, but eventually it was announced that they would meet Bolton at the County Ground on the first Sunday of February.

A week later Swindon's young Scottish keeper, Jimmy Allan, threw a spanner in the works. The *Evening Advertiser* carried the story under the headline 'Devout Jimmy says "Never on a Sunday".' It went on: 'Jimmy Allan, Swindon Town's 19-year-old goalkeeper, threw the Sunday soccer experiment into turmoil today by refusing to play because of his religious beliefs. The young goalkeeper dropped the bombshell when he told Town boss Les Allen that he would not play in the first Sunday game against Bolton Wanderers this weekend.'

Allan had signed with Swindon at the age of 16 and had only recently battled his way up from third-choice keeper to the number-one spot. By the end of January 1974 he had played in 32 successive games, he was established; but, as he told the *Evening Advertiser*: 'I am a member of the United Free Church of Scotland, and I have been brought up to regard Sunday as a day for religious activities only. I have talked over the possibility of Sunday football with my father, and he told me that he would rather I did not take part. And I would like to respect his wishes.'

Town's manager Les Allen told the press that he respected the keeper's beliefs, but nevertheless attempted to change Jimmy's parents' minds. He failed and Allan's absence meant that Alan Spratley got his first-team debut.

Jimmy Allan was the first professional to refuse to play on a Sunday. It was a brave stand that cost him his regular place for a couple of years. Not until the 1976–77 season was he firmly re-established as the club's number-one keeper, going on to make more than 430 appearances – a remarkable figure considering that his career was cut short in 1983 by a manky elbow, smashed in a game against Rochdale.

Sunday soccer proved a flop. Less than 9,000 turned up for the Bolton game and it was to be another eight years before Swindon took the Sunday option again. Interestingly, this time Allan played. With hindsight, the keeper, who now lives and works in Devon, says of his refusal to play back in 1974: 'My beliefs were very strong, but also I was very inexperienced in life. My father was keen that I shouldn't play, that I should stand up for what I believed in. I did that.' He says that he had widespread backing from both supporters and players alike – 'The players were glad because they didn't want to play themselves on Sunday. It mucked their week up.' Yet despite the fact that his beliefs were just as strong eight years later, he decided to play on a Sunday. 'I had grown up more and found that even if I was playing in the afternoon, I could still go to church at night. The situation had changed, clubs were playing on Sundays, and besides, things come along like mortgages.'

Son of God, come down from the cross*

Following a complicated set of instructions scribbled hastily on the front of an old newspaper, I eventually pulled off the main road and rattled my car up a pock-marked dirt-track to the stone-arched entrance of a neat, but decaying former guest-house somewhere in the middle of Wiltshire. Guinea fowl, chickens and weeds overran the garden and in spite of an early morning mist that had blotted out the sun, the house sat quiet and dark.

As I looked for a bell and a sign of life, a large silhouette rose behind the window and beckoned me round to the back of the house. David Icke was expecting me.

Icke, for the uninitiated, is a former Hereford and Coventry City goalkeeper whose career was finished by debilitating rheumatoid arthritis at the age of 21, launching him on an odyssey that took him to the top of sports presentation at the BBC, the top of the Green Party, and then, after a mystical conversion in Peru, to the top of the tabloid press 'nutters' league.

He looks younger than his 43 years, but the neat, curly, trademark locks of the former *Grandstand* presenter have long washed away and been replaced by lank grey hair that demands the urgent attention of an enthusiastic barber. The house that we

*Matthew 27:40

enter has a slightly unlived-in feel, for the Ickes had only just moved there from their long-term base on the Isle of Wight. It's a big change for a family that made themselves infamous on an island of rather conservative mores.

Intuition brought the Ickes to this spot. 'If you relate it to goalkeeping, anticipation was one of my abilities. The ability to start to move in a certain direction in an apparently no-hope situation, somehow intuitively you know where the ball is going to go . . . this is how we got here, pure intuition.'

Icke's press-cuttings over the last five years expose two types of interview with the man who, dressed in turquoise ('the colour of wisdom and love') once declared himself the Son of God and predicted the disappearance of Cuba, the Isle of Arran and the White Cliffs of Dover by the end of 1991. Style one is the 'I'm a really clever journalist and I'm going to prove it to you by taking the piss' type interview; style two is the old cliché 'I was a real cynic, but you know the man has got a point' type interview.

And let's be clear here and own up. Sticking Icke in the Holy Goalie chapter is an exercise in slight and contrived cynicism, for the former 'turquoise one' emphatically dismisses religion as 'psychological fascism'. He is, nevertheless, a keeper who has gone public and laid out his spiritual mindset for all to see and for most to mock. There are few people in Britain who have been so publicly ridiculed as Icke; in an earlier age he would have been burned at the stake, and at times it must have seemed preferable.

The man can fairly talk. We agreed an hour-long interview, but three and a half hours and barely half a dozen questions later, I'm finally walking back through the stone arch to my car.

If nothing else, Icke is an exceedingly focused man. Examine the evidence: (i) As a child he had seen football as salvation and, seeking to escape a lonely life and an abusive father, he determined to become a professional keeper. This he achieved. (ii) When interviewed by BBC television over the impact of having his career curtailed at such an early stage, he had been so impressed by the technology that he had decided that this was for him and, within a very short space of time, he was not only a trained news reporter, but also a regular presenter of *Grandstand* and the World Snooker championships. (iii) Within six weeks of setting up a branch of the Green Party on the Isle of Wight he was a national spokesperson for an organisation soon to achieve 15 per cent of the vote in the European elections.

In many ways Icke fulfils the cliché of the goalkeeper as a loner. As a child he preferred his own company to mucking about in the streets with other kids. 'I liked to play alone with little push-along trains. I did this for hours every day. I loved steam trains and I dreamed of being an engine driver.' Such reclusiveness would see him crossing roads, with nerves in his stomach, to avoid having to say hello to other children and people he knew. It was something he carried with him through countless childhood football trials and games, but he sees his early love of soccer as the first stage on his journey towards self-confidence.

'My experience of goalkeepers and goalkeeping is that we think more than other players,' he says emphatically. 'It's an expression of the fact that although you're part of the team you're actually on your own to a very large extent. To be a really good keeper what you need is self-confidence. If I'd have been what I am now as a person, with the same ability and body as I had then, and without the arthritis, I'd have at least played in the Premier League . . .'

Icke is big on psychics and psychic intuition and believes that the world is one gigantic mind. 'All energy is consciousness, all consciousness is energy' is a particular mantra of his. It's a world where all things – humans, chickens, the walls to his house and the wedding ring on his finger – are magnetic energy evolved to a different point. These different energies store information from which 'good' psychics can read a projected, but not unchangeable future.

A Scottish clairvoyant told Icke. 'You know why people like Gary Lineker always seem to get in the right place at the right time? It's because they're psychic. They don't realise they are. What they are doing is tuning into the projected future a split-second before it becomes the now . . .' And Icke agrees: 'I think there's a lot of psychic, intuitive stuff going on in football all the time among players who are head and shoulders above everyone else. Bobby Moore was the classic intuitive footballer.'

Icke is big on fear, too, which he sees as a controlling mechanism of the human race; overcoming the fear in his life has been one of his big challenges and, in a peculiar way, one of his pleasures too. Where some goalkeepers might have found the chants and taunts of the fans unsettling, Icke got a secret kick. 'Away supporters always used to wind me up. I used to love it. My great orgasmic experience in football was being away from home, where the goal net was very close to the crowd and there's a full house, you're 1–0 up, under pressure, and the crowd behind you are willing the ball in. I had one or two games like that and it's like an orgasmic experience – you're on such a flipping high.'

Icke always wanted to be a goalkeeper. He made it into Leicester Boys under-14 team and suddenly there was interest from all over the place. He was offered trials by Nottingham Forest, Arsenal, Liverpool, Millwall and Leicester City. Being a supporter of the last-named he was naturally curious about their approaches, but saw any chance of progress blocked by a senior team that boasted England's number-one Gordon Banks as the first-team keeper and a very young Peter Shilton in the reserves. He shifted his attentions to Coventry and, having passed a trial, joined the club in 1967. Thus began a short and painful career that eventually took him to Hereford and then, crippled by the agony in his legs, to the dole queue.

He still feels bitter about this period. It wasn't just having his career snatched away from him, it was the treatment meted out by the club. Hereford were on a roll, climbing divisions and winning big Cup games, making money. Home crowds topped 12,000 and Icke was part of the success, but he complains they 'did the dirty on me'. Two weeks after the doctor told him he wouldn't play again and just as the press interest in him waned, the club terminated his contract, a promised testimonial game never materialised and Icke and his wife Linda were left with £36 in the bank and a mortgage of £66 a month.

But let's face it, it's not football that Icke is famous for, it's not even really for reading out the scores as they came in at 4.45 on a Saturday afternoon. No, it's that moment in March 1991 when, having resigned from the Green Party, he flew into Gatwick with a message for the world. At a specially convened press conference a turquoise Icke, 'eyes blazing with the passion of a man with a mission', announced that he had been given the title of Son of God by a being called the Godhead. Icke's 'spiritual companion', Canadian Mari Shawsun, was to be called the Daughter of God and his wife Linda the Spirit of the Angel of God. 'We three form a triangle and along with my children, Kerry and Gareth, we are going to save the world from what would otherwise be certain destruction,' he told the gathered press.

He predicted the birth of a new baby Jesus; numerous environmental disasters and revealed that Saddam Hussein was dead. In this country, he proclaimed, Kent would be hit by a surge of energy damaging the Channel Tunnel, and the project would never be completed. 'Many people will think that I am out of my mind, a lot of people in this room will do so, but they are going to be proved wrong.'

Icke's final prediction was at least partly right, for he was devoured by a voracious press pack seething with bloodlust. 'The loony Gospel of Saint David', blasted the *Daily Mirror*, which urged readers to join the 'Potty Party': 'David Icke was offered another mission last night . . . to become the Raving Loony Green Giant party's first MP . . . Party chairman Stuart Hughes, who runs a Torquay hotel called Fawlty Towers, said: "He's the man for us." And Dr Heather McKee, psychiatrist at London's Charing Cross Hospital, joked after hearing of the new Son of God: "Sometimes we have wards full of them."'

For a brief moment Icke was everywhere. The papers were full of him: the *Evening Standard* warned its readers to 'Beware the Ickes of March', *Today* ran 'My turquoise mission of love to save the world, by David Icke'. On television Wogan humiliated him and in nightclubs stand-up comics built new material around him.

What was going on? Much was made of visits Icke made to a psychic called Betty Shine and visitations he received from the Ancient Greek philosopher Socrates, but Icke insists that the role of Shine was exaggerated. More important to him was that, having never knowingly met a psychic in his life, he was suddenly bumping into them all over the place.

Urged on by both a powerful personal intuition and one of these psychics to go to Peru, Icke upped and left, despite knowing little more about the country than that their soccer team had once beaten Scotland in the World Cup. Here, in the ancient Inca capital of Cuzco, Icke had a supernatural experience involving a hilltop, strange voices, a circle of stones and lots of rain, thunder and lightning that changed his life and presaged the 'Turquoise period'.

It's a time which he looks back upon with resignation. He claims to have learned two important lessons: 'Firstly how easy it is to get large numbers of people to think what you want them to think. Most people were laughing at me, not for what I was saying but for what I was supposed to be saying. And, secondly, I let go of the fear of what other people thought of me and I walked out of prison. I realised what the prison was, the prison is what other people think of you.'

He admits now that with hindsight the Turquoise period was a very good publicity stunt, though only at a subconscious level – 'at the time I was just thinking "What's happening to me? I feel the need to say this".'

Five years later he is on an almost perpetual speaking tour, addressing big meetings devoted to bringing 'suppressed material into the public arena'. The Turquoise period, he claims, was integral to this. 'Being ignored is the worst nightmare. If I'd taken the straightforward approach I might have got two pars in *The Guardian*.' As it is he gets interviewed constantly all over the country, on local radio stations and in the local press, 'They're talking to me not despite the Turquoise period but because of it.'

He claims to have built a 'platform of notoriety' for himself, from which he is currently fighting allegations that he is spinning 'a fantastical tapestry of far-right conspiracy theories' *(New Statesman,* 23 June 1995). He responds robustly to such charges. 'I said in 1991 that this process is going to go: ridicule, condemnation, acceptance. I've had the ridicule, and now I'm in the condemnation, with people trying to dub me a far-right Nazi, which is actually what I'm exposing to be running the world.'

For Icke we are moving into an important era; no matter that Cuba still exists, the White Cliffs of Dover still stand and Eurotunnel, on its better days, continues to shift thousands of passengers to and from the continent. 'If you look at information that is being gathered psychically all around the world, everything points to this decade being a time of tremendous changing weather patterns and colossal geological events. At the time that I was saying all this in 1991, I didn't know any of it, I was just in a fog.

'One thing's for sure, the weather patterns of the world are changing well beyond anything the greenhouse effect would have made happen by now and I think it's magnetic vibrational change that's changing the weather and I think we're in for a pole shift as well.

'I see the future in amazingly positive terms, the present restrictive prison is in the process of collapsing and the world financial system will go, and it will go, when it does go, very quickly. Coming out of that is a very different world, the kind of world we can dream of – and I think it's going to happen in our lifetime.'

Making a football analogy Icke says, 'Football is a microcosm of life. Most of the people involved in football are sitting in the flipping stand watching others do it. Most people in life are sitting in the stand of life watching others do it. If you are out on the pitch, however, it is an amazing vehicle for evolution. Someone who is not involved would go through months, maybe years, to experience the emotional, physical and mental highs and lows that a football match can give you in 90 minutes.'

Icke has clearly decided to take part in the football match of life and, in recent years, has taken to playing the occasional game of football itself once again too. Apparently his performances for Ryde Sports in the Jewson Wessex League were impressive, but a rival club expressed no jealousy, claiming, 'We are more interested in making a profit than signing one.'

The Gorsedd of Bards

I had forgotten about Dai Davies. That was until a story in the *Daily Mail* sought to pour scorn on a newly awakened spiritualism in the former Welsh international goalie. In an article entitled 'Dai the Drop is keeper of the faith', the *Mail* reported: 'It is often said that goalkeepers are a breed apart – and former Everton star Dai Davies is doing his best to reinforce the image. He says he has undergone a spiritual conversion, becoming a medium and acquiring a penchant for reincarnation.'

According to the story, Davies underwent a transformation after visiting the pyramids and he was quoted as saying, 'If anyone believes I'm off my head then all respect to them. But there are fairies somewhere with tremendous energy. I can sense angels.'

A few days later I was arranging an interview with David Icke when he suggested I get in touch with Davies too. 'They call him the David Icke of Wales now, you know. He's into all sorts of things like aromatherapy and flotation tanks – all sorts of new-age nonsense. They say I'm into all that, but I'm not.'

So it was that on a cold but bright winter's day I found myself driving through a deliciously frosty North Wales to the gorgeous little town of Llangollen. Autumn had finished late and golden leaves clung doggedly to tall and abundant trees, giving the valley a rustic brown tinge. In the town centre an old steam locomotive, boasting its own Santa's grotto, billowed thick smoke into the crisp blue sky.

Dai was waiting for me at the Llangollen Holistic Health Centre, where he had just finished the morning session of a 'Feldenkrais – awareness through movement' class. Since leaving football Davies has run a Welsh bookshop in Mold, but now specialises in remedial massage and runs a flotation tank at the centre.

He greeted me with a huge smile and a firm handshake with hands the size of watermelons and the grip of a Black and Decker Workmate.

Dai Davies, 'Dai the Drop', had loomed large in my childhood. One of my brothers was a fanatical and overtly sad Everton supporter (so much so that as a 12-year-old he would go to the barber's with a Typhoo Tea picture of Joe Royle and demand his hair be cut in the same lacklustre style). Dai was an erratic genius of occasional brilliance and rather more frequent clumsiness. In addition to the nickname 'the Drop' there would be catcalls of 'Dracula' from the terraces, referring to his fear of crosses, but as prepubescent youths we thought it owed more to his lack of front teeth which emphasised his fangs.

Back at Dai's bachelor pad, where he has been living since separating from his wife Anne, the former goalie rustles up a baked potato and stirfry – I refuse an offer to join him on the grounds of being a confirmed chip-butty-and-Daddy's-Sauce kind of man. He talks over the wok of matters of the mind, body and soul, reincarnation and how we choose our parents before we are born. When I express some scepticism, but disguise it by confessing to a mind as closed as a South Wales coal-pit, he examines my spine with those big hands of his and declares: 'A bit of a parson's stoop, but apart from that I'd say you were rather open-minded. One day you will understand.' He also tells me that he detects a psychic element to me, the sign being, apparently, a well-bent forefinger.

When I reveal I am deaf in one ear (the result of measles at the age of five), Dai pokes my chest, tells me I should see a healer and demands to know what it was that I had been trying to avoid hearing all those years ago. When I express an interest in interviewing a goalkeeper whom I hadn't realised had died a while back, Dai suggests straight-faced that I find a good medium and interview him through the ether.

Nevertheless, there's a plausibility to Davies that overcomes my inner distaste for all things lentil. He speaks with conviction and humour and without ostentation. Most of all he speaks like a man who knows what he is talking about.

The son of a footballing miner, he first realised his goalkeeping potential when his elder brother Tomi and mates shunted him into goals and out of the way. Soon he was amazing them with his abilities and before long was playing for both Ammanford United and Ammanford Town. From there he went on to play professionally for Swansea and Everton and was capped 52 times for Wales.

Davies is intensely proud of his Welshness. In his autobiography *Never Say Dai*, he writes of his father's failure to make it at Wolves and Sheffield United: 'The only consolation is that a professional footballing career for him might have meant I was born an Englishman!' When, in 1978, the authorities refused to play the Welsh national anthem before a game against England, Dai was one of the leaders of a 15-second protest. 'We just stood there after the England team broke, as if listening to our own anthem. It will always stand out as my greatest moment, because we stood as a team. Just 20 years ago the English had the audacity not to recognise the Welsh national anthem.' The next year it was played.

In 1978 he was honoured by being made a Gorsedd of Bards for his services to the Welsh language at the National Eisteddfodd in Cardiff. 'If I'm known for anything it's for being the goalkeeper who played for Wales and who spoke Welsh.'

Despite his international success Dai's career had its ups and downs. On his début for Everton he scored an own-goal in the first 15 minutes; one more game and it was three and a half years before he played for the first team again. In the meantime he went on loan to third-division Swansea and after blunders in his first couple of matches he reached his nadir – a first-division keeper dropped from a third-division team.

The 1975 Home International Championships were a nightmare. Against Scotland he took five steps with the ball in his hands and conceded a goal from the resulting free-kick. Having never beaten England at Wembley, Wales were leading 2–1 with a minute to go when Davies missed a Brian Little cross and watched as Johnson tucked in the equaliser. Days later he missed another cross against Northern Ireland and Wales lost 1–0 and took the wooden spoon. 'Dai the Drop' was a nickname that, unlike the ball, was beginning to stick.

But Dai had learned a valuable lesson early on in his career playing in front of a hostile Molineux crowd for Swansea's youth team. 'I'd come from a little village, I was 16 at the time, it was the biggest crowd I'd ever played in front of. I had my back to thousands of Wolves supporters, most of them skinheads, who with verbal abuse belittled me, my parenthood – I was a stupid bastard, I was Welsh, a hillbilly, a sheep-shagger – and I took it personally and went to pieces, everything these yobboes shouted hurt. From that moment on I determined never to let it affect me again.'

Not that learning a lesson is the whole picture for Davies. When I asked him if such intimidation and barracking by the crowd made Eric Cantona's kung fu foray onto the terraces at Crystal Palace all the more understandable, he agreed but added, 'If you actually look at Cantona's astrology chart, that is him anyway, he just simply can't help it, it's part and parcel of his being, his make-up, of his life on this earth at this time.'

But Davies feels he learned to cope with most things. 'I had knives, billiard balls, lead balls thrown at me, but the only thing that caught me was a coin at QPR – a tuppenny piece – which hit me with such velocity that I went down.'

Ironically, one of his fondest memories of football is from just such an incident. In the days when teams thought twice about visiting Northern Ireland because of the Troubles, Wales mulled it over and decided to play in Belfast. Somebody threw a bottle onto the pitch, which Davies picked up. 'There was a photographer wanting to take a picture and I just put it behind my back and quietly gave it to a policeman. Quite a few of the crowd recognised what I'd done and I received nice letters because of it.'

In another projectile incident, one manager, whom Davies refuses to name because of possible libel action, instructed him to carry a sharp piece of metal onto the field and to fall to the ground claiming to have been hit by it in the hope that the game would be declared void. Davies refused.

The tall Welshman is a thoughtful individual who has given time to pondering the nature of goalkeeping. 'I don't think you'll find a lot of goalkeepers saying that they are crazy, or that other keepers are crazy. You certainly have to be different though, because you are the only person who can use your hands to hold the ball. And you have to be tough both physically and mentally; when the opposition score not only are they rejoicing, but all your team-mates are looking at you almost saying "Oh bloody hell!"

'Goalkeepers never get kissed. I've got false teeth, so I'm ugly anyway! But when your team scores you are at your most vulnerable, certainly as a last line of defence, because what normally happens is that most of the outfield players have had a chance to congratulate the scorer and are therefore on a high. You say to yourself, "Great, it's gone in," but then – click – you have to switch off and be ready. Discipline. Organise. You don't have time to jump for joy and fly with the pigeons.

'People say goalkeepers are mad, but they are quite profound thinkers. The nature of the beast is that they have to memorise a lot of things – penalties, corners, strengths and weaknesses – there's a mental rehearsal goes on. They're not daft; they're often very, very bright and more sensitive, because letting a goal in hurts. You have to overcome that hurt, overcome that pain and find something that keeps you sane otherwise you will actually go off your head.'

Dai's new path for his life began when his wife started suffering from panic attacks and they went on holiday to Egypt. He entered the king's chamber of the main pyramid and was emotionally moved. It led him to a voracious reading spell and realisation that he had to alter his way of life.

On the *Daily Mail* piece he expresses disdain: 'That came out because of a 40-minute radio piece I did in Welsh. *Wales on Sunday* translated it from Welsh into English, misinterpreted it, and did a piece which upset quite a lot of my friends. I just shrugged it off as I normally do, I wouldn't give it any more energy. The *Daily Mail* and other newspapers picked it up from there.'

In addition to the work down at the holistic centre, Dai commentates in Welsh on the occasional match. 'I had a four-year break from soccer, and now I'm back with greater enthusiasm. Part of my life that's been wonderful has been that I could go away from the game completely and discover that there is something more to life than just football. I didn't read a paper, I didn't watch the telly. It was brilliant.'

On my return home I decided to follow Dai's advice and try and interview a dead goalkeeper through the ether. I determined that rather than offending any relatives by contacting the recently deceased keeper that Dai and I had discussed, I would try and get in touch with the long-dead Leigh Roose. From the local newspaper I selected Medium Mabel and, resisting the temptation to ask her what a large Mabel was, I put my proposal to her.

'I don't go into a trance for just anybody, you know,' said Mabel. 'It's not the sort of thing I do at the drop of a hat. I'll need an item of clothing or a memento of his too.'

'What about a photograph?' I asked.

'Oh, I'm not sure . . .'

'And £25?'

'I'll think about it and call you back.'

She never did.

5 ... But is it art?

The artist is an exhibitionist by profession.
VINCENT VAN GOGH

On and off the field, goalkeepers are artists. Their performances between the posts may often be more Jackson Pollock than Michelangelo, but away from the turf goalies and culture can make a coupling as natural as Gilbert and George, René and Renata or perhaps Creutzfeldt and Jakob. If you're an outfield player your cultural and artistic icons may stretch only as far as Des O'Connor (Northampton Town) or Rod Stewart (Brentford second team), but if you're a goalkeeper you can sit back and perhaps dream of one day winning the Nobel Prize for Literature (Albert Camus), writing an internationally acclaimed book about sexual obsession (Vladimir Nabokov) or becoming a film super-star and marrying Brigitte Nielsen (Sylvester Stallone).

For the goalkeeper is a man of cultivation, wit and talent. John Ewart, who was capped in goals for Scotland against England in 1921, had an on-field reputation for excessive daring and an off-field name for his linguistic abilities (fluent in French, German and Russian) and his musical talents (he played the piccolo, the flute and the violin).

Once again it may stem from the same motivations that gave us the spiritual keeper – all that time to think, all that time to keep occupied and perhaps a little time to pen a song, rehearse a scene from a forthcoming movie or advance a chapter in your next intellectual blockbuster.

The world of literature is peppered with keepers. *Catcher in the Rye*, it is said, was originally intended as a cereal about goalies, *Not Far From the Madding Crowd* a book planned by Bert Hardy (but never completed) and the poem *Not waving, but clowning* was a poem by the little-known keeper Steve Smith.

It's Camus and Nabokov, though, who were the two literary giants of goalkeeping. Camus, the French-Algerian existentialist, played soccer in the 1920s as a youngster with Arab boys and a ball made of rags. Later he played more seriously for his university team in Algiers. For the future Nobel laureate, soccer's first and most vital lesson stayed with him until his death: 'I quickly learned that the ball never came to you where you expected it. This helped me in life, above all in the metropolis, where people are not always wholly straightforward,' he wrote in *France Football* in 1957.

In the same article he remembered his youthful days of anxious desperation when he was eager to get out and play: 'I fretted with impatience from Sunday to Thursday, for training day, and from Thursday to Sunday, match day. So I joined the university men. And there I was, goalkeeper of the junior team.'

The goalkeeper's position, he acknowledged, was tough: 'We used to play hard. Students, their fathers' sons, don't spare themselves. Poor us, in every sense, a good half of us mown down like corn!' And the trepidation of certain games lived on in his mind. 'The hardest team was Olympic Hussein Dey. The stadium is beside the cemetery. They made us realise, without mercy, that there was direct access. As for me, poor goalkeeper, they went for my body. There was Boufarik . . . that great big centre-forward (among ourselves we called him Watermelon) who always came down with all his weight, right on my kidneys, without counting the cost: shin massage with football boots, shirt pulled back by the hand, knees in the distinguished parts, sandwiches against the post . . . in brief, a scourge. And every time Watermelon apologised with a "Sorry son" and a Franciscan smile.'

Camus owns up to getting Watermelon back for his attentions 'but without cheating' and acknowledges the debt he owed to soccer – 'For, after many years in which the world has afforded me many experiences, what I most surely know in the long run about morality and the obligations of men, I owe to sport.'

Camus received his Nobel Prize in 1957 for a body of work that included such classics as *The Plague*, *The Outsider* and *The*

Rebel. He was killed in a car crash in 1960. Rod Stewart probably hadn't even met Maggie May by then, never mind woken her up.

Vladimir Nabokov, the author of *Lolita*, had more mixed feelings about his goalkeeping experiences. He readily admitted to being crazy about the position and, writing in his book *Speak, Memory – An Autobiography Revisited*, acknowledged that he loved the glamour that was attached to it in his Russian homeland. 'Aloof, solitary, impassive, the crack goalie is followed in the streets by entranced small boys. He vies with the matador and the flying ace as an object of thrilled adulation. His sweater, his peaked cap, his kneeguards, the gloves protruding from the hip pocket of his shorts, set him apart from the rest of the team. He is the lone eagle, the man of mystery, the last defender.'

But in his Cambridge days Nabokov found the English 'dread of showing off and a too-grim preoccupation with solid teamwork' knocked his interest in the game and his performances dipped. The conditions didn't help either, for there were 'esoteric days, under dismal skies, with the goal area a mass of black mud, the ball as greasy as a plum pudding, and my head racked with neuralgia after a sleepless night of verse-making. I would fumble badly – and retrieve the ball from the net.'

Sleepless nights of verse-making! As the ball drifted to the other end, young Vlad would use the excuse for a nap and a daydream. 'The far, blurred sounds, a cry, a whistle, the thud of a kick, all that was perfectly unimportant and had no connection with me. I was less the keeper of a soccer goal than the keeper of a secret. As with folded arms I leant my back against the left goalpost, I enjoyed the luxury of closing my eyes, and thus I would listen to my heart knocking and feel the blind drizzle on my face and hear, in the distance, the broken sounds of the game, and think of myself as of a fabulous exotic being in an English footballer's disguise, composing verse in a tongue nobody understood about a remote country nobody knew.'

At least he had the sense to realise that 'Small wonder I was not very popular with my team-mates'.

Not only do keepers make great literary figures, they also make great literary subjects. The loneliness, the eccentricity, the ostentation have all held a fascination for writers in a way that no other sporting position can match. No surprise then that there is no novel called *The Left-Back's Fear of the Throw-In* or *The Centre-Forward's Surprise at the Corner*, but there is one called

The Goalie's Anxiety at the Penalty Kick by German author Peter Handke in which the reader is subjected to such profound conversations as:

> He couldn't watch that way for very long, answered the salesman; you couldn't help but look at the forwards. If you looked at the goalkeeper, it seemed as if you had to look cross-eyed. It was like seeing somebody walk toward the door and instead of looking at the man you looked at the doorknob. It made your head hurt, and you couldn't breathe properly any more.
>
> 'You get used to it,' said Bloch, 'but it's ridiculous.'

Indeed. Wherever he's encountered, the image of the keeper is invariably that of the dolt, the dubious, the untrustworthy, the slack and the ever so wacky. Alan Sillitoe reinforces this in his classic, *The Loneliness of the Long-Distance Runner*:

> From an animal pacing within the prescribed area of his defended posts, the goalkeeper turned into a leaping ape, arms and legs outstretched, then became a mere stick that swung into a curve – and missed the ball as it sped to one side and lost itself in folds of net behind him . . .
>
> 'That goalie's a bloody fool,' Lennox swore, cap pulled low over his forehead. 'He couldn't even catch a bleeding cold.'

As does Rudyard Kipling in his poem, *The Islanders*:

> Then ye returned to your trinkets; then
> ye contented your souls
> With the flannelled fools at the wicket or
> the muddied oafs at the goals.

In literature, nobody chooses to play in goal, for it's an admission of failure – of both rejection and dejection. Soccer in Roddy Doyle's Booker Prize-winner *Paddy Clarke Ha Ha Ha* is played on the streets of Dublin's fictional Barrytown:

> The smack of the ball against the gate was a goal. Goalkeepers scored about half the goals. We tried to change the rules but the goalkeepers objected: they wouldn't go in goal if they weren't allowed to score goals. The useless players went in goal but we still needed them.

127

In Barry Hines' *A Kestrel for a Knave*, young working-class outcast Billy Casper has no interest in school and even less in school football. He's the whipping boy for teachers and pupils alike and in one memorable scene his true social inadequacies are fully exposed, when once again he's put in goal by the ferocious Mr Sugden. Casper has his own way of dealing with it:

> Billy gripped a post between both hands, inserted one raised foot into a square in the side netting, then, using this as a stirrup, heaved himself up and grabbed hold of the crossbar. He hand-over-handed it to the middle and rested, swinging loosely backwards and forwards with his legs together. Then he let go with one hand and started to scratch his armpits, kicking his legs and imitating chimp sounds. The bar shook and the rattling of the bolts turned several heads, and soon all the boys were watching him, the game forgotten.
>
> 'Casper! Casper, get down lad! What do you think you are, an ape?'
>
> 'No, sir, I'm just keeping warm.'
>
> 'Well, get down then, before I come and make you red hot!'

A Kestrel for a Knave made a successful transition to the silver screen as the Ken Loach film *Kes*, the football match being gloriously played out with Brian Glover giving a wonderful performance as the overbearing Mr Sugden.

The Goalkeeper's Fear of the Penalty was a lesser hit, but was much respected on the art-house circuit. Constantly verging on the pretentious, the film, adapted from Peter Handke's book, is nevertheless the most sinister manifestation of the goalkeeper as a dangerous psychotic yet produced – Harald Schumacher included. Goalkeeper Josef Bloch leans against a post and watches the ball go into his net. He claims offside, scuffles with the ref, is sent off and knocks a team-mate to the floor. Later in the film he has sex with a woman called Gloria who works in the box-office of a local movie-house. At this point Bloch reveals his true horror by standing up in a pair of skimpy white underpants – how could Gloria now fail to realise the danger she was in? Those pants were never in fashion anywhere west of the Ukraine. She doesn't clock them and instead listens to Bloch as he tells her about being a professional goalkeeper and how he once stood in a puddle in the wrong corner for an own-goal. He strangles her, falls asleep and then travels across a bleak German landscape to a desolate frontier town – as you do. Here he fills out the space between the killing and the final credits by engaging the locals with banal conversation and participating in the occasional brawl with disaffected ruffians.

More accessible and assuredly more enjoyable is the old favourite *Escape to Victory* in which Sly Stallone is a prisoner-of-war hell-bent on breaking camp, who ends up pulling off a stunning performance between the posts, falls in love with a raven-haired beauty and is made a French national hero. For once the keeper is the sensible one, a cool dude using football to escape, but there's a catch, of course – he's a North American and doesn't understand the rules of the game. So for the first reel Stallone's character, Hatch, stalks the set complaining about the effect that soccer is having on his life and his desire to split camp – 'This frigging game is wrecking my life, sir!', or 'You couldn't pay me to be in that team'.

Naturally, though, he comes good and goes in goal for a team led by paunch-plagued Michael Caine in a big game against Nazidom's élite players in Paris.

With the half-time score standing at 4–1 to the Germans, the plan is to escape down a tunnel dug by the French Resistance – but there's pride at stake and the team decide to abort their plan and play on. Stallone, being the brash American, cannot believe it, and for once the goalkeeper is given his true value, when Michael Caine announces, 'We cannot go back without the goalie.' Stallone's Hatch, a sucker for the compliment, gives in.

Back on the pitch the plucky Allied lads pull the score back to 4–4, but with seconds left on the clock, Ossie Ardiles puts in a soft tackle and the Germans are awarded a penalty. The rebellious crowd sing a hearty 'Marseillaise', Stallone walks out to meet the penalty-taker, man to man, eyeball to eyeball, like heavyweight boxers about to go 15 rounds. He saves the penalty, the crowd breaks onto the pitch and the Allied players escape (no doubt to victory).

It was a tough assignment for Stallone, tougher than he believed possible. Overconfident in his ability, he challenged Pele to an off-screen penalty shoot-out, betting that he'd be able to save at least one of them. He didn't, but the power of the only one he got to broke a finger. This, added to two badly bruised knees damaged in training, meant that he returned to the USA describing himself as a 'walking blood-clot'. There was no sequel.

Goalies in films have resulted in one of the most bizarre film titles of all time and no, it's not *Honey I've Narrowed the Angles*, but a little-known Czech production called *The Goalkeeper Lives in Our Street*. Potential sequels in the Prague pipeline include *The Ref's Gone Down the Pub* and *The Milkman Lives Two Roads Down, Third on the Right*.

It's when we move into the world of music that the goalkeeper suddenly plunges perilously close to the Des O'Connor level. Somebody told me that Pavarotti used to specialise between the posts, but it turned out that the posts they meant were Domingo and Carreras – his hometown local newspaper were only too proud to tell me that this was no modern singing Foulke, no 'O Goalie Mio' had ever been hummed by big Luke. No, the Big P had resisted filling the goals and had spent his time dribbling up and down the field in local junior leagues. (The Italians were proving a problem: I heard elsewhere that novelist and intellectual Umberto Eco had done time in the nets and was considering a new novel, *The Name of the Goals*, but he replied, '*Mai stato portiere, mai scritto la citazione che mi attribuisce, mai giocato a calcio, neppure da piccolo. Mi spiace.* Which, roughly speaking, means he's never played football, never mind in goals.)

But back to music. For the proud bearer of the singing goalie's jersey we have to cross the sea (and no, it's not Val Doonican) to Spain. Here the son of a Madrid gynaecologist grew up in awe of Spain's greatest-ever goalie, the 'Man in Black', Ricardo Zamora, and decided that one day it would be him. We are, of course, talking about Julio Iglesias, he who began the Beguine, and is possibly Spain's greatest, and certainly its most successful, musical talent.

If it hadn't been for an unfortunate car crash when the young Julio was a mere 19 we'd never have heard his singing voice – but we might have seen him in goals for Real Madrid, for Julio was a natural in the nets, which he saw as a wonderful way of grabbing the centre of attention. It was crucial to his youthful development since as an averagely ugly kid with severe self-loathing, football gave him a foothold on a ladder of self-confidence which he has climbed and climbed and climbed. Talking with hindsight about his schooldays at the College of the Sacred Heart, Julio says, 'We would play alone, just the priests and myself . . . I was, permit me to say in modesty – yet the same time with pride – the best goalkeeper in the history of my school.' Yep, plenty of self-loathing there, plenty of lacking in the self-confidence stakes.

Julio used to watch the great Real Madrid team of the early 1960s training and worked his way into the goalie's shirt of the junior reserves. At this point, as he approached 20, his unofficial biographer Jeff Rovin says in *Julio!*, the future crooner had three goals in life: 'to graduate from law school and join the diplomatic corps: to become a semi-professional soccer goalie, a dream he'd nurtured since childhood: and to fall in love with as many women as humanly possible – two a day if he could have his way.'

A legendary 3,000 women further down the line, it seems that Iglesias was to achieve only one of those ambitions – depending on your definition of love – because very soon this 'athlete on the soccer field and in the bedroom' was to be on the receiving end of some very bad luck. Speeding in his car he had his first, but sadly not his last, smash hit – a tree. Confined to a hospital bed, the gift of a guitar weaned him off shin-pads and Deep Heat and into the music world. He wrote a song *'La vida sigue igual'* ('Life Continues all the Same') and won the Benidorm Song Festival of 1968. It was a moment from which he has never looked back – the statistics, if not the music, say it all. In 1970 he won the Eurovision Song Contest for Spain and it is reckoned that by 1990 he had sold more than 100 million albums.

That first Benidorm Song Festival appearance was a significant moment, too, because he met his old idol Ricardo Zamora and was able to thank him with the words: 'You see what I've done, Don Ricardo? Well, it was your example that enabled me to do this. I couldn't achieve it in soccer, so I'm going to be as good as you are – only in music.'

History doesn't record whether Zamora took this as a compliment.

6 Débuts, disasters and Scotland

TONY: *Chalky White. Oh well, we've had it. We won't get a draw with him between the sticks. Biggest score in history. Ninety minutes of kick-offs and goals. He's useless, that man. He stands there leaning up against the goalpost measuring himself. He can't see what he's doing, that's his trouble. Not only can't he see them coming – he has a job finding them once they're in. Wandering about the back of the net poking around here and there . . . he kicked his hat out twice last week . . .*
FROM *Hancock's Half-Hour – 'The Football Pools'*,
BY RAY GALTON AND ALAN SIMPSON

It seemed that everybody who watched English football in the 1960s knew that, under no pressure, Gary Sprake had thrown the ball into his own net while playing for Leeds United. And, like hippies at Woodstock, most of us claimed to have been there when it happened.

Sprake was an erratic keeper, mixing slack concentration with undoubted ability and it is possible that he perpetrated this particular blunder more than once. What is certain is that he did throw the ball into his own goal in front of an Anfield crowd of almost 40,000 supporters.

Standing well off his line to receive a back-pass from Jack Charlton, Sprake collected the ball and went to chuck it to his full-back Terry Cooper. As he reached the instant of release he realised Cooper was being threatened by an opposing forward and changed his mind – too late. The ball bounced backwards out of his hands and bobbled into the net.

On the Kop a stunned and disbelieving silence held the crowd momentarily, as they took in what they had just seen. A collective giggling started up and then finally a massive guffaw of appreciation. The despairing keeper sank to his knees and held his head in his hands – most of the spectators were surprised he didn't drop it!

It was a minute before half-time and, as the teams walked off for the break, the normally fiery Leeds skipper Billy Bremner ran over to his keeper and commiserated with him. Over the PA system 'Careless Hands' played to the delight of the Liverpool fans. The local *Echo* newspaper called it 'one of the most freakish goals ever seen'.

Sprake's blunder was a very public mistake, a public humiliation in front of one of the country's largest and most unforgiving crowds. It speaks volumes for the Welshman's strength that he was able to continue, and by all accounts play superbly.

This is not really surprising. Sprake was a good goalkeeper, occasionally even a brilliant one, but behind the formidable barrier that was the Leeds defence of the late 1960s and most of the '70s he was inclined to lapses of concentration – one story going that he even had to pinch himself continually to make sure he stayed alert.

So keen had Leeds been to get Sprake into their team in 1962 that when their first-choice keeper Tommy Younger was injured and forced out of a game at Southampton, a plane was specially hired to get the 17-year-old Sprake to the Dell. Thus began a successful career, but one that is remembered to this day more for slips, botches and bungles than spectacular shot-stopping. At times it seemed that so conceited, arrogant and confident were the Leeds team of Bremner, Hunter, Clarke and Giles that they felt they had to give everybody else a chance – Gary Sprake was that chance. Few will remember that at just 19 Sprake became the youngest goalkeeper to play for Wales and that he went on to win 37 caps; few will remember that he played 507 times for a great, if rather tedious, club side; but most of us will have our favourite Gary Sprake blunder story – such as the time he dived over a slow-rolling ball in the 1970 Cup final, the ball trickling through his legs against Liverpool, the harmless high ball that floated gently through his arms into a gaping net.

But this is the essence of goalkeeping. We all make mistakes at work, but unless you happen to be prime minister or a manufacturer of dodgy nuclear weapons, few people's errors have the ramifications of those made by a goalie. Football may be a team game, relying on strategies and co-operation, spirit and understanding, but within it the work of the goalkeeper is a very isolated, often lonesome and always responsible ordeal. Above all else, the goalkeeper knows that he is the perfect scapegoat and that any fumbling, fluffing or failing will lead to instant mortification.

It really doesn't have to be his fault. Take the case of David Seaman and the 1995 European Cup-Winners' Cup final. Just three weeks earlier Seaman had been a semi-final hero, borne shoulder-high by jubilant team-mates as he pulled off three stupendous saves in a penalty shoot-out with Sampdoria. Those saves had single-handedly taken Arsenal to a final against Spanish club Zaragoza.

Extra-time was all but over in the final, the ball was near the halfway line and Seaman was being attentive on the edge of the box, quite possibly contemplating another imminent penalty shoot-out, when Zaragoza's Nayim suddenly launched the most speculative of long-range shots – and it was long, fully 50 yards or more. But from the second it left his boot it was a goal. Lost high in the glare of the floodlights it came down at an angle so acute that Seaman was left flailing hopelessly. The ball was in the net, Zaragoza were Cup-winners and Seaman was disconsolate, downcast and tangled in the netting like a discarded marionette.

Oh, how we laughed! Arsenal beaten in the last second of a Cup final by a former Spurs player and their goalkeeping hero turned villain. A moment to savour for all those who hate Arsenal (99.998% of the adult population). But wait a second, I digress. Why was Seaman the villain? He was most certainly branded thus in some circles, but what was he supposed to do? He was in the correct position for the most likely eventuality, ready to sweep any swift attack by Zaragozan forwards. While the shot was a shot and a legitimate attempt on goal, the fact that it was so accurate and so powerful and that it went in was a fluke. Seaman couldn't do anything about it. He was no more, and probably less, to blame than the Arsenal midfielder who allowed Nayim the second it took to tee it up. Yet when that ball hit the goal, almost everybody's eyes were on Seaman – those of his players, those of the supporters, those of the millions of viewers watching at home on television – although probably not those of Nayim who was buried under the bodies of ten ecstatic team-mates.

(The great Pat Jennings disagrees with me. 'He was too far out,' he told me. 'I spent the night commenting for RTE and telling the audience what a great keeper Seaman is, that he's the best in the country. But there is no doubt that for the goal he was too far off the line. He'd done brilliant all night, but that's what goalkeeping is all about . . .')

Goalkeeping is about saving your team, keeping the ball out of the net at any cost and that's it really. When you don't do it don't expect any thanks. David Seaman let in two goals that night, and while he may have got a consolatory pat on the back from his captain and manager there would have been little praise for 119 minutes of stalwart work. Goalkeeping is all about vulnerability and strength. It's a position where glory and ignominy, fame and infamy, life and death are separated by the width of an inflated pig's bladder flying towards you at 90 m.p.h.

There is no more detached figure on the field of play than the goalie – identified by a different-coloured shirt to his team-mates, able to handle the ball, controller of his own defined patch of turf and with the expectations of all riding on his back.

And, like in other areas of life, a goalkeeper is never more vulnerable than when he makes it for the first time. In that first game for the first team many a career has been made and a significant number shattered.

Just ask Milton of Halifax Town. Put yourself in his position. You've been playing in the reserves for a couple of years, you're still very young, but you've got ambitions. Then, just after the New Year, the first-team keeper who is also the captain sustains a thigh injury and the moment you've been waiting for arrives – you're in the team. How excited do you get? Do you get tickets for your family and friends to come and sit proudly in the stands? Do you wave to them as you jog out onto the pitch? Does a little thrill run through you as your name is announced over the public-address system? Do you become anxious as the referee gets the game under way with a shrill toot on his whistle? Was this what happened to Milton of Halifax?

Well, when you've finished answering all those questions, here's another: imagine how you would feel if, 90 minutes later, you were plucking the last of 13 goals from the back of your net? Downcast? Dejected? Demoralised? For this is what happened to young Milton in his first game. Called up in January 1934 to play at Edgeley Park against Stockport County, Halifax were on the end of what the local *Daily Courier and Guardian* called an 'AMAZING GOAL AVALANCHE'. In front of 6,000 spectators on a cold and windy afternoon, Milton received a baptism of fire. Incredibly, though, at half-time the score was a mere 2–0 – 11 goals were plundered from Milton's charge in the second half. It was the biggest score of the season and the worst defeat Halifax had ever suffered.

In truth it wasn't until the seventh goal that Milton could be faulted. He went down to a low shot which would have gone past the post and popped it up to an oncoming Stockport forward. Fifty-seven minutes had gone, Milton had been beaten five times in the 12 minutes since half-time. The eighth was no fault of the keeper's, but the ninth was, according to the *Courier*, when Downes, a Stockport forward, 'from a position a few inches from the dead line, smashed in a shot which, to the amusement of everybody, flew into the net. Milton, of course, was badly out of position. Downes could not repeat his shot if he tried all day.'

Both the 10th and the 11th were down to the keeper, too, and for the 12th he failed to clear a corner, gifting it to the opposition. The 13th was crashed in on the final whistle.

How must Milton have felt?

On Monday 'Pioneer', writing in the local newspaper, was outraged – 'Thirteen-nil! What was this – a football match or a whist drive?' – but the reporter attempted to exonerate the young débutant, praising him for keeping the score down to just 2–0 at half-time. In a section of the article headlined 'MILTON NOT TO BLAME', Pioneer went on: 'One player in the Halifax team had my wholehearted sympathy and only one. He was Milton, the unluckiest goalkeeper who ever made his bow in league football. Milton performed well and everybody on the ground had a good word for him [though Pioneer doesn't elaborate on what that word was]. Some of his saves were brilliant, and though he might have prevented three or four goals, these errors were chiefly due to inexperience.'

Of course, being responsible for three or four goals might under normal circumstances constitute a disaster. In the context of 13 goals, the four down to the keeper pale into the vicinity of insignificance. Nevertheless, even though Pioneer concluded in his article that 'Milton was the best player in the Halifax team', it was to be over a year before the hapless keeper made another appearance for the first team. This time he conceded only three against Southport and must have been well pleased at reducing his goals-against average to a relatively humble eight.

But Milton was far from the only débutant disaster area. Step forward Dennis Murray of Crewe Alexandra. His big moment came in September 1951 and, having been promoted from the reserves, did he grasp the opportunity with both hands? Well, if he did, it's about all he did grasp on a cold afternoon in Lincoln. He certainly didn't get too close to the ball. By half-time his Crewe side were 5–0 down. When 90 minutes finally arrived, Lincoln had put another six past Murray. 11–1! Just how depressing could it get for a new goalkeeper? The local paper, the *Crewe Guardian*, was kind to him, but not that kind: 'Murray showed that he is not yet experienced enough for Northern Section football, but it was unfortunate for him that he had to play against a team which had struck such brilliant form. It would be unfair to make him the scapegoat of this defeat, for the Crewe defence generally was hazed and bewildered by the rapid-moving and sharp-shooting Lincoln forwards.'

Murray was dropped back into the reserves and only ever made one more full appearance for the club.

But I asked just how depressing could it get for a new goalkeeper. Surely not much more than it must have been for Les Surman of Charlton Athletic. Surman made the leap from youth-team football to the senior side in late December 1965; he was 18 years old and had been plunged into a team already struggling to avoid relegation. The omens were bad. Athletic were on a run of poor results and now they had a string of injuries in the lead-up to an important game against Portsmouth at Fratton Park. A whole raft of youngsters had to be blooded in one go and Surman was in for the newly purchased Noel Dwyer who had pulled out following a heavy fall in the previous game.

He didn't get any time to think that this might be his day. The game was just 18 seconds old when Billy Bonds decided he should give the young greenhorn behind him a feel of the ball. It was a horrific mistake, for Surman stood transfixed on the goal-line and watched the gently headed ball trickle into the back of his net. It was to be the first of three the keeper would concede that day and the *South East London Mercury* told it like it was: Surman 'had a nightmare of a first half, in 20 seconds or less pulling the ball out of the back of the net. And he could have saved the other two goals with a little more experience.'

But this was exactly what Surman was not going to get. He had been at the club for two years, and on his début Charlton had lost 3–1, only 3–1 – he hadn't conceded 13, he hadn't conceded 11, he had conceded just three, but he'd blown his big moment. Charlton never picked him again.

The saving grace for these keepers was that their moments of misery were in front of relatively small crowds. It could have been worse – they could have been labelled blundering fools on their international débuts in front of 50,000 spectators like, well, like Pat Kelly of Northern Ireland. His big night came in 1949 when he was called up to face the Scots in Belfast. It was a night that no doubt he would love to have forgotten and equally, no doubt, one that he was never able to. The final score was 8–2 to Scotland. Kelly was to blame for five, a penalty made it six, leaving just two genuinely deserved Scottish goals. It was Northern Ireland's first international since the formation of the Irish Republic and the *Irish News* and *Belfast Morning News* reported pessimistically that 'without the assistance of the 26 counties-born players there will be no future for the IFA in the international arena'.

This time it genuinely was down to the keeper. Northern Ireland had matched the Scots in the outfield and for large chunks of the game demonstrated better skills and outshone the team that obliterated them. Only the Irish goalie, for whom the night was a litany of disasters, had a stinker. Within minutes of the kick-off Kelly had accidentally knocked his own centre-half over when both jumped to clear a header – 1–0. Mere seconds later he completely misjudged an attacker's intentions and presented him with an open target – 2–0.

There was a lull, followed by a seemingly harmless lob. Kelly jumped and came down with hands full of nothing but fresh air – 3–0. Steel, the scorer, was not a little ashamed by what he had seen and he returned to the halfway line with his head in his hands. The fourth was a good goal and the fifth a penalty.

Half-time arrived and on the restart a reinvigorated Northern Irish team looked set to make a game of it, scoring two goals before the hour had passed. The Scots were beginning to sweat – that is, until they remembered their secret weapon in the Irish goal. On the 70th minute Morris chased a long ball but gave it up when he saw the keeper coming for it. Kelly came out to clear, but for reasons known only to himself, he froze on the spot. Morris took up the challenge once again and it was 6–2.

If the seventh was a good goal, the eighth was the most ghastly – listen to the voice of the *Glasgow Herald*, which echoed the feelings of many Scots who found themselves embarrassed at accepting such a gift: 'Morris, off his balance, swung his boot and just managed to trundle the ball at Kelly, whose lamentable effort to save was received in complete silence. Not even the most raucous-voiced of the tartan-bedecked Scots desired any such goal.'

The final whistle couldn't come soon enough for Kelly, but he presented a sorry picture as he walked, shamefaced and alone, the 200 yards to the dressing-room. The Irish supporters watched in silence as his faltering steps carried him out of the international arena for ever. One player – Jimmy Cowan, the Scotland keeper – stayed on the pitch to comfort him and presumably tell him something like 'Come on, mate. It's not all that bad.' If he did, he was lying.

Not surprisingly, Kelly didn't play for Northern Ireland again, although it's not known whether it was because he wasn't picked or whether he just couldn't face it.

Of course, the serious side to this is that it doesn't take long for a goalkeeping career to go completely down the pan. A couple of bad performances and you start to lose the confidence of the players in front of you and, probably even more importantly, you start to lose confidence in yourself. Goalkeeper after goalkeeper, in interviews and in their memoirs, talk about the importance of getting into a game early, feeling the ball, feeling the rough and tumble and pulling off a good save. All this gives confidence – a performance-enhancer that, if it came bottled or in tablet form, would be a banned substance. So it is with a goalkeeper's career. A couple of good, sound or even spectacular early performances can become the foundation stones of a solid future. Early poor performances, or even satisfactory performances for a poor and losing team, can lead to the abyss of oblivion opening before you quicker than you believed possible.

Take a look at the careers of a couple of Wolves players in the 1920s. What a promising footballing future lay in store for Freddie Bryce when he signed for Wolverhampton early in 1928.

But within a fortnight of his début, his goalkeeping dreams were over.

Directors of the club had spotted him in fine form for Flint and bought him on a month's trial to deputise in an emergency for first-choice Canavon. That emergency arose at the end of January when Wolves visited Preston. It was to be a stirring game of football in which for 45 minutes the Preston forwards pummelled the new keeper, taking a 4–1 lead into the break. Nevertheless, Bryce was singled out for his good performance and given a rousing cheer when he came out for a second half in which the Midlanders very nearly rescued the game, eventually losing 5–4.

The local press were wowed, Wolverhampton's *Sporting Star* headlining with 'BRYCE'S FINE "KEEPING" DEBUT AT PRESTON'. Wolves manager Major Buckley was praised for his foresight in finding the new goalie, although in its words of acclaim for Bryce there was a note of caution: 'on his initial display [Bryce] is a good one, but a bigger man with Bryce's capabilities would be preferable. He earned high praise at Preston.'

Bryce would have done well to have remembered the fickleness of both the press and the footballing world. Two weeks later he again stood in for Canavon on a disastrous afternoon at Fulham. Seven goals zipped past him and the paper that had so recently welcomed him called him uncertain and, in a telling note for observers and a chilling warning for the keeper, the paper added: 'Up to date Bryce has made three appearances, and the goals scored against him have been five, six and seven.' (The six were lost in a game for the reserves.) Bryce's contract with Wolves was not renewed and his career in top-flight football was over – it had lasted from 21 January 1928 until 4 February – a total career spanning 15 days, three days less than the number of goals he had conceded.

A couple of years later in December 1929 Billy Walker made a disastrous début for Wolves. In front of 20,000 on a wretched afternoon at the Hawthorns, Wolverhampton went down 7–3 to a rampaging West Bromwich Albion. In the light of what has gone before, it should be no surprise that this story too is going to conclude with the words 'and the goalie didn't play first-team football ever again'. In this case, though, it was particularly unfair, for it seems that Walker had a cast-iron alibi – he wasn't on the pitch for most of the game. With the score at 3–1 the keeper collided heavily with the Albion attacker, Glidden. The

Albion man limped away, but Walker remained prostrate in the mud, a broken leg the price of his valour. He was stretchered away and ended up in Wolverhampton's Royal Hospital. 'It was a dual misfortune for Walker, as it was his first appearance in the Wanderers Second Division eleven and he was doing well up to the time of his mishap,' reported the local paper.

He recovered from the injury, but never from the blow to his career. After a few more months at the club he sidled off to Bridgnorth and that was that.

The flip side to the disastrous entrance into senior-level goalkeeping is, naturally enough, the sensational start to a career or sensational début for a club. Belgian Marc de Clerck made one for Aberdeen in August 1980 and Tony Coton another for Birmingham City four months later. De Clerck had been bought from the Dutch team Twente Enschede and had only played just over 20 minutes for Aberdeen when, as the local papers reported, he 'heightened the sense of farce, the situation almost entering the realms of slapstick' by drop-kicking to the edge of the Berwick Rangers penalty box on the first bounce. The ball flew over the upstretched arms of the Berwick keeper as he dashed out to collect it and landed in the net on the second bounce. De Clerck had scored. The *Aberdeen Press and Journal* predicted that 'the exotic combination of a Belgian keeper, transferring from a Dutch club to a Scottish one and scoring a goal on his début against another Scottish League club in a match on English soil sounds excellent material for football-quiz compilers.'

Coton's impact was rather more immediate. Birmingham's game with Sunderland was barely 48 seconds old when the 19-year-old débutant saved a penalty. The ball had bounced awkwardly into the area and caught defender Joe Gallagher on the arm. The referee immediately pointed to the spot. There were no protests. Hawley stepped forward and slammed a firm shot towards the right-hand corner of the net. Coton predicted correctly and magnificently tipped the ball out for a corner. Birmingham went on to win the game 3–2 and Coton went on to make a successful career at Birmingham, Watford, Manchester City and Manchester United.

It's infamy that lingers, though, it's the memory of mistakes that lurk in darkened corners and pounce just when you thought it was safe to step onto the pitch once again. Of course, it affects all players – who will forget Chris Waddle's penalty miss in the shoot-out with West Germany at Italia '90? Or, only seconds into the game, Stuart Pearce's back-pass to a San Marino forward, in England's crucial and ultimately futile qualifier for the USA World Cup?

But the goalkeeper is particularly susceptible. Former Chelsea and England keeper Peter Bonetti has a theory. 'Yes, we are vulnerable, because if we make a mistake everyone remembers it. You could be playing well for 89 minutes and make a mistake in the last minute and they'll remember you. Whereas a forward can do the reverse – he can have a stinking game for 89 minutes, score in the last minute and be the hero because you've won 1–0. It's definitely always been the Aunt Sally position.

'Other players have always got someone behind them to back them up, correct their mistakes if they make them in the outfield. We don't, we haven't got anyone behind us making up for our mistakes, and they're always analysed in depth and stand out more.'

Bonetti should know. More than a quarter of a century after the event he still gets asked questions about one game in June 1970 – though it would be fair to add that these days the questions come mainly from people like me. The game in the frame was the quarter-final of the World Cup, the stage was Leon in Mexico and the opponents West Germany.

'I accepted that I played badly. I was the first to hold my hand up and say, "Yes, I made a mistake in the game," and that's it,' claims the keeper.

Bonetti was the understudy to Gordon Banks in a widely fancied England squad that had come to Mexico as world champions. It was a role that Bonetti had carried out in the 1966 World Cup, too, but he'd also won six caps in his own right before that fateful day.

'It's funny how people just remember your bad games. The only one they ever remember me for is the one in Mexico which we lost. That was my seventh cap, yet all the other games I played in we won – all six and I only conceded one goal . . . So it makes you laugh when people say to you, "Oh yeah, you're the one that played in that Mexico game".'

Although Bonetti was Banks' understudy, he never really expected to get a game. Banks was having a good World Cup and, in contrast to Bonetti, is still remembered to this day for a remarkable save that he pulled off against Pele in the first round.

But crisis hit the England camp when Banks was struck down by Montezuma's revenge after drinking a bottle of dodgy beer on the eve of the big game. The next morning he seemed to have recovered and was well enough to be included in the team, but at the pre-match team meeting he collapsed and, amid panic and uproar (there were all sorts of allegations about Latin American conspiracies and deliberate nobbling), Bonetti was drafted into the team. There was next to no time to prepare – one moment Banks was in, the next Bonetti was walking out onto the pitch.

In many ways part of the problem lay in the fact that it all started off too easily for the keeper – England strolled to a 2–0 lead – and Bonetti had little or nothing to do. That is until within a space of a few minutes he firstly reacted too slowly to a shot by Beckenbauer and then shortly after was caught out of position for a shot by the West German captain Uwe Seeler. A demoralised England team were beaten in extra-time and Bonetti took the lion's share of the blame. Hugh McIlvanney summed it up in *The Observer*: 'Sir Alf's team were out because the best goalkeeper most people have ever seen turned sick, and one who is only slightly less gifted was overwhelmed by the suddenness of his promotion.'

Bonetti was, and remains, stoical about the criticism. 'I've got a hardened skin to it. If it had pissed me off I wouldn't have been a professional. It's the nasty people around you – I got jeered about it every time I went to an away game after that and there were people chanting about it, but if you're a professional you've got to put up with this sort of thing. Just like when you have good games and people write well about you, you've got to expect that when you have bad games they will write bad things about you.

'It was ironic since only two months prior to that I helped Chelsea to win the Cup, I had two of my best games in the final. Two months later you have one game where things don't go so well for you and people remember it. That is life, I'm afraid.'

Bonetti had sufficient self-confidence and self-assurance to pick himself up after Leon and continued a successful career with Chelsea that, when he retired in 1979, spanned a full 20 years. He is now a goalkeeping coach, having come back to football after a four-year interval spent working as a postman, librarian, helping the undertaker and running a guest-house on a remote Scottish island.

Scotland the grave?

Yuri Gagarin came home from the first manned spaceflight in April 1961. The *Daily Mirror* greeted the Russian astronaut and his spaceship *Vostok I* with the huge headline, 'WELCOME BACK TO EARTH'. In London violent clashes broke out after a massive 'Ban the Bomb' march. Meanwhile in Israel, Adolf Eichmann stood accused of the slaughter of six million Jews in the Second World War. In Florida 5,000 American-sponsored counter-revolutionaries were preparing for a farcical invasion of Cuba. In Lucca, Italy, jazz trumpeter Chet Baker was about to be sentenced to 19 months' imprisonment for possession of drugs and, back in Britain, *What's my Line?* was put off the air by a strike of BBC electricians.

It was a crucial moment in the history of the world, in so many ways a turning point – but if you happened to be Scottish there were more significant matters to be dealt with: how to recover from a 9–3 defeat by England at Wembley and how to get your hands around the throat of a man called Haffey.

That afternoon, 15 April 1961, has become the most extravagant symbol of one of the enduring traditions of goalkeeping folklore – the almost supernatural incompetence of the Scottish custodian. It's a tradition that says that Scotland is to goalkeeping what Bosnia is to peacekeeping. It's a tradition that says that if a Scottish goalie walked in front of a double-decker bus it would go between his legs, and it's a tradition that continues by saying that when the rest of his international team-mates are practising swerves, dribbling through cones and throwing medicine balls at each other, the hapless Scots keeper is doing a specially designed exercise – ball-retrieval repetitions.

In the popular consciousness – though probably only the English one – the abiding images of the Scottish keeper are of a man wrapped around a goalpost, legs flapping like the torn shreds of an old kite caught on an electricity pylon, or a man tangled in a mass of netting like some cast-off from a failed Houdini experiment. The word that's most commonly applied is 'butterfingers'. It's also a tradition that says that Wembley is the graveyard of Scottish custodians and that it is here that the Scots come to bury their keepers.

But is it fair? Is it a tradition that has a firm grip on reality or the slippery Flora-coated fingers of an old Frank Haffey?

There are many instances that the advocates of the tradition would put forward in addition to the 1961 débâcle. The afternoon in September 1885 when Arbroath put 36 goals past the despairing fingers of the keeper of a team called Bon Accord for one. It was the first round of the Scottish Cup, and even before the kick-off it was reported that the difference in class between the two teams was apparent – Bon Accord turning out in a variety of different-coloured shirts, working trousers supported by braces and no boots. In contrast Arbroath were kitted out in neat maroon shirts and white shorts.

Nevertheless, Bon Accord's luckless keeper, Andrew Lornie, could hardly have expected what was about to befall him. In a game described by the *Arbroath Guide* as 'the most amusing football match ever seen', the home team forwards ran amok, putting 15 past Lornie before the whistle for half-time.

Lornie was ordinarily a right-half with no experience of goalkeeping – he had agreed to fill in in the absence of Bon Accord's normal keeper. It is said that he wasn't to blame for a good 20 of the goals, but it is nevertheless also rumoured that he retired from the game soon after, a tad embarrassed at his inclusion in the record books.

At the other end, the Arbroath keeper Jim Milne had the quietest afternoon of his career – he didn't touch the ball once. On a day that saw the heavens open, not only on his opponents, Milne sought refuge from the rain under a spectator's umbrella and lit up a pipe. Mmmm, Condor!

It didn't help the reputation of Scottish goalkeepers, nor indeed Scottish football in general, that on that very same afternoon, less than 20 miles away, Dundee Harps were putting a mere 35 goals past Aberdeen Rovers' goalkeeper. For a brief, euphoric moment they must have believed that they were about to enter the record books for the highest tally of goals ever scored.

And then there's Joe Crozier. The official Scottish records don't recall him as the national team's most unfortunate keeper – but that's what he was. Joe, who played for Brentford, was called up twice by his country during the Second World War, but for unofficial internationals against the 'auld enemy', designed to lift morale – which they most certainly did if you happened to be a Sassenach. Crozier watched forlornly as eight crashed past him at Maine Road in 1943 and was probably even more downcast as a further six were rattled in just four months later at Wembley. An international keeper with an average of seven against – Crozier must have been relieved that the games weren't credited in the official annals.

But wait, there's another – Freddie Martin. His overall average may well have been less than seven, but in two games in 1954 and 1955 he picked the ball out of the net 14 times, too, first against Uruguay in the World Cup finals and then against England at Wembley.

There was no blame to be laid at his door for the Uruguay defeat; the team as a whole were outplayed and outsmarted, as the *Glasgow Herald* reported the South Americans 'rubbed our faces in the dirt'. It was different against the English, though, for Scottish expectations were high, *The Scotsman* asserting that even though the Scots were, man for man, significantly shorter than their opponents, it would be a case of 'guid gear gangs intae sma' bulk'. But Martin and his defence, led by the delightfully named Harry Haddock, had a nightmare, being roasted by the talents of Stanley Matthews and Nat Lofthouse. A normally reliable Martin was indecisive, gifting a first goal and then, with the score at 2–1 to England, he fumbled a ball on the ground and let Don Revie in. It was a decisive mistake. Within minutes England were 4–1 up and coasting. The Scots were despondent, as one football correspondent reported on the mood afterwards: 'First impressions as I heard them expressed by the dejected Scots supporters as they streamed away from the stadium, were that the side should be tossed overboard and a new start made.'

As late as 1984 Scottish matches were continuing to slip into the sublime. In an early round of the Scottish Cup, Stirling Albion stuck 20 past Selkirk in front of 250 spectators. At 18–0 the Selkirk coaching staff held up number cards for every one of their players in an attempt to substitute the whole team. Richard Taylor, the Selkirk custodian, may have been described in the match programme as 'very brave and a good reflex goalkeeper', but speaking to the *Stirling Observer* following this shambles of a mismatch, 'he did admit . . . that perhaps he had not found his right position yet'. The match ball was given to him as a memento of the game, but as the same paper commented, 'Did he really need reminding of what it looked like after picking it out of the net so often?'

It was 1961, though, that was the big one. Six years after losing seven goals to England, Scottish supporters could be forgiven for thinking that their nightmare had come true. Never has a game been more successful in wounding national pride than the 9–3 hammering of April 1961. There are several reasons for the longevity of its survival in the national psyche: the sheer scale of the defeat, to the team the Scots would least like to be defeated by; the truly inept performance of the team's goalkeeper; and the presence of one Jimmy Greaves in the victorious England team. This was the game that both conceived and delivered the legend of the Scottish goalkeeper.

It was a match that the *Sunday Express* described as a 'nightmare massacre . . . this Sassenach cakewalk', and it began with a 20-yard volley from Bobby Robson that saw Scottish goalie Frank Haffey diving seconds too late.

By half-time Haffey and his team-mates were three down, but not out. Denis Law had had a goal disallowed for offside, and within minutes of the restart Scotland had scored twice. They were within an ace of pulling it back when a controversial goal settled the day. From a free-kick which the Scots argued was taken yards from where the offence had been committed, the men in blue were forced to watch in agony as the ball trickled from Haffey's hands and rolled inches across the line. There was to be no looking back for the English.

There may, of course, have been mitigating circumstances for such a heavy loss. One of the stories doing the rounds at the time was that the reason Scotland lost was down to the colour of the ball – orange, the colour of rampant Protestantism. In the sectarian Protestant/Catholic split that is Glaswegian football, it was said that there was no way a Celtic goalkeeper was going to hold onto the thing and no way that Rangers full-back Bobby Shearer was going to kick it away! England merely exploited this religious divide.

Under a vicious parade of nine painful photos, the *Sunday Express* filled their back page with the headline 'The man who let through 9 goals'. Haffey is seen grounded, stranded, despairing, clutching, flailing, crawling, sprawling, agonising and failing – identified in the most cruel and graphic of ways as the man responsible for what the paper called 'a slaughter in the spring sunshine'.

It was all rather tough on Haffey, an isolated figure as he left the field. He wasn't the first-choice keeper for the game and was clearly out of his depth. But despite his inappropriateness for the big match, the greater part of the blame should surely have gone to a misfiring Scotland team in which others were most certainly more culpable.

Haffey had been drafted in to cover for Tottenham's Bill Brown on the basis of being a competent if somewhat erratic Celtic keeper. He was a likeable, big-hearted man prone to both blunders and pranks, but also playing decent football in a club not at its best. Anecdotes of his goalkeeping eccentricity abound: how even as a youngster, playing Boys' Guild soccer, he had shocked his team-mates when, in an attacking position, they were put off by the sound of music emanating from their own goal. Turning to look back, they found the young Haffey sitting on his crossbar singing his heart out. It was a favourite trick even in adulthood, according to Stuart Cosgrove who in *Hampden Babylon* writes, 'In more than one crunch game when the pressure was off and the ball was in the opposition's half, Frank would climb on to the bar and endear himself to the Celtic faithful by pretending to sleep on the woodwork.' The blunders were, naturally enough, part and parcel of the man too. One story tells of how, against Hearts, a 40-yard speculative shot from Johnny 'Jumping Jack' Hamilton passed through Haffey's legs as he bent down to collect it. Whatever the truth, the fact is that when he stepped onto Wembley's turf, he stepped out of his class and in so many ways will never be forgiven.

In actual fact the press were mixed in their treatment of the young goalkeeper. Monday's *Daily Record* didn't know which way to look. Under a picture of Haffey leaving the field at the end of the game, the paper talked of a national disgrace, adding, 'He's just been beaten more times than any Scottish international keeper in history . . . so no wonder Frank Haffey's so unhappy as he leaves the pitch at the finish.' But in another article it dredged up the ghost of goalkeeping failure past – Freddie Martin, the man who had conceded those seven goals to England in 1955: 'Only one man can really understand the goalkeeping nightmare that was Wembley for young Celtic keeper Frank Haffey . . . And no doubt Martin will join us as, with Scots footballers everywhere, we send a "cheer up" Monday morning message to young Haffey saying, "Don't worry, Frank. Just try to forget it."'

In the *Daily Telegraph*, Welshman Donald Saunders debated whether it was the ineptness of the keeper or the brilliance of England's Johnny Haynes that was the decisive factor in the massacre: 'Always the English will believe the genius of Haynes earned glorious victory; Scotsmen will for ever blame Haffey's shortcomings for ignominious defeat.' He concluded, though, that 'England would have destroyed Scotland on Saturday whoever had been in goal.'

There was no ambivalence to Hugh McIlvanney's searing condemnation in *The Scotsman*:

> *Greatest humiliation in the 90 years of international football*
> It was a night (in West End pubs later) when most preferred to identify themselves with Rangers or Celtic rather than Scotland, although the representatives of Parkhead were not rushing to defend the performance of Haffey.
>
> The young goalkeeper's was the biggest personal tragedy on a day when there were no shortage of them. He might have saved at least four of the goals, including the vital first in the eighth minute . . .
>
> After that mistake he erred with the clumsiness and regularity of a substitute in a second-class works team. Admittedly, the actions of some of the players in front of him were liable to convince him that he was, in fact, in such a side.

Haffey seemed to exacerbate his reputation, not least of all because he didn't seem to realise the degree of his disgrace. He may have looked a downtrodden, lonesome figure as he trudged off the field, but just minutes later he was astonishing his team-mates by singing happily in the bath. It was almost as if he knew that this was the final chance he was ever going to get of playing for Scotland and, despite the enormity of the calamity, he was darned well going to enjoy every last minute of it. As the team bus pulled away from Wembley it was attacked by a mob of outraged Scots. Bottles, cans and stones rained down on the coach, but as his colleagues cowered below their seats Haffey beamed radiantly and waved with all the aplomb of passing royalty.

Later that day he rubbed it in further by posing for television cameras in front of Big Ben as it chimed for nine o'clock. 'What's the time?' 'Nine past Haffey', became the joke of the day.

Some didn't see the funny side. At Glasgow's Art Gallery and Museum in Kelvingrove a young man threw a lump of sandstone at Salvador Dalí's famous crucifixion painting *Christ of St John of the Cross* and followed up by tearing the canvas straight down the middle. Word went around town that as he was carted off to

Barlinnie prison he told the police, 'I'd had a few drinks in me at the time, and I thought it wis a picture o' big Haffey swingin' fae the crossbar!'

Haffey's career in Scotland was not to last too much longer. He wasn't selected for the national side again and although he played 200 times for Celtic, including giving a great performance in the 1963 Scottish Cup final against Rangers, he soon headed off to a new life in Australia where, after playing for clubs with exotic names such as Hakoah, St George, Budapest and Sutherland, he began moderately successful careers as both a cabaret singer and radio disc jockey.

However, perhaps the most significant figure in the Scottish goalkeeping legend was not even playing for the Dark Blues that day. He was in fact tormenting them. Jimmy Greaves had the pleasure of popping a hat-trick past Haffey as part of his contribution to the drubbing. More importantly, though, it's through his subsequent media career as obnoxious television slaphead that Greaves developed his theme of the Scottish keeper as a hybrid Frank MacSpencer. Whenever a Scottish keeper made a mistake – as all keepers do – it would be highlighted by Greavsie and whenever they didn't it would be highlighted as an aberration, a miracle or a mistake. Whenever an English goalkeeper made a mistake of sufficient hilarity to be worth a few seconds airplay, or whenever a foreign keeper achieved the same, Greaves would, and does, follow up with, 'He's good enough to play in Scotland, Saint' or 'Give Andy Roxburgh/Jock Stein/Willie Ormond/Ally MacLeod a call – I think we've got him a new national keeper'.

In such a way do myths take on lives of their own. It's like you never see a Morris Minor Countryman until you buy one and then suddenly everybody's got one. You never noticed a bad Scottish keeper (as distinct from any other nationality keeper) until it's pointed out at every turn, and all of a sudden myth and reality blur into one. So is there a generic term for Scottish goalies – a flock of sheep, a herd of cows, a murder of crows and . . . and a bungle of Scottish custodians?

Granted, some goalkeepers playing before the Tartan Army were meat and drink to Greaves – Stewart Kennedy, for a starter, who seemingly trawled for the ball against England with his goalnet. Five passed him in a pathetic Wembley spectacle in 1975. But is there any substantial truth to it? Take a look at the evidence.

Even in the aftermath of the springtime slaughter there were influential voices calling, if not for Haffey's exoneration, at least to have the blame redirected. The *Glasgow Herald* pointed its finger not at the keeper, but at the more experienced Anglo-Scots in the team: 'Not for the first time Mackay and Law must be charged with putting their own whims and fancies before the good of the team as a whole,' it reported. If Dave Mackay's performance had 'any connection with common-sense wing-half play,' wrote Cyril Horne, 'then I'm the Queen of Sheba.'

Even back in those far-off wartime friendly games of 1943 and 1944, the keeper on the wrong end of eight goals had an unexpected sympathiser – his England counterpart. Frank Swift, having stood at the other end watching the carnage, was moved to comment, 'I was glad that afternoon at Maine Road that it was Joe Crozier in the Scottish goal and not yours truly. I had no wish to test my skill against this goal-hungry line. Lawton was shooting too accurately for any goalkeeper to stand much chance of saving his shots.'

Indeed it was true. This was an unstoppable England team led by the 'terror of the Scots' – Stanley Matthews – and the insatiable Tommy Lawton. In the face of such a ravenous attack, Crozier was actually saluted as a hero, for it was said that he had done well to keep the score down to single figures in 1943 and was completely blameless four months later for any of the goals.

Nevertheless, Crozier did let in 14 goals in two games, as did Freddie Martin – isn't that sufficient proof? Well, maybe, but what about Gil Merrick? Where was his Scottish citizenship when he stood between the posts for England and conceded 13 goals in two games against Hungary? Stewart Kennedy may well have looked ridiculous in 1975, flailing his arms like a windmill on speed, in the face of an England onslaught led by Gerry Francis, but did Ray Clemence really look any more sensible when, a year later, Kenny Dalglish nutmegged him at Hampden to give Scotland a 2–1 win?

For the truth is that in the final analysis goalkeepers are only really as strong as the team in front of them. Blaming the keeper for a heavy defeat is to ignore the role of the defence and the forward play of the attackers. Sometimes in Scotland this can have even more significance than usual: when Jim Baxter scored twice against England at Wembley in 1963, he determined that he was going to be the first Scotsman to score three goals on

England's own turf – even if it meant putting one past his own goalie, Bill Brown. He alerted his dismayed keeper to the possibility, but was forced to abandon his outrageous plan when England pulled one back.

Keepers, as we have seen, make easy scapegoats, but when it comes down to statistics Scotland fares no better, but certainly not much worse, than England. From the very first international played by Scotland through to the end of 1991, the average number of goals conceded by Scottish keepers is just over one per game. From the very first international played by England through to the end of 1991 the average number of goals conceded by English keepers is just over one per game. Ooops, Jimmy, surely shome mistake!

Nevertheless, this myth of incompetence is all-pervasive and powerful. It means that instead of referring back to a magnificent line of Caledonian keepers with pride, modern Scottish custodians are constantly forced to respond to the footballing equivalent of 'When did you stop beating your wife?' It has clearly got to some of them.

Alan Rough in his autobiography talks of one particular occasion when he came south to play against England and met Bob Wilson, the English-born telly presenter and former keeper who had played twice for Scotland, after qualifying for the team through his father's birth-right. Wilson wound Rough up, reminded him of past disasters, Scottish goalkeeping horror stories and asked him whether he was afraid of what might happen to him. Angry, Rough 'let him know that past events were no concern . . . It was out of character for me, with ten caps to my name, to ask him how often he had played international football. The truth is I was fed up with hearing about this so-called jinx on goalkeepers. From the time the team arrived in the South, I seemed to hear nothing else and I have to confess that I did not sleep as well as usual on the eve of the game.'

Scotland lost 2–1, Rough being blameless as England scored from a penalty three minutes from time.

Jim Leighton has had enough of it too. In 1996 the Hibernian and Scotland keeper told *Goal* magazine, 'I feel a lot of this rubbish started when Frank Haffey let in nine goals at Wembley because, to be fair to us, we have only really had four regular goalkeepers for the good part of 25 years: me, David Harvey, Alan Rough and Andy Goram. Nobody is going to tell me that we are all terrible. Then, of course, we had all that stuff that Saint and Greavsie did. Really horrible sarcasm, that's what their programme was all about. It wasn't funny, especially if it was about you personally. Remember, as well, that at the time England were lucky enough to be able to field two exceptional goalkeepers in Shilton and Clemence. So maybe we suffered by comparison.'

Leighton is correct. His own goalkeeping may have undergone a bit of a crisis mid-career, when a couple of very public mistakes resulted in him losing his place firstly in Manchester United's FA Cup final replay team and secondly the Scottish national team, but Leighton is a fine goalkeeper in what is actually a fine goalkeeping tradition.

From the game's earliest days Scotland has produced keepers of the highest calibre, keepers like H.G. Rennie, the finest keeper of the first decade of the 20th century – a man who was so keen to be involved in the game that he could often be found further upfield than his defence, but who was, nevertheless, famed for his sound judgement and positioning; or Dumbarton's James McAulay, who, as we have seen, in the pioneering days of goalkeeping, the 1880s, became the first man to earn the title 'Prince of Keepers'. Keepers like Ned Doig of Sunderland and Scotland, who won six caps and was described in his day as being 'as cool as a cucumber between the posts'; or Daniel McArthur, the brilliant Celtic keeper who won three caps in the late 1890s despite being a mere waif at 5ft 5in and tipping the scales at no more than 10st.

In later days, too, as football developed, Scotland continued to provide keepers of quality: Jimmy Cowan, who won 25 caps in the 1940s, and who trained under Rennie at Morton; Jerry Dawson, one of the country's regular keepers in the 1930s; even later, Bill Brown of Dundee and Spurs, a fine and distinguished keeper of the highest calibre; and Ronnie Simpson, whose professional career stretched from 1945, when he wasn't even 15, until 1970 and who made his international début at the ripe old age of 36.

The list could go on, but the point is this: the next time some little fella with a bald head and a tatty moustache tries to tell you about the standard of 'Jocks' between the posts, wag your finger at him, shake your head and say, as politely as possible, 'Tut, tut. Not so, my man, I think perchance that you are mistaken,' and then ask him where he was when Geoff Hurst was putting three goals away in the 1966 World Cup final.

On the other foot

Of course it isn't all misery and imminent disaster for goal-keepers, of whatever nationality. It's one of the schizophrenia-inducing properties of the custodianship of the nets that, in that moment when catastrophe is looming, salvation and glory can be so close at hand. And, yes, good saves are remembered, lauded and discussed, but nothing is more talked about and nothing is more savoured than the phenomenon of the goalkeeper who scores.

One of the most famous instances of this occurred in the 1967 Charity Shield match between the FA Cup-winners Tottenham Hotspur and League-winners Manchester United. Eight minutes into the game Pat Jennings, in the Spurs goal, punted the ball and, borne by a stiff breeze, it flew, and flew and flew – right over the heads of the Man United defenders and out of the grasp of their wrong-footed keeper Alex Stepney. The goal caused a sensation.

Jennings had only sympathy for his opposite number. 'It's one of those things that you dread happening to you,' he told me. 'Once the defender lets the ball bounce like that, the keeper is left stranded in no-man's-land. I felt really sorry for Alex Stepney. In my early days I used to get told off a lot for overkicking the ball. Fifteen years ago I went to Japan and every time I kicked the ball out you could hear the crowd going "Whoooo" in awe. Nevertheless, the ball going into the net from a kick-out by a goalie is more the fault of the defenders than anybody else. I played for almost 24 years and always felt that there must have been a good chance of me being on the receiving end of one of those. I was lucky, Alex wasn't.'

Stepney remembers the incident as his 'most embarrassing moment'. In his autobiography, he recalls: 'I hardly knew a thing about it. Play was at the other end of the field and as Pat made his long clearance, kicking out of his hands, the ball seemed to be dropping into the area where Bill Foulkes would be expected to clear.' For some reason, though, Foulkes let the ball pass and Stepney, who had moved out to the edge of his box, was caught on the hop. 'The ball bounced in front of me,' he continues, 'and soared in a long, slow, agonising arc over my head and into the goal.'

Fortunately for Stepney's reputation, it was one of those incidents that tend to get laughed off as a freak. And he himself was to discover what it was to have the boot on the other foot a few seasons later, when he was in the remarkable position, possibly unique for a goalkeeper, of being Manchester United's leading scorer as the season hit Christmas.

His goalscoring talents (if scoring twice from penalties can be called a talent) were first noticed in a pre-season friendly against a Spanish team that went to a sudden-death shoot-out. Stepney saved one and stepped forward to finish the game off. A seed had been planted in the idiosyncratic mind of United boss Tommy Docherty and it had bloomed when the usual spot-kicker, Willie Morgan, was injured before the season started.

Leicester City and Peter Shilton were to receive the first Stepney penalty. An astonished Filbert Street went quiet as it realised that Stepney wasn't ambling down the field to invite the referee around for tea and biscuits after the game – he was going to take the spot-kick. Peter Shilton was equally surprised, as Stepney continues: 'When he saw me pick up the ball and place it on the spot he never said a word. He's too professional for that, but the look on his face said everything. I drove the ball well wide of him to score the first goal of my career.'

When your goalkeeper is your top scorer and he's got the grand total of two, you know that you've got a problem. Manchester United did have a problem: by the end of the 1973–74 season they were no longer in Division One.

Even if it had been the most natural thing in the world, and despite the claims of so many keepers that they could do a better job than their forwards, not all goalies would relish the prospect of taking a penalty – despite the fact that it could mean instant glory. For some the offer of scoring a goal might be rejected out of laziness – why leave the warmth of your own goal when somebody more qualified could do a better job anyway? For others it may be the responsibility, the fear of missing, the fear of embarrassment and the fear of finding the ball saved, cleared and flying over your head towards an unprotected net at the other end of the pitch. Frank Swift had his own reason. During the war he played for an RAF XI at Shrewsbury and, with his team winning 5–0, his side were awarded a penalty. Responding to shouts from his team-mates, Swift ran the length of the pitch and, without stopping, blasted the ball first time. The power was stunning, the ball ripping the back out of the net and hardly slowing before it smashed into the face of an old man who was leaning against the railings behind the goal. As the man picked up the pieces of his shattered dentures, Swift vowed never to take another penalty in his life.

Fifty years later in the UEFA Cup, Peter Schmeichel of Manchester United dashed upfield for a final-minute corner against Rotor Volgograd. United were losing and it may have been a last gasp act of desperation, but as the ball floated into the box, the big Dane with the red hooter rose above the mêlée and nodded it home with all the assurance of a budding Dixie Dean. It wasn't enough to save United – the match ended 2–2 and the Russians won on away goals – but as John Motson probably said, 'That'll give them something to talk about in the pubs of Manchester for quite some time.'

Rule changes, however, have made it more likely in the 1990s that goalkeepers will score, though not necessarily in the manner of the great Dane. When, in 1995, the rule permitting three subs on the bench was loosened so that one of them no longer had to be a cover for the keeper, it was possibly the dawn of a new era. Managers are faced with a straight choice: at a time when more and more keepers are getting sent off for professional fouls, do they risk omitting a keeper from among their substitutes and face the possibility of having to put the burly full-back in goal if the keeper receives a red card? Or do they play it safe and leave an extra goalie on the touchline? In many cases the answer has been to gamble with three outfield players.

In other cases, though, where managers persist with a keeper on the bench, the possibility arises, where two subs have already been used, that the keeper might be called on to play in the outfield if a further injury occurs.

Alan Fettis of Hull is a case in point. Unable to play in goal because of an injured thumb, he nevertheless went on the bench for a game at home to Oxford in December 1994. When Hull's centre-forward was taken off, Fettis entered the fray and, with two minutes to go, met a perfect cross perfectly and scored. Later in the season he did the same against Blackpool – this time his striking skills earning him an outfield place in the starting line-up.

In the long run it's a development that may bring with it the further enhancement of the ball skills that keepers had to hone when they were barred from picking up back-passes; in the short term, though, another consequence has been the bizarre sight of veteran keepers like Les Sealey playing up front for West Ham in the dying moments of a Premier League game against Arsenal.

Not that scoring goalkeepers are by any means a new phenomenon. In fact, considering how rare it should be – 100 yards from the target, 11 opposing players in the way, lack of ball skills and so on – the goal from the number 1 is, and always has been, a remarkably common occurrence and isn't as exceptional as perhaps it ought to be.

Penalties have, of course, always been a good source of goalie goals. Back in 1911 James Brownlie, the Third Lanark custodian, ran the length of the field to take a penalty against Motherwell. He missed, but scored off the rebound. In the 1923–24 season Arnold Birch of Chesterfield set a goalkeeping record by putting five goals away, while keeping up the responsibility of minding his team's nets. All of them were penalties, but hey, they all count!

Sixty years down the road another Chesterfield keeper, Jim Brown, scored from a 97-yard drop-kick to help his team beat Stockport County. Once again the wind caught hold of the ball and helped it to fly over the head of County's keeper Salmon, who singularly failed to jump like his namesake. It was the second such goal that Brown had scored; two years earlier he had tucked one away for the Washington Diplomats in a North American Soccer League game against Atlanta.

Possibly one of the most courageous goals was scored by Arsenal's custodian Frank Moss, back in 1935. Moss seems to have been a 1930s version of Bryan Robson – if there was an injury around he'd pick it up and stick it in his collection. Arsenal had spotted him at Oldham Athletic where he had lost his place in the first team after breaking his nose. No sooner was it mended than the Gunners pounced. In March of 1935 he was playing in front of 50,000 at Goodison Park when, going up for a corner, he dislocated his shoulder and collapsed in agony. Following a lengthy delay, Moss was carried from the pitch and Hapgood, the full-back, went in goals. Despite a brilliant performance, including many fine saves, the defender caused a great deal of hilarity when, every time he took a goal-kick, he forgot that he was now the goalkeeper and ran up-field to his old position, leaving an empty net behind him. These were the days when no substitutes were allowed and, in spite of the fact that after 45 minutes Arsenal were a goal up, they started the second half with one Frank Moss at outside left.

With his shoulder heavily strapped, Moss was a revelation, going close to scoring on two or three occasions before, in the 75th minute, he latched on to a pass from Ted Drake and tucked it into the back of the Everton net. Arsenal were two up. Moments later he provided an inch-perfect cross which really should have been converted and then he hobbled off the pitch in distress for a bit of attention.

Up on his feet again he strolled onto the pitch and immediately gave away a free-kick for re-entering the game without permission. Then, coming within a whisker of scoring another, he injured his shoulder once more and retired from the game for good. He'd done more than his bit, the papers called him the hero of the day and Arsenal won the game thanks to his efforts.

7 Days like these

Almost from the moment of its invention the position of goal-keeper came under attack: restrictions on movement, restrictions on handling, proposals on the size of the goals. It's almost as if in some conspiracy of embarrassment, football's ruling authorities sought to stuff the goalkeeping genie they had released in 1871 back into the bottle.

Examine the evidence: once, like buffalo, goalkeepers could roam freely, handle the ball at will in their own half and still get back to make glorious saves. But, as with their four-legged North American counterparts, they were pushed back and back until finally they found themselves corralled to the limits of their own penalty areas. Then, from the late 19th century, keepers were forced to face penalties, usually brought about by the mistakes of others – a contest of wills maybe, an opportunity for instant glory perhaps, but who else on the pitch has to stand guard while from 12 yards away a striker blasts the ball at them at the speed of a bullet? Not punishment enough? Until 1905 keepers could attempt a save from anywhere within six yards of their goal-line. In 1905 they were forced back onto the line. Still not punishment enough? Well how about 30 years after spot-kicks were introduced, goalkeepers being forced to remain still until the kick is taken, thus allowing the penalty taker time to decide which part of the keeper he'd most like to maim?

Of course there are those who would say that keepers get everything they deserve and that they are their own worst enemies. In evidence the detractors might quote the behaviour of

J.F. Mitchell as he faced the first-ever penalty in an FA Cup final.

Mitchell was an amateur who kept goals in spectacles for Preston North End and, in spite of his myopia – which had once led to him leaving the pitch before a game was over, giving the opposition a free goal – he had played for England in the 1920 Olympics and in several amateur internationals. Midway through the second half of the monstrously tedious 1922 Cup final between Preston and Huddersfield, Mitchell found himself confronted with the spot-kick, after Smith was tripped in the box by Hamilton.

Mitchell's reaction? As Smith prepared to take the kick, the goalie ran frenziedly along the line like a man possessed, jumping in the air, hopping, skipping, waving his arms and howling in a frantic effort to distract the kicker. Unperturbed, Smith drove the ball below the wailing keeper and, in the words of the *Athletic News* correspondent, 'took no notice of this spring-heeled-jack business and thus fulfilled the idea of retribution . . .'

Mitchell's mischief was rather frowned upon as not the sort of thing a gentleman does, one newspaper complaining that he behaved like 'a man highly strung', and it was only a matter of a few years before the rule change was introduced limiting a keeper's movements.

This process of pinning back the keeper has continued to the present day. As Eddie Niedzwiecki, the former Wrexham, Chelsea and Wales keeper who now works as reserve-team manager for Chelsea, told me, 'There were so many changes in the game when I was a keeper. They used to say you had to be daft to play in goal, but I'm not so sure – by the time that I retired I thought you'd need an A-level to cope!'

In the 1990s, over 120 years of passing back to the goalie as a means of sound defence were wiped out at a stroke, and keepers were barred from picking up the ball when it deliberately came back to them from the foot of a team-mate.

Now, as we approach the millennium, the debate has focused on the need to score more goals. This is not judged to be a product of the poverty of attacking skills on show; no, it's because the poor old keeper is doing his job too well. Football is becoming boring, or so the argument goes, because of its lack of goals, and there are only two ways to improve this. First of all you could lighten the ball, change its aerodynamics, make it fly with the speed of Concorde and the unpredictability of a European space mission. Secondly, you could spread the posts. Anybody who has ever watched NBA basketball, where points are scored with alacrity and rarely a moment passes without the lead changing hands, will be aware that this thinking is a result of the ascendancy of a North American value system that says a game that finishes 0–0 must have been dull (as opposed to a game which finishes 136–134, which must have been exciting).

Furthermore, now that football has become a truly big-business concern, with flotations on the stockmarket, megabucks being splashed out in the war for TV rights and transfer fees spiralling into orbit, there must be a real fear that the days of the showman/eccentric goalkeeper are numbered. The grey suits that run today's football are men for whom a suspect goalkeeper is an added risk to an already frequently risky investment. Rough-edged keepers need not apply. As Brian Glanville wrote some years back:

> By the very nature of his art and duties, the goalkeeper is inclined to be an explosive and temperamental fellow who reads his stage if he is to function properly. This stage is increasingly cluttered with the boots and bodies of his fellow defenders; a situation which is growing worse rather than better . . . What we see before us, a manifest sign of the times, is the transformation of the goalkeeper from flamboyant individual into a grey company man.

There may be some truth in what Glanville writes and for those of us who like their heroes to be occasionally vulnerable, prone to tragedy and susceptible to the unexpected, there can be no bigger proof of our pudding than the appearance of the goalkeeping coach – can there?

When future historians look back on our century, it may turn out that we lived through a far less significant period than we are willing to admit. The lasting developments of our age may add up to very little: the ability to destroy ourselves many times over, the rise of the motor car, the invention of the computer, Salt and Lineker crisps and the concept of modern sport.

In the later stages of the 20th century, modern sport, from synchronised swimming to rugby union, has sought to hone its skills in the search for perfection. The rewards justify the effort. So too with soccer, and as coaches have become ever present in athletics so have they become indispensable to football. The need for coaches for goalkeepers, like everything about goalkeeping, just took a little time to be recognised.

So are coaches there to eradicate the Foulkes, Rooses, Haffeys and Higuitas of the future, to iron out the creases and give us silky slick teams?

If anybody should know about differences in goalkeepers now and a few decades ago it's Peter Bonetti – the 'Cat' of Chelsea. Bonetti grew up playing football with his mates in the park and, like so many future keepers, had no desire to be a goalie until he found himself plonked there by a disciplinarian sports teacher. After his mother wrote to Chelsea requesting a trial for her son, Bonetti found himself joining the club on the same day as other soon-to-be-famous newcomers – Terry Venables and Bobby Tambling. He is now the goalkeeping coach at Leicester, Wolves, Watford, Bristol Rovers and Reading to name but a few.

'I made my début against Manchester City at Stamford Bridge in April 1960 – I was 18. Denis Law was playing his first away game for City and there were 40,000 there to see us,' he told me. 'It was very unusual, because in those days there weren't many youngsters or teenagers making their débuts or even playing first-team football. It wasn't the norm then. Certainly now teenagers are playing regularly for the first team. In those days they used to rely more on the experienced players.'

Bonetti is the first to admit that things are different now. 'Football in general has changed considerably in the sense that a goalkeeper is now more of an athlete. The game's speeded up no end, which means you've got to be physically stronger.'

'The Cat' was not a big keeper, but he was famed for his agility and spectacular saves; had he been born a decade or two later there's a chance any aspirations he had of becoming a keeper would have been laughed at on size alone. 'The physical side has really changed,' he says. 'You very rarely see any small goalkeepers these days. They're all six-foot-three, six-foot-four guys. And the little guys like in my day, there's not many of them around. I coach one at Leicester, Kevin Poole, a brilliant keeper, very agile – reminds me a lot of myself – and he holds his own.

'Back in the '60s you had loads of them; you had the likes of Springett, Hodgkinson, Hopkinson . . . all on the small side; playing for England. Now you'll very rarely get an England goalkeeper who's under six foot.'

According to Bonetti, the other big difference is the speed of the game. 'It is so much faster now, not so much skill in it and so you've got to be physically stronger to cope with it.'

Coaching wasn't an automatic choice for him. After leaving Chelsea he lived a rural idyll on a small Scottish island, but chucked it in in 1983 when the isolation meant that in order for his children to go to school they had to live away from home. For a while he was like a fish out of water, pondering what his next move would be: 'I thought why not specialise in goalkeeping coaching? I remember ringing up Bob Wilson. He was doing it at Arsenal and he said, "You won't earn a living from it, you'll just do one day a week, two days a week," but I had to start somewhere so I called Chelsea.'

It took off from there and he found an immediate and receptive audience. 'Ask any goalkeeper in any club and they love being coached . . . there is a need for us because it means keepers can develop things they can't do with the rest of the players.'

He starts with the basics: 'You develop the technique first and foremost. If they've got a poor technique then you correct it – if their stance is poor or their positional play is poor, you sort it out. The rest is just speeding them up. Working on handling every day, making them better.'

The back-pass rule has added a new dimension to the game and for Bonetti the initial fears that it would ostracise the keeper further from the game have been unfounded. 'I wish the back-pass rule had been round in my day. I like the skill side of it, I think it's great. It's made the keeper more of a last sweeper than before. You could say you weren't so involved before it, in some ways. When I'm coaching I do a lot of footwork because a keeper needs to be confident of his skill. They have to touch the ball, control the ball at a bad height or pace or whatever.'

And what about coaches ruining the game, reducing the element of risk? 'It's like anything else – why do athletes have coaches? Why do tennis players have coaches? Because the coaches see things you're not doing right and they correct you. I wish I had had a coach. I feel I could have been a better player because all I used to do was train with the outfield players. Even now it's only the clubs with a bit of extra money who take on specialists to train their keepers because many other clubs still feel it's a luxury. But it pays dividends.'

The fear remains, though, that the drawing in of the goal-keeper from his lonely isolation could lead to his continued transformation into the 'grey company man' highlighted by Brian Glanville.

But is it really time to despair? In an age when the repeated claim that there are no characters left in football resounds around pubs and clubs alike, is it time to fret that the apportioning of a more general role to the custodian will be the death knell of the last position guaranteed to give us those characters we so crave?

Of course not. No matter what they try to do, no matter how they try to get to him, the keeper's spirit shines through, indomitable to the last. The nature of the job would have it no other way; and its most overarching components – vulnerability and responsibility – persist, and with the stakes so high, the money interest so large, their magnitude is multiplied.

Besides, as we have seen, goalkeepers are wise old birds – the thinking man's footballer – and in so many ways the rulings that have been imposed on them from on high have been subverted to their own ends. As Peter Bonetti pointed out, the back-pass rule, so obviously intended to reduce a goalkeeper's influence on the game, has had the opposite effect. The opportunities for keepers to exceed themselves have actually increased exponentially at the stroke of a pen. The chance of running out to clear a back-pass under pressure and missing or miskicking; the chance of kicking out badly and incurring the full-blown wrath or amusement of the crowd; the chance to amble out of the area with the ball at his feet and take the equivalent of a free-kick in his own time from somewhere near the halfway line; and the chance to develop sufficient ball skills not only to cope with back-passes but, when needed, to be plunged into attack and show that lazy bastard of a centre-forward just exactly what is expected of him – all have been enshrined and endorsed by the back-pass rule.

It only takes one exception to break a rule, and when it comes to modern-day goalkeepers who err on the flamboyant rather than the grey, the world is full of exceptions. The eradication of the modern-day goalkeeping eccentric? There's more chance of Graham Kelly being bitten by a daffodil.

A light that never goes out

Just like Weebles that wobble but won't fall down, no matter how many restrictions are put on a goalkeeper's activities, no matter how many knocks individual keepers take and no matter how athletic and professional they have to become in order to survive, it seems that the oddball goalkeeper will always bounce back.

There's a direct thread stretching back to the pioneer days of idiosyncratic net-minders, through the Foulkes, Trainers, Herbie Arthurs, Rooses and Hillmans, that pulls taut on the keepers of today and, as the line winds its way to the modern era, it passes through an illustrious (some would say infamous), crew: Swift, Macedo, Sprake, Icke, Davies, Borota, Burridge, Quiroga, Sealey, Southall, Grobbelaar, Campos of Mexico, Varelli of Sweden, Higuita . . .

And every so often when there's a bite on the line, a tug at the heartstrings or a pang on the conscience, and one of today's custodians feels the need to step forward and explain just exactly why he is or isn't one post short of a goal, it's as if all of the ghosts of goalkeepers past can be heard jangling in the wind.

Frank Swift emphatically denied being mad in his auto-biography, but in another place talking about goalkeepers in general, he surmised that if keepers had a predilection for dottiness then it must be because 'they have to spend their lives watching the people in front of them trying to play football'.

The big thing about big Frank was that he was big, in every sense of the word. He was a giant of his era – a Jolly Green Giant – whose presence commanded both respect and admiration during a football career that straddled the Second World War; a physical giant, over six foot tall and with a hand span of all but 12 inches. Derby and Sunderland's Raich Carter, one of England's finest inside-forwards, said of him: 'He looked so big in goal that it was almost like trying to put the ball into a matchbox.'

Not that this made him impervious to the occasional glitch. In 1934, at the age of 19, Swift was so overcome with Cup final nerves that, on the final whistle, as he bent down to pick his cap out of the back of the net, he went all dizzy and fainted. Minutes later, collecting his winner's medal, the King asked him how he was and commended his performance. At the start of the 1949 season big Frank, who was by now well into the twilight of his career, was placing what was possibly exactly the same flat cap into the back of his net, when it was joined by a ball. The game was seven seconds old and Preston had scored while Frank was bending over. In truth, Frank had caught a glimpse of it coming his way and had hurriedly tried to adjust to the long shot from

Langton, but the ball had bobbled, bumped and beaten him. It was the quickest goal ever scored.

When Frank's footballing days were over he turned those huge hands to journalism. It was to be the death of him. In February 1958, acting as a hack for the *News of the World*, Swifty was sent to cover Manchester United's European Cup quarter-final with Red Star Belgrade in Yugoslavia. He was one of 23 passengers killed when the BEA jet that carried him plummeted to earth in a snowstorm near Munich. Around him died the flower of English football, but Big Frank was as keenly missed as the Busby Babes who perished at his side.

At Fulham in the 1950s, Tony Macedo was a different kettle of fish, a keeper who perhaps didn't achieve as much as he should have, other than that he won sufficient love, affection and tolerance from the faithful that they would forgive him his foibles and forget his failings for those moments of glory that he bestowed on the club and for the glow that he gave them as they poured out of the game when the 90 minutes was up. Frank Keating captures the spirit of 'the Fulham gloveman' in his book *Long Days, Late Nights*: 'When Tony Macedo was good he was very, very good – but when . . . but we loved him. He once lost us a semi-final of the Cup. But we knew he'd got us there in the first place. He was a magnificent madcap.'

And there it is in a nutshell, like some crazy love affair; we the paying public are willing to tolerate the downs – the goofs, the fumbles, the unnecessary mistakes, the unprovoked miskicks, the jokes, the arguments – so long as the ups tip the scales, so long as the passion, the spectacular and the flamboyant outweigh the disaster that invariably comes as part of the package. We know that there can be a price to pay, but we also know that the good things in life rarely come cheap.

Petar Borota was another. The art-student son of a Yugoslav army general, Borota joined Chelsea in March 1979 from Partizan Belgrade at the knockdown price of £70,000. He was good, sometimes very good, but his antics and extravagances were often too much for Geoff Hurst, the Chelsea boss. Hurst told the press after one particularly frenetic game against Cardiff that his Yugoslav bargain would be the death of him: 'If I'm here three or four years, I won't live to 43.' Hurst was joking; that afternoon he had reason to be happy as Borota's performance had helped push Chelsea to the top of the Second Division, but one could understand the manager's sentiments. Chelsea had won the game 1–0, their winner coming just five minutes before time. In the preceding 85 minutes Borota had had two sets of stitches put in his head, he had dribbled the ball out of his area nine times, nutmegged a centre-forward, headed it out, chested it out – in fact, it seemed he had done everything to keep Chelsea in the game apart from catch the bloody ball.

It was a fine line that Borota trod every time he took to the pitch, but to try and tell him differently, to try to instil some sense and some steadiness into the guy, would have been futile – the probability was, too, that any success would have made him worse than useless as a goalkeeper. Not that that stopped his manager having a go. 'I tell him about it three or four times a week and it doesn't matter how many times I tell him to relax, he is still tense,' Hurst told the *News of the World*.

Late in 1979, when asked whether he hoped he would survive as long as another P.B. at Chelsea, Peter Bonetti, Borota laughed and predicted that he didn't have the stamina. 'Peter's hair is grey. Ten years ago it was black like mine. I have some grey coming. I say, "Peter, are these the Chelsea goalkeeper's colours?"' His prediction was right. In 1981 he boarded the bus to nowhere, stopping only briefly at Brentford, Benfica and FC Porto.

When it comes to voyages into obscurity, though, there's one goalkeeper whose long march might only have taken him from Workington to Dumfries, but it makes Mao Zedong's equivalent look like a trip down the Seven-Eleven. John Burridge has a professional career that has spanned four decades and more than 20 clubs. The journey that began at Workington in 1967 has taken in Blackpool, Aston Villa, Southend, Crystal Palace, Queens Park Rangers, Wolves, Derby County, Sheffield United, Southampton, Newcastle United, Aberdeen, Hibs, Dumbarton, Falkirk and more, many more. At 43 in 1995 he played his first game in the Premier League, for Manchester City; the way things are going for him, who is to say he won't play there again? Here is a man in the Leigh Roose 'Have gloves will travel' mould, who for the first time in almost 30 years found himself without a senior-level game on Saturday afternoons in early 1996 – that is, until Queen of the South seized their opportunity and snapped him up. A man who changes his clubs like most of us change our socks, who knows where he'll be by the time that you read this.

The secret of his longevity must surely be in his fitness – he's an obsessive trainer whose batteries will still be driving his motor long after the Duracell bunnies have banged their last drum. Not many people would, for example, complain that the autocratic taskmaster Ron Saunders was soft – Saunders had, after all, won his macho spurs by wandering around with a broken neck for a year – but Burridge did, having a bust-up with his boss when his demands for extra training were not met. While at Southampton he would entertain the crowd with his pre-match stretches and strains, a warm-up to shame the best of us. But even he could push it too far – before a game with Wimbledon, he went though his routine of hand-stands, back-flips, walking on his hands when something in his thigh popped and, by the time the whistle went for the start of the game, he was a crock and one of his defenders was called upon to take all the goal-kicks.

Stories about Burridge, who in addition to being the keeper for Queen of the South is the goalkeeping coach at Newcastle United, are legion. How he goes to bed at night with his keeper's gloves on; about a weekly ritual of watching *Match of the Day* in full kit with a ball grasped in his hands; and about going to the hairdresser's with a picture of Peter Shilton and insisting on having the same perm. In March 1996 he told the *Sunday Times*, 'People thought I was odd. Nobody said anything specific, but you get the message. I'm not a nutter. I'm just totally dedicated, in a way that is beyond most people's comprehension . . .'

Sometimes you can be fooled by the apparent ordinariness of the goalkeeper, but when you look deeper it's this very facet of his character that becomes his significance. Modern footballers are the demi-gods of the new age, and Neville Southall is one of the best at his trade, but you wouldn't think so to look at him. Here's a man who made his début for Llandudno Swifts in the Welsh League (North) at the age of 14, a man who left school to work on the bins and to demolish gun emplacements for the local council. Here's a man who worked in the Ritz café Llandudno and later as a hod carrier on building sites. Yet here also is the man who went on to become Wales's most capped goalkeeper, but who quite clearly can't see what all the excitement is about. When Everton won the 1995 FA Cup, Southall decided to forego the traditional banquet and night-out in London, got into his car and drove back up the motorway to his home in North Wales. It wasn't that he was being a miserable bastard, it was just that he disliked the fuss and the obligation; besides there was probably

Blind Date and *Casualty* to catch up with on telly. His manager Joe Royle was moved to comment: 'All keepers are mad and Nev is no exception.'

In the search for a quiet life he has eschewed controversy, but therein lies a problem for goalkeepers – they might want to be Steady Eddies, but trouble will actively seek out those not actively seeking it themselves. In Everton's opening home game of the 1990 season, Southall walked out of a half-time team talk and sat down against his goalpost on an empty pitch – Everton were two goals down to Leeds at the time and it looked like the sit-down protest of a badly disgruntled goalkeeper. As he sat there alone, a fan ran on the pitch and remonstrated with him. The press had a field day, deciding that Southall's behaviour was a public expression of a private feud with the then Everton boss Colin Harvey. According to *The Times*, 'the football was overshadowed by a staggering gesture of dissent' from Everton's 'disaffected keeper'. *The Times*, like other newspapers, reported that Southall was known to be fed up with his club and eager to leave – 'the breach is surely irrevocable' it proclaimed. Colin Harvey tried to play down the issue, insisting that his keeper had just gone out for a breath of fresh air. Players union chief executive Gordon Taylor was more forthright: 'His conduct was unprofessional and not fair to his team-mates, his manager and the fans who pay his wages . . . his action was not good for the profession and we do not want any more displays like that.'

Southall has always insisted that the press got him wrong, that in fact he needed some time alone, to get his head together, to refocus his thoughts and sort out his mind for the game ahead. By Tuesday he had made a public apology and had had a week's pay docked – almost £3,000 – as a fine for his misbehaviour. It really wasn't to be a very good week for the Welshman. On Wednesday night in a midweek match at Coventry he was warned by the police for using foul language after home supporters complained at the way he was shouting instructions to his own players.

Six years down the line, at the age of 38, Southall's explanation would appear to have been vindicated: he is still the Welsh national keeper, still one of the best in the British game and that irrevocable breach between him and Everton, so confidently predicted by *The Times,* has yet to become a reality.

Southall is a man without frills, often lampooned by team-mates as a scruff. Even that moment when the fan invaded the pitch to interrupt Nev's goalmouth 'protest' had a more mundane explanation: 'He tiled our bathroom once,' commented the Everton keeper. 'He said, "Don't worry, it can't be that bad!" I laughed and said I wanted his hat, but then the bizzies took him off.'

In the final analysis it appears that Southall is fundamentally determined not to be fazed by the excesses of the game. He summed up his attitude in an interview for *FourFourTwo* magazine in April 1996: 'I just live my own life. I please myself. It's the only way.'

If banality is the watchword of Southall's eccentricity, for much of his career he was forced to share the city of Liverpool with a goalkeeper for whom there were frills and thrills aplenty – Bruce Grobbelaar. But as the man from Zimbabwe's career draws ever nearer to its close, the glorious years of showmanship and football artistry have been somewhat dulled by allegations of match-fixing and corruption. Doubts and suspicions may leave a bad taste in the mouth, but they should not be allowed to tarnish almost two decades of erratic goalkeeping, wonderful saves and eccentric good humour from a man who has simultaneously fought and promoted the image of goalkeeping 'Prince of Clowns'.

Bruce Grobbelaar, one suspects, would like nothing better than to be remembered as a great professional goalkeeper. At times he has come close to achieving this, but Grobb is a man whose experiences of the 'real world' have given him a perspective on life that helps him to realise that some things are more important than football.

He was born in South Africa in 1957 but moved north to Rhodesia at the tender age of just two months. In the 1970s he fought for the government side in the then Rhodesia's long civil war. In the bush and on the border with Mozambique, Grobbelaar fought the rebels of Mugabe and Nkomo who were attempting to bring an end to white rule. Many of his colleagues died and one of his best friends was gunned down as he stood just five yards from the future Liverpool keeper. 'If war teaches you anything it is the appreciation of being alive,' he said in one interview. 'Losing a game is not a tragedy after experiencing border raids and having to eat beetles because you are out of rations. I will never apologise for laughing at life and enjoying football.'

In another interview he said of his military experiences, 'The memory of those days puts everything into perspective. After a mistake at Liverpool, I may get down but at least I'm not dead.' His autobiography carries a moving dedication: 'To all my friends who died in a needless war'.

He joined Liverpool in 1981 following a tortuous route that took him to Vancouver Whitecaps and Crewe Alexandra, but found that he wasn't immediately welcome on Merseyside. The Liverpool team he joined wasn't obviously short of a goalkeeper – Ray Clemence, one of England's finest, was the incumbent – so when Grobbelaar announced that he had no time for reserve-team football and that he had his eye on Clemence's place, it was treated by his team-mates as nothing less than the arrogant claptrap of a foreign braggart. One of those colleagues, Alan Hansen, later recalled that in the early days Grobbelaar did nothing more than get the other Liverpool players' backs up: 'The consensus of opinion among established players was a sarcastic "he's a really shy lad – needs to be taken down a peg or two".'

But it was Grobbelaar who was proved right. Within weeks Clemence was playing for Spurs and the Zimbabwean jungle-fighter, who had just been on honeymoon with his best man rather than his wife – her job as an air stewardess had meant she had had to fly to Barbados – was Liverpool's first choice.

Not that it was all one big smooth ride. The first years were characterised by silly mistakes and reckless mishaps, which at times tried the patience of the Kop to its limits. Grobbelaar won new nicknames – 'Bruce Dropalot', 'The Clown' and 'Jungle Man'. With time, however, he established himself as one of the favourites not only of the Anfield Kop, but of football supporters up and down the country. The man made a speciality of combining great natural talent with sublime unpredictability. Week in week out Grobb would defend his line with staunch skills and superb flair, but there was always a doubt at the back of the mind – as each week passed, so the inevitable rush of blood would come inexorably closer, and the question that hung in the air was would he get away with it? Would he get away with a dribble up the field, a tackle by the corner flag, or an attempt to take a high cross 16 or 17 yards from his goal-line? Inevitably there were times when he didn't and the mistakes were spectacular – a fluffed attempt at taking a cross against lowly Peterborough; a feeble dribble out of goal in Moscow; a miskick on the run against Sheffield Wednesday – all resulted in goals against and, this being the Liverpool of the 1980s, all were caught on film for the nation to gloat and chuckle over.

His is extrovert, robust and, yes, sometimes reckless goalkeeping that was (and hopefully will continue to be) a joy to watch. The cause is probably a personality flaw for which we should be grateful, for Grobbelaar is quite clearly an extrovert even when he's not going for the ball. Hand-stands and cartwheels are nothing to him; banter with the crowd just good humour; using an umbrella on the pitch in the rain little more than a sensible precaution; throwing oranges and assorted fruit back at a Spanish crowd who have been pelting him all game nothing less than fair retaliation.

The proof of the pudding is in the eating: with Grobbelaar in goal Liverpool won six league championships, three FA Cups, three League Cups, the European Cup-Winners' Cup and were runners-up in the European Cup. This would not have been possible with an incompetent between the sticks. It needed a keeper of top-class ability and nothing less. As Liverpool's most successful manager, Bob Paisley, said of him, 'I will accept those wayward moments in return for his qualities and I would not change him for any goalkeeper in the First Division [Premier League]. Had he not been committed to Zimbabwe, I am sure he would have eventually taken over from Shilton in the England goal.'

The human side of Grobbelaar came to the fore when he was confronted with two of the most horrific tragedies in football's history – the Hillsborough disaster and the Heysel massacre. Both catastrophes severely challenged his perspective on life. At Hillsborough in 1989, where 96 supporters were crushed to death in the stand behind him, the keeper argued with and swore at police in a frantic attempt to get them to open the gates and relieve the pressure on the suffocating masses. In the sad weeks that followed, Grobbelaar made a visible public stand to help and comfort the bereaved. The terror of the events had filled him with a grief and a shock that were nothing new – four years earlier, rioting Liverpool fans had caused the deaths of 39 supporters in the Heysel Stadium. He had considered quitting the game and, comparing it to his time in the army, said, 'During that dusty war, I saw sights which made me despair, but they were nothing compared to Heysel. Screams shrieked through my ears, only this time it was not war but a football match.'

In 1994 allegations were made that Grobbelaar, along with the Wimbledon goalkeeper Hans Segers, John Fashanu and a Malaysian businessman had been rigging matches for financial gain. In his first game for Southampton after the accusations were made public, Arsenal fans waved tenners and sang 'Brucie, Brucie, give us a goal'. All very amusing, but there is no doubt that the allegations have cast a dark shadow over the Zimbabwean's career. They also leave it uncertain as to how history will judge the man and how deeply our respect for him has been wounded. Bruce has endeared himself to the British (and Zimbabwean) footballing masses, built up a rapport, created an affection; that he may have been cheating at the same time feels like a gross betrayal of trust.

For whatever reason, the goalkeeping careers of Swift, Macedo, Borota, Burridge, Southall and Grobbelaar are over or nearing their final curtain. What about the new generation of goalkeepers?

Shaka can

It was a cold and crisp day at Durham's Main Castle sports centre, a building so ugly it resembles nothing less than a huge, green crab left marooned as the winter floodwaters of the River Wear receded. It probably won many awards back in the 1960s, but there again so too did Centrepoint, Jimmy Saville and Pickety Witch.

Inside the secondary modern complex, Premier League leaders Newcastle United were completing their Wednesday morning training session and star players were beginning to disgorge at random. Outside, small clumps of autograph-hunters hung around the wrong doors waiting for their heroes to pen their names and pose for pictures.

I sat in the dismal reception area. Shaka Hislop was keeping me waiting while he took a post-training shower. It was probably for the best – the water would almost certainly have ruined my tape-recorder not to mention drench my notebook. I could do without that.

Young boys with Newcastle Brown stars emblazoned across sweatshirts milled around, refugees from a hectic game of five-a-side. Les Ferdinand wandered through, stopping for a quick chat with a member of the United coaching staff. A short and sweat-sodden Kevin Keegan skulked by and cast an admiring glance at the suit worn by his central striker. His eyes said it all: 'So this is what you did with all that transfer money'.

I fought back an overwhelming desire to fire questions at him: 'Mr Keegan, Mr Keegan . . .' about that miss against Spain in 1982, about that Highbury bust-up with Bruce Rioch and, most importantly, about that bike crash in BBC's *Superstars* that had endeared him to the nation in a way that only the likes of Gary Lineker and Mr Blobby have managed in subsequent years.

But no, I was here to meet a goalkeeper, and as I sat waiting I pondered once again the nature of the modern game. Was there really still a role for the madman on the line? Or had big money knocked the tolerant stuffing out of the game's heart?

It was an appropriate place to be having such thoughts: Newcastle, in so many ways, epitomise the British game as it enters the 21st century. Under the leadership of Keegan and using the wallet of Sir John Hall, the Toons of Tyneside have bought their way to the top. Shaka Hislop, price-tag £1.6 million, is just another example of the fact that when it comes to football, money can buy you almost anything.

And who better to talk to than a goalkeeper who not only soars to the top of his goal-net, but who has, in his own small way, helped others reach the outer limits? Shaka Hislop has dabbled with space travel at the Washington DC headquarters of NASA. Who better to talk to about goalkeeping in the modern age.

A tall silhouette emerged from the changing area: it was Shaka, a gentle giant of a man who, at 6ft 6in must be one of the tallest players in the league. We shook hands and sat down. My tape-recorder started up, made a slack grinding noise, a low whistle and faltered to a halt; tape spewed out. Fingers, thumbs, wires, microphone and headphones tangled in a panic of apologies. Who needs a shower to damage equipment like this? I threw the recorder to the ground and apologised again. Shaka stayed calm. I produced a pen and then a second one that worked – an embarrassed bead of sweat emerged from my harassed brow. I prepared for a session of near-indecipherable speed writing.

Shaka Hislop's arrival at Newcastle has not been totally conventional. Born in London to Trinidadian parents, he moved to the Caribbean at the age of two. Here soccer became the love of his life, and striker his favoured position. However, with just nine or ten years under his belt, he went to an under-12 trial in Tobago. 'The coach said, "You, you're the tallest, you're the goalkeeper." I'd never played there before, but I made the zonal team, then the national under-12s, under-14s, under-16s and under-19s.'

At times he still craves the glory of the goalscorer. 'Yeah – really I must admit I miss playing up front. I think that every keeper wants to be a striker. Every keeper thinks that it's easy to score – especially as we *know* how easy it is to score! When I see a striker miss, I think I could have got that – it's like we think that we can score a hat-trick every game!

'You really do have to be mad to be a goalkeeper. When you think about it, there are ten players against me whose sole purpose is to get the ball as close to me as possible and hit it as hard as possible. To volunteer for that sort of punishment, yeah, maybe the goalkeeper has got a screw loose. They're not all mad, but there is something in it.'

He won a US soccer scholarship and went to Howard University in Washington DC. The soccer club paid his tuition fees while he studied mechanical engineering – hence the connection to the space race. 'I did an internship at NASA for three months in the summer of 1991, based at their HQ – it was part of my mechanical engineering degree and it was great fun, I really enjoyed the experience. I have to admit, though, that, like their rockets, much of it went over my head, but I learnt a lot at the same time.'

Shaka was spotted by Reading and while he quickly became a firm favourite of the fans, standing in front of antagonistic opposition supporters brought its problems. 'It's very hard at first and takes some getting used to – but you can't run away from it, you're always within earshot. Still, I seem able to blank these things out.'

There are new issues affecting today's goalkeepers, though. One of them is racism. As one of the country's few black goalkeepers he has inevitably suffered the taunts of idiots in the crowd. 'Racism is a problem. It does come up – but you can't follow your first instincts and climb the fence to sort it out. I have a job to do and, I don't know if it's a good thing, but I can blank these things out. The most important thing is to deal with it mentally and then, when you can, let people know how you feel about it in other ways such as through interviews and anti-racism schemes that have been set up. Things have changed over the last decade – the situation's improved dramatically, but there's still a long way to go – further than the authorities would like to believe.'

Another issue for Shaka and his profession is the high price put on his head. In the past, transfer fees for goalkeepers have been notoriously low, but that's all changed and it brings its own pressures. 'Newcastle forked out a lot for me, but I had nothing to do with it. At the same time I am aware that it's their money that paid for me and that they will want to see a return on their investment. The step up from a small club like Reading was scary at first. But everybody made me feel welcome and it helped me settle into both the team and the town more quickly. From being very nervous about the whole thing, it became a very pleasant experience.'

This pressure was compounded by the fact that when he moved north he was moving to a club where expectations of success are high and where goalkeeper Pavel Srnicek had just been voted the supporters' player of the year. 'I wasn't put off by the situation with Pavel. I came here with my eyes open and knew exactly what I was walking into. I took it as another challenge that I had to overcome.' After just two games in the first team Hislop tore a muscle taking a goal-kick and Srnicek became top dog again.

Like most good goalies, Shaka has his own personal coach; his is 'Budgie' Burridge. To Shaka, the rise of the personal goalkeeping coach demonstrates the fact that the approach to his chosen career is now perhaps more professional and more serious than it might have been in the past. 'The goalkeeper is more recognised as integral to the team and particularly to the successful team. The modern game demands a quality athlete between the sticks; goalkeepers need to be increasingly light on their feet.'

In this context Shaka repeats the goalkeeping mantra – no less true for the frequency that it is chanted – 'You feel more vulnerable as a goalkeeper, anyway; you're not allowed to make mistakes, you're not allowed to be human. Ninety-nine times out of a hundred, you make a mistake and it ends up in the net – everybody else has the luxury of being able to get away with theirs.'

As I got up to leave, I remembered a rumour I'd heard that his name wasn't Shaka at all, but Neil. 'It's true that my first name is Neil, but my father thought that I should also have an African name to reflect my African heritage, so he named me after the first Zulu king. I've always been called Shaka. Not many people know about Neil.'

'We do now,' said a voice from the next table, followed by a sharp giggle from a group of apprentice boys.

Rough girls

Football is all very well as a game for rough girls, but it is hardly suitable for delicate boys.
OSCAR WILDE

'Hello, this is Pauline, the Queen – I'm sorry I'm not here, but please leave a message after the long beep . . .'

The answerphone of Pauline Cope, England women's number-one number 1 and self-proclaimed head of state. I wanted to find out whether to be a goalkeeper in the fast-blossoming women's game you had, like the men, to be a breed apart. I had a result already and I'd neither met her nor spoken to her. England's keeper – 'Copey' to her friends – aspired to being Princess Di's mother-in-law. Nuff said!

To further my quest I headed off to Surrey Quays and the home of Fisher Athletic to catch the women's league match between Millwall and Wolverhampton Wanderers. Twenty-seven-year-old Copey is captain and keeper of Millwall, and on a bitterly cold March afternoon I watched the Lionesses of South London devour the Wolves by five goals to nil.

Pauline, hair tied in a long and tidy ponytail that stretches down her back, spent most of the game 50 yards behind her defence, but they couldn't miss her – nobody could. Shouts of 'Blue ball!', 'Unlucky, girls!', 'Come on, liven up!' 'Never on your Nellie!' detonated across the windswept field like minor sonic booms – and like when a dog barks in the night, you felt like leaning over and shouting 'Shut up!' even though you knew it would have no effect. I wondered whether there were ever any complaints from the workers in Canary Wharf.

Her own voice aside, it was a quiet afternoon for Pauline. A few kicks to the halfway line and a couple of crosses to make safe.

Early in the first half she went for a high cross and, in successfully clearing the ball, flattened her own defender. Late in the second half a punch clearance sent an attacker's head flying off towards her own half, her body crumpled to the floor. Pauline was barely troubled. Only one save stretched her, a spontaneous deflection around the post. Wolves were well beaten and Copey had hardly broken into a sweat.

I don't know why the quality of the football surprised me, but it did, particularly that of Millwall who played neat one-twos and avoided any temptation to drop into a long-ball game. It deserved a much bigger crowd than the 30 or so that were there. In a tree next to the main stand a young boy perched, watching with enthusiasm. Somebody should have called him down, told him that it was free inside and that there was plenty of room.

Women's soccer in this country really took off during the late 1980s and it's reckoned that there are more than 15,000 women playing for 500 clubs. Despite sporadic attempts by the male authorities to stamp it out, it's been around a long time, though – a representative game between north and south being played as far back as 1895 – but it's been a hard struggle for survival. In 1902 the FA prohibited men from playing against women, but, spurred on by advances made during the First World War, the female game grew to new heights of popularity in the immediate post-war years – one game in 1920 between Dick Kerr's Ladies (of Preston) and St Helens' Ladies attracting a crowd of 53,000 to Goodison Park. Women's football was getting bigger crowds than many of the lower-division men's games and the Football Association didn't like it. Its response was brutal. In 1921 it banned women from playing on league grounds – a ban that remained until 1972 and which effectively smothered the women's game at birth.

This probably explains why women playing football in this country are such an anomaly – in Norway, a country with one eighth the population of Britain, 44,000 women play football (more than the men); in the USA there are over three million women players. The situation here may yet change, encouraged no doubt by the formation of the Women's National League in 1991, consisting of 30 teams split into three divisions.

I arranged to meet Pauline at the merchant bank in the City where she has worked as a receptionist since the age of 17. Leaving the 20th century behind on the ground floor, I stepped into a world where all was pinstripe suits and black waistcoats. Pauline greeted me with a big smile and an even bigger handshake – who said Pat Jennings had the largest hands in football?

We talked in an office overshadowed by the dome of St Paul's. Pauline's a good-humoured, enthusiastic Cockney, proud of her Peckham roots and her West Ham allegiances and even prouder of her reputation as one of the most flamboyant characters of women's football. 'I am the joker of the team,' she says with a big grin. 'There are others, but I just seem to be the loudest – and I think you'll find that they all agree.'

She started playing at the age of 12, park games with her brother Johnny and his mates. 'At first they thought, "Oh God, we've got a girl playing",' she remembers. 'But I used to go every week and soon they were picking me before my brother! He never envied me, though.'

Like most goalies, she began as an outfield player and went in goal at the age of 14 when the team's first-choice didn't turn up. In her late teens she got bored of keeping and played a couple of seasons at centre-half. An England under-21 scout spotted her and she got selected as a centre-half/goalkeeper.

Even now, with her full England caps into double figures, she sometimes gets bored of standing between the sticks. 'I don't want to go out there and score goals, I just want to make my presence felt, because there's times in our games when my players are getting pushed off the ball and I want to just put myself about a bit, to let people know that I'm on the pitch.'

In a travesty of a cup game against Maidstone United the ball didn't come anywhere near her in the first half and, her patience wearing thin, she moved up to the halfway line for the second half. When the ball arrived at her feet she needed no encouragement to dribble through the entire Maidstone defence and score. Hers was just one of 15 Millwall netted that afternoon.

After ten years at Millwall, the last two playing in the outfield, she headed off to Highbury for a season and won glory as goalkeeper for Arsenal's double – league and cup – winning team. She also won her first cap for England. When colleagues at her workplace saw her on Sky television's coverage of the Women's FA Cup final many attitudes changed. 'I've got people saying to me, "I see you in a different light, I didn't realise you was that good and we've got more respect for you."' A year earlier she had tried to get a kickabout with the company team, but the boys had refused to let her play. Days after the final, the works team approached her and asked her if she fancied a game. She wasn't about to mince her words: 'I told them to poke it! They didn't want me before, but now they'd seen me on telly . . .'

Her Arsenal days were short-lived and after 'a bit of a disagreement' she returned to Millwall. 'That's one thing about amateur football – you can leave when you like,' she added coyly.

My short experience of women's football had taught me that it was every bit as skilful and competitive as the men's game – it's also just as aggressive. If the Wolves match had been relatively clean, it nevertheless had its share of sly digs and frosty glares. Pauline confirms the impression. 'Everyone goes out to win and there's a lot of real rivalry in the league. When we play Arsenal we do or die to win. We don't hold back in tackles and if someone gets fouled we all join in. If anyone squares up to someone we jump in and help them out – to split them up, if they're going to pick on one they're going to pick on the whole team. We're in there for each other.'

(As far as Arsenal are concerned, it's not just on the field either. After the Gunners beat the Lionesses in the 1996 London Cup final, all hell broke out. The winners' trophy was smashed in a brawl, and one Arsenal player was knocked unconscious by a flying teapot.)

The skills she needs to employ are the same as in the men's game too. Pauline's height and build mean that she dominates her box and the odds are on her winning most 50:50 balls. 'Even in training I hear comments like "Sod running into you!" In a game there's many times when I think their centre-forward's shanked it a bit. It's like I'd think twice about running into Peter Schmeichel!'

She's not in the Peter Shilton 'bollock-everybody-no-matter-what' school though. She may be a foghorn on the pitch, but she considers herself fair. 'To be truthful, if I've made a mistake I won't blame anyone except myself, I might even put my hand up and say "sorry, girls", so that they know it was my fault and nobody else's. In the women's game if a defender loses the ball she'll get up and say "I'm really sorry, Copey". I feel guilty shouting at her because she knows she's done wrong. It's different if she's just got up and walked away, then I'd really rollock her!'

She rates David Seaman and Peter Schmeichel as the best two keepers in the country, but her real hero is Trevor Brooking – even though he's a notoriously crap goalie. Her eyes go watery when she thinks about him. 'He's always been my hero. If I win the lottery I'll probably give half to him. I love him to bits. When he played his last game at Upton Park I was there and I cried my eyes out. Every time he's on the telly my family phone up and say, "Quick, Trev's on the telly".'

What about this stuff about having to be mad to be a goalkeeper? Does it translate across to the women's game? Copey has no doubts. 'You do most definitely have to be crazy to be a goalkeeper.' What's more, she can prove it. She may still get a little nervous when playing for England, but that doesn't mean she suddenly goes all demure. England played Italy away just days before we met, and as the women lined up in the tunnel before the game, Pauline noticed that Italy's best player, their superstar Carolina Marachi, was wearing her hair up. Quick as a flash Pauline was leading a chorus of 'She's got a pineapple on her head, she's got a pineapple on her head' to the music of 'He's got the whole world in his hands'. It caused great hilarity among the English team. 'The whole team were singing and I looked back and saw Ted [the manager] was doubling up in pain. He could not stop laughing. I'm sure she must have known. I think she understands English. It doesn't bother me. She scored against me. Bitch! But never mind.'

One of Pauline's problems is that she gets uncontrollable fits of giggles. On her England début her best mate Lou Waller scored a blinding own-goal against her. Seaman might have been distraught, Walker downcast – but Copey? 'I said, "Lou, whatever you do, don't laugh, because Ted's going to kill us." So I've got my back to her and I'm trying not to laugh, but I couldn't stop. I don't mean to, it just happens.

'This season, playing for Millwall, we had a free-kick in our box, so I said to my sweeper "Leave it, I'll take it", but I kicked it and it hit her right on the back of the head. It really tickled me and I couldn't move for laughing. My stomach was hurting me so badly, but the game was still going on. I shouted "For Christ's sake, don't let that ball come near me", because it would have gone in. I tell you I must have been laughing for about 20 minutes.'

Copey has a big effect on her team-mates, although sometimes living up to her reputation can be a bit of a strain. 'Even for England games I'm the one that's shouting, "Wakey wakey, come on we can do this". Anyone needs cheering up it's always "Go on, Copey, go over there and say a few words".

'I am a constant joker and it's just in me. If I go to the football now and I don't joke, they all go "what's the matter?". I've got to keep it up now.'

But it's perhaps on the team bus that she comes into her element. 'All the naughty ones grab the back seats. There used to be only about four, but now I've got a big clan at the back. I'll start off the chanting and singing.'

'Does this mean that you are the Paul Gascoigne of the team?' I ask.

'No, he's the Pauline Cope of Glasgow Rangers.'

'Pauline Gascoigne?'

'No thanks! Pauline Brooking maybe!'

8 A parting shot

A question lodged in the back of my mind, like an unwelcome auntie at a 21st birthday party demanding to know who had slipped the ecstasy tablet in Uncle Albert's Drambuie: if you've got to be mad to be a goalkeeper, how come some of the greatest were so normal? It was a question I put to former Spurs, Arsenal and Northern Ireland keeper, Pat Jennings.

'Well, what you're saying, that's rubbish!' exclaimed the Great Pat. 'I'm not crazy. People look at these things from the outside and see what goalies have to do – diving at other people's feet and diving into a crowd of flying boots. There are dangers, but you don't see them. Risks are different than for other players and the pressure is on in a goalkeeper's early days, but you don't have to be mad.'

And there it is in a nutshell. The Great Pat has spoken and who am I to disagree. He, of course, speaks the truth, the whole truth and nothing but the truth – you don't have to be crazy. Absolutely not. There are some very sane people who have played between the sticks, people like, well, like . . . It's unlikely, for example, that the government might see merit in a Care in the Community access course for keepers, but this wasn't really the point in the first place. I was never questioning whether mental illness was an essential element of a goalkeeping job specification, coming just below 'Able to catch white globe travelling at speed' and above 'Can kick to the halfway line'. No, the questions posed at the beginning relating to that rare condition *lunaticus goalkeeperus* are gentler and perhaps more clearly espoused in the old pub plaque 'you don't have to be mad to work here, but it helps' – do you have to be a bit different, a bit special perhaps, or even a breed apart to be a goalkeeper?

It's here that I would part ways with the Great Pat. There is something different about the goalkeeper; there is something different about his or her role in the game compared to everybody else's, something about the way they relate to their team-mates, about the way they are integrated into a team plan, about the way they are trained and about the conditions under which they work. Time and again, vulnerability is mentioned by goalkeepers as one of their major concerns. All goalkeepers talk of the mental as well as the physical strains of the game and the need to be strong in both. Ball smashed at you, feet raised to you, studs thudded into you, elbows swung at you, fans baying at you, fans despairing of you – all are pressures faced by the keeper. During the course of a game, keepers get a lot of time to cogitate such matters, to build them into nightmarish phantoms on days when things aren't going well, or to dismiss them as part of the job when things are fine. There wasn't a keeper I spoke to who in one way or another didn't say 'The thing is, if a full-back makes a mistake, so what? If I make one, then nine times out of ten, it's a goal and I'm in trouble.'

Showmanship, eccentricity and oddballism are nothing less than some goalkeepers' mechanisms for survival. Clowning with the crowd, fooling with the ref, exploding at other players, writing a Nobel Prize-winning book, all act as a keeper's safety valve. The pressures of the job demand such behaviour; to bottle them up would be nigh on disastrous.

In Jim Hossack's book *Head over Heels*, Dave Cumming, goalie for Scotland and Middlesbrough in the 1930s, expresses what must be a common goalkeeping sentiment: 'In my day there were many great sharpshooters who could bamboozle goalkeepers with all kinds of tricks. I used to dream of getting revenge on guys like McGrory, Dean, Ted Drake, George Stevenson and Cliff Bastin. They'd be stuck in the goal while I played the same tricks on them and left those pathetic individuals standing like fools in a net bulging with balls I had put there . . . then I'd fall out of bed and realise that all dreams must end.'

I too have a dream (more a recurring nightmare) in which a long way off on the horizon I can see terrible events – a slaughter, robbery, bombs, that sort of thing – and they are getting ever closer no matter how much I run. I never know whether I'm going to survive or die when they reach me (and because I always wake up in time, hopefully I will never have to). At times goalkeeping must be like this. The ball is at the other end, bouncing around; you desperately attempt to stay alert – and then there's a break. The opposition are streaming towards you and your defenders are falling by the wayside. Until it reaches you, you don't know whether you are about to experience a moment of glory or a moment of complete dejection. It must be very disconcerting.

As for whether you have to be a bit dotty in the first place or whether the position makes you so, it's difficult to say, and I'll take the Liberal Democrat route on this by surmising that it's probably a bit of both. Certainly there is enough evidence to show that some of the loopiest net-minders have been ready-mixed when they put on the gloves, but certainly there's enough to the job to send anyone round the bend.

Whatever the cause, the eccentricity of the goalkeeper is a positive boon to the game, a ray of hope in an era when slick football and professional values are called for by pundits who, with their next breath, lament the demise of the character in the modern game. There is no doubt that, in spite of an optimism born of the oddball goalkeeper's resilience, the modern game would like to be rid of what it sees as its sore thumbs, its rough diamonds. What this is to ignore is the crucial fact that goal-keepers who are entertainers are almost always highly competent, often brilliant goalies, whose amusing side is an extra to, not a substitution for, class.

It is a sad fact that in the future we may have to look abroad for our light relief: to Sweden where Varelli mixes brilliance with buffoonery; to Mexico where Jorge Campos has scored almost as many goals as he has saved, refuses to play in garish shirts that are not designed by himself and who has signed to Los Angeles Galaxy in the USA as both keeper and centre-forward; and to Colombia where René Higuita behaves like, well, like René Higuita . . .

Nevertheless, the tradition of the eccentric goalkeeper is too precious to let slip without a fight. The time is right to begin a rearguard action for its preservation and its future encouragement. Nothing is more crucial than ensuring that new talent continues to squeeze through the pipeline and that young aspirants to the clown's shirt have mentors to look up to. Perhaps a set of guidelines could be adopted by football clubs. A first draft might include the following eight points:

i. Shouting Practice
Ten minutes a day before the mirror. Begin with easy exercises ('Mine', 'Yours', 'Offside') and build up to the more complex set of phrases ('Come on, ref, get a bloody grip', 'Right, right, right, left, left, stop – shit, right which sonofabitch ducked?', 'I said, leave it, plonkhead, what have you got – shit for brains?').

Ask yourself: do you scare yourself? Be honest. If the answer is no, try harder, watch old videos of Les Sealey or consider playing midfield.

ii. Names
Guaranteed success only comes with the choice of a good name. Yes, you can get games if you happen to be called Ian Bennett or David James, but things become so much easier if you are blessed with a monicker like Perry Digweed or Bruce Grobbelaar. Even better, an eastern European twinge to your calling card is certain to push you several steps up the goalkeeping ladder, and it's a virtual requirement for the Premier League. Kharine, Ogrizovich, Immel, Myklosko, Bosnich and Srnicek have already been taken, but Yeltsin and Gorbachev have yet to be booked. Be warned though, Ivan Denisovitch has had his day. Get in now while you can. Better still try a composite – Perry Myklosko has that surefire goalkeeping feel to it.

iii. Nicknames
Almost as important as real names. Don't wait for your team-mates to come up with one or you'll end up with something really interesting like Jonesy or Banksy. No, turn up for your first training session with one prepared, so that when the boss asks you to introduce yourself to the rest of the team, you can say 'Call me "The flying pink blancmange/the praying mantis/el bloko/ Jurgen Klinsmann".' That way they're bound to notice you and from the very start you'll have made an impression. Incidentally, 'Clumsy', 'Butterfingers' or 'Dracula' are not good choices of nickname.

iv. Weight
All the sensible advice says that you have to be fit, strong and athletic to make it in the keeper stakes. Forget it! Get going on

those Curly Wurly sandwiches and oven chips. Remember some of the finest examples of goalkeeping talent have been horizontally challenged in the lower chest/upper pelvis region. Join a tradition that includes Fatty Foulke, Tiny Joyce, Happy Jack Hillman, Tommy Lawrence and Joe Corrigan. Don't just talk about disposable waist, get one!

v. Speed

Often cited as a factor as critical to goalkeepers as it is to centre-forwards, your aim should really to be to improve your slow running for those rare occasions when your team is winning and you've got half an hour to eat up on the clock. Don't forget goalkeepers are only allowed to carry the ball for four steps; if you learned to count above three at school or have a GCSE in Applied Mathematics, give up now.

vi. Hardness

Even if your liver is well past lily, try and give the impression that Iron Mike Tyson is nothing but a chicken who wouldn't go two rounds with your baby sister – it's okay, he's in the States, he's probably never heard of soccer and he's almost certainly never heard of you. The chances are you're safe. Of course, if anything goes wrong, don't blame me.

vii. Kit

There are three schools of thought on this one. The first is the Campos strain – make your own and make it lurid. Advantages? You can be seen anywhere and everywhere, you are absolutely guaranteed to get noticed. Disadvantages? You can be seen anywhere and everywhere, you are absolutely guaranteed to get noticed, particularly by oncoming strikers who will be better able to decide where to put their shots.

The second is the old-fashioned green shirt. Plain and natural, a Neville Southall favourite; some might say it's a little boring, others that it's retrospective fashion chic, harking back to the glory days of the '70s. Advantages? Good, solid, down-to-earth, easy to hide in the long grass. Disadvantages? Those Glitter Band and Chicory Tip tapes you'll have to play in the Porsche on the way home.

Finally, there's the third, dirty option, which can be combined with either of the above. Claim that you are superstitious and never wash a winning kit. Let that mud cake in. Advantages? Once you're on a winning streak it will continue, as both attackers and defenders avoid coming anywhere near you. Disadvantages? Lack of close friends, the probable need to take a hammer to your kit round about April time, the fear that sooner or later you're going to lose a game and then you'll probably need a new Hotpoint.

viii. Aloofness

Be an enigma. Not one of those things the doctors give you to put up your bottom, but have a certain detachment, a separation from your team-mates. Advantages? A good goalkeeping attitude that may well result in a literary prize or a bishopric when you retire. Disadvantages? Accusations of being a *Guardian* reader by your team-mates and no invitations to go and tap off with some birds down at Slinky's nightclub and wine bar.

There's one final question I'd like to leave you with. In researching this book I wrote over 200 letters and made innumerable phone calls. When my interview with Higuita in London fell through, I made arrangements to meet el Loco on his own patch, Medellin. Just ten days before I flew out to Colombia, the message came through that there were only certain questions that he was willing to answer. A couple of days later I started to hear rumours that he would want paying. The rumours crystallised into a demand for $7,000 and I cancelled my plane ticket.

Somewhere deep inside I should have been happy, for after all Higuita was just taking me at my word, wasn't he, right down to the enigmatic aloofness. Bollocks I was.

Of the 200 letters I wrote, the Pope replied, but Peter Schmeichel, Neville Southall, Bruce Grobbelaar and Les Sealey never did . . . so who is closer to God?

Bibliography

Camus, A., article in *France Football* (1957)

Cosgrove, S., *Hampden Babylon: Sex and Scandal in Scottish Football* (Canongate Press, 1991)

Croall, J., *Don't Shoot the Goalkeeper* (Oxford University Press, 1976)

Davies, D., *Never Say Dai* (Siop y Siswn, 1986)

Davies, G.M., and Garland, I., *Who's Who of Welsh International Soccer Players* (Bridge Books, 1991)

Doyle, R., *Paddy Clarke Ha Ha Ha* (Martin Secker and Warburg, an imprint of Reid Books, 1993)

The Football Association, *Women's Football* (1994)

Forsyth, R., *The Only Game: The Scots and World Football* (Mainstream Publishing, 1990)

Galton, R. and Simpson, A., *Hancock's Half-Hour: 'The Football Pools'* (1959)

Hamilton, I., *The Faber Book of Soccer* (Faber, 1992)

Handke, P., *The Goalie's Anxiety at the Penalty Kick* (Eyre Methuen, an imprint of Reid Books, 1977)

Hines, B., *A Kestrel for a Knave* (Michael Joseph, 1968)

Hossack, J., *Head Over Heels: A Celebration of British Football* (Mainstream Publishing, 1989)

Icke, D., *In the Light of Experience* (Warner Books, 1993)

Inglis, S., *Soccer in the Dock: A History of British Football Scandals, 1900 to 1965* (Willow Books, 1985)

Keating, F., *Long Days, Late Nights* (Robson Books, 1984)

Lamming, D., *Who's Who of Scottish Internationalists* (Association of Football Statisticians, 1982)

Leatherdale, C., *Scotland: The Quest for the World Cup* (Two Heads Publishing in association with Desert Island Books, 1994)

Longford, Lord, *Pope John Paul II* (Michael Joseph/Rainbird, 1982)

Matthews, T., *Golden Greats of Wolverhampton Wanderers: The Goalkeepers* (Sports Leisure Concepts, 1990)

Nabokov, V., *Speak, Memory* (Weidenfeld and Nicholson, 1966)

Sir Norman Chester Centre for Football Research, *Women and Football* (1993)

Parry, P., and Lile, B., *The Old Black and Green: Aberystwyth Town FC, 1884–1984* (Aberystwyth Town FC, 1987)

Pickering, D., *The Cassell Soccer Companion* (Cassell, 1994)

Rough, A., *Rough at the Top* (John Donald Publishers, 1988)

Rovin, J., *Julio! The Unauthorised Biography* (Bantam Books, 1986)

Rowlands, A., *Trautmann: The Biography* (Breedon Books, 1990)

Sillitoe, A., *The Loneliness of the Long-distance Runner* (Pan Books, 1959)

Small, Revd L., *The Holy Goalie* (Pentland Press, 1993)

Stepney, A., *Alex Stepney* (Arthur Barker, 1978)

Swift, F., *Football from the Goalmouth* (Sporting Handbooks, 1949)

Wilson, B., *You've Got to be Crazy* (Arthur Barker, 1989)

The following publications were extremely useful in the research of this book:

Aberdeen Press and Journal
Arbroath Guide
Athletic News
Birmingham Daily Mail
Burnley Express and Advertiser
Crewe Guardian
Cricket and Football Field (Bolton)
Daily Mail
Daily Mirror
Daily Record
Daily Telegraph
Edinburgh Evening News
Esquire
Evening Standard
Express and Star
The Face
Football News
FourFourTwo
Glasgow Evening News
Glasgow Herald
Goal!
Grimsby Daily Telegraph
The Guardian
Halifax Daily Courier and Guardian
Irish News and Belfast Morning News
Kentish Mercury
Lancashire Evening Express
Liverpool Echo
Liverpool Football Echo
London Evening News
Manchester Evening News
New Statesman
News of the World
The Observer
The People
The Scotsman
Sheffield and Rotherham Independent
Sheffield Daily Independent
Sheffield Daily Telegraph
South East London Mercury
Sporting Star (Wolverhampton)
Sports Argus (Birmingham)
Stirling Observer
The Sun
Sunday Express
Sunday Telegraph
Sunday Times
Sunderland Football Echo
Swindon Evening Advertiser
The Times
Today
Total Football
Viz
When Saturday Comes
Woolwich Gazette
World Soccer

Index

Allan, George, 40, 41
Allan, Jimmy, 111, 112
Allen, Les, 111
Arthur, Herbert 'Herbie', 33, 34, 35, 165
Ashcroft, James, 36, 37, 50, 72
Asprilla, Faustino, 10, 100

Baker, Chet, 144
Baker, Howard, 31
Baldwin, Stanley, 109
Balfour, A. J., 43
Banks, Gordon, 18, 24, 115, 142, 143
Bartram, Sam, 20, 21
Battiston, Patrick, 74, 75
Baxter, Joe, 151
Baynton, Jack, 30
Beattie, Dick, 91, 92, 93
Beckenbauer, Franz, 143
Bennett, Ian, 76, 77, 79, 186
Birch, Arnold, 157
Björk, 76
Blyth (Hibernian), 63
Bonds, Billy, 137
Bonetti, Peter, 142, 143, 162, 163, 164, 167
Borota, Petar, 165, 166, 167, 173
Bosnich, Mark, 75, 186
Bound, W. S., 49
Boyle, Peter, 43, 44
Bremner, Billy, 96, 133
Brodie, Chic, 19, 56, 57, 58, 69
Brown, Bill, 148, 152, 153
Brown, Jim, 157
Brownlie, James, 157
Bryce, Freddie, 139, 140
Burridge, John, 165, 167, 168, 173, 176

Campos, Jorge, 165, 185, 187

Camus, Albert, 124, 125
Canavon (Wolves), 140
Cantona, Eric, 121
Carrott, Jasper, 24
Carter, Raich, 165
Chapman, Herbert, 52
Charlton, Jack, 132
Clemence, Ray, 151, 153, 171
Clerck, Marc de, 141
Connor, James, 32
Cooper, Terry, 132
Cope, Pauline, 177, 178, 179, 180, 181
Corrigan, Joe, 187
Coton, Tony, 141
Cowan, Jimmy, 139, 153
Crozier, Joe, 145, 151
Cubillas (Peru), 95
Cumming, Dave, 184

Dalglish, Kenny, 151
Davies, Dai, 118, 119, 120, 121, 122, 165
Dawson, Jerry, 153
Digweed, Perry, 186
Ditchburn, Ted, 70
Docherty, Tommy, 155
Doig, Ned, 153
Downie, Robert, 30
Drake, Ted, 158
Dwyer, Noel, 137

Eco, Umberto, 130
Edwards, Alf, 52
English, Sam, 64
Escobar, Andrés, 99
Escobar, Pablo, 98, 99, 100, 101
Ewart, John, 124

Fashanu, John, 173
Fettis, Alan, 156

Francis, Gerry, 151
Fry, Barry, 76, 77
Foulke, William, 31, 35, 37–46, 56, 69, 73, 85, 94, 130, 162, 165, 187
Foulkes, Bill, 154
Fowler, Robbie, 76

Gascoigne, Paul, 182
Gauld, Jimmy, 89, 92
Giles, Johnny, 133
Gillespie, George, 30
Glanville, Brian, 161, 164
Goodall, John, 37
Goram, Andy, 152
Greaves, Jimmy, 147, 150, 153
Greenhoff, Brian, 71
Grobbelaar, Bruce, 18, 70, 71, 72, 77, 165, 170–173, 186, 188
Guevara, Che, 18

Haddock, Harry, 146
Haffey, Frank, 144, 147–152, 162
Haggo (Dumbarton), 60
Hancock, Tony, 132
Hansen, Alan, 72, 171
Hardy, Bert, 125
Harper, William, 31, 69
Harvey, Colin, 169
Harvey, David, 96, 152
Hart, C. E., 29
Haynes, Johnny, 148, 149
Herriot, Jim, 17
Higuita, René, 9–13, 18, 22, 97, 100, 101, 102, 103, 162, 185, 188
Hillman, 'Happy' Jack, 36, 85, 86, 87, 88, 165, 187
Hislop, Shaka, 173, 174, 175, 176, 177
Hume, Cardinal Basil, 107, 108
Hunter, Norman, 133

Hurst, Geoff, 154, 166, 167
Hussein, Saddam, 115

Icke, David, 18, 23, 24, 112, 113, 114, 115, 116, 117, 165
Iglesias, Julio, 130, 131
Iremonger, Albert, 37

James, David, 186
Jennings, Pat, 18, 135, 154, 179, 183, 184
Jesus, 15, 107, 115
John Paul II, Pope, 18, 108
John, Roy, 30
Jones, Gwyn, 90
Jones, Jack, 47
Joyce, 'Tiny', 56, 69, 187

Kazadi, Muamba, 21
Keegan, Kevin, 174
Kelly, Pat, 138 139
Kennedy, John 'Diver', 30
Kennedy, Stewart, 150, 151
Kinnaird, Lord Arthur Fitzgerald, 27, 28, 29, 30, 31, 43
Klinsmann, Jurgen, 75, 186

Lato (Poland), 103
Law, Denis, 147, 151, 162
Lawrence, Tommy, 187
Lawton, Tommy, 22, 151
Leighton, Jim, 152, 153
Lineker, Gary, 114, 174
Little, Brian, 120
Lloyd, Marie, 47
Lofthouse, Nat, 146
Lofthouse (Blackburn), 34, 35
Lornie, Andrew, 145

McArthur, Daniel, 153
McAulay, James, 30, 153
McDougall, Ted, 57
Macedo, Tony, 165, 166, 173
Maciel, Juan Carlos, 103
McGrory, Jimmy, 64
McIlvanney, Hugh, 143, 149
Mackay, Dave, 151
McLeod, Ally, 95
McManaman, Steve, 71
McPherson (Alloa), 63
MacPherson (Nottingham Forest), 87
Maley, Willie, 66
Marindin, Sir Arthur Francis, 29, 30
Martin, Freddie, 146, 148, 151
Matthews, Stanley, 146, 151
Maturana, Francisco, 101
Meiklejohn, Davie, 65
Mello, Rosemary de, 104, 105, 106
Meredith, Billy, 85, 88
Merrick, Gil, 151

Merriman, Colonel, 29
Milla, Roger, 101
Million, Esmond, 89, 90, 91
Milne, Jim, 145
Milton (Halifax Town), 135, 136, 137
Mitchell, J. F., 160
Molina, Claudia, 99, 102
Molina-Yepes, Carlos, 99, 101, 102
Montgomery, Jim, 24
Moore, Bobby, 114
Moss, Frank, 157, 158
Murray, Dennis, 137

Nabokov, Vladimir, 124, 125, 126
Nayim, 134
Needham, Ernest, 38, 44
Niedzwiecki, Eddie, 17, 160
Nielsen, Brigitte, 124

O'Connor, Des, 124, 130
Olivier, Laurence, 78
Ortega, Daniel, 99

Paisley, Bob, 172
Pavarotti, Luciano, 130
Pele, 24, 104, 129, 142
Phillips, Brian, 90
Platini, Michel, 74
Platt (Liverpool), 58
Poole, Kevin, 162
Preud'homme, Michel, 24

Quiroga, Ramon, 103, 165

Raikes, G. B., 109
Redknapp, Jamie, 13
Rennie, Harry G., 30, 33, 36, 153
Revie, Don, 24, 146
Ridge (Ecclesfield Town), 73
Rioch, Bruce, 174
Robinson, Jack, 35, 36
Rodriguez Orjuela, Miguel, 98
Rojas, Roberto, 104, 105, 106
Romario, 104
Roose, Leigh Richmond, 30, 37, 46–54, 69, 123, 162, 165, 167
Rough, Alan, 95, 96, 97, 152
Rowan, Archibald, 31
Royle, Joe, 119, 169
Runcie, Archbishop Robert, 107

Saunders, Ron, 168
Schmeichel, Peter, 16, 71, 156, 180, 188
Schumacher, Harald, 74, 75, 128
Scott, Elisha, 36
Scott, Walter, 33
Sealey, Les, 157, 165, 186, 188
Seaman, David, 134, 135, 180, 181
Segers, Hans, 77, 173

Senna, Ayrton, 59
Shearer, Bobby, 147
Shilton, Peter, 18, 71, 93, 94, 95, 115, 153, 155, 168, 180
Shine, Betty, 116
Simpson, Ronnie, 153
Small, Leonard, 109, 110
Socrates, 116
Souness, Graeme, 72
Southall, Neville, 165, 168, 169, 170, 173, 187, 188
Sprake, Gary, 70, 132, 133, 165
Spratley, Alan, 111
Srnicek, Pavel, 176, 186
Stallone, Sylvester, 78, 124, 129
Stein, Jock, 95, 96
Stepney, Alex, 21, 71, 154, 155
Stewart (Burnley), 34, 35
Stewart, Rod, 124, 126
Street, Tina, 93, 94
Surman, Les, 137, 138
Sutcliffe, John, 31
Swift, Frank, 22, 109, 151, 155, 156, 165, 166, 173

Tambling, Bobby, 162
Tann, Bert, 90
Taylor, Gordon, 77, 169
Taylor, Richard, 146
Thomson, John 'Jock', 63–66, 69
Thorpe, Jimmy, 61, 62, 63, 68
Thwayi, 39
Tomaszewski, 24
Trainer, James, 31, 32, 94, 165
Trautmann, Bert, 66, 67, 68
Trevis, Derek, 56
Tubilandu, Dimbi, 21

Utterson, James, 62, 63

Valderrama, Carlos, 10
Varelli, Thomas, 165, 185
Venables, Terry, 162

Walker, Billy, 140, 141
Ward, Mark, 71, 72
Warner, Jimmy, 81, 82, 83, 84
Wayne, John, 68
Wells, H. G., 47
Wilkinson, Joshua, 59, 60, 63
Williams, Charlie, 37
Williams, Keith, 90
Wilson, Bob, 152, 163
Wilson, Peter, 65
Wood, George, 96
Wright, Alex, 62, 63

Yashin, Lev, 18
Young, Willie, 96
Younger, Tommy, 133